Digging Up Mother

Digging Up Mother

A LOVE STORY

Doug Stanhope

Foreword by Johnny Depp

Da Capo Press
A Member of the Perseus Books Group

Set in 10.5-point Goudy Oldstyle Std

Cataloging-in-Publication data for this book is available from the Library of Congress.

First Da Capo Press edition 2016
ISBN: 978-0-306-82439-5 (hardcover)
ISBN: 978-0-306-82440-1 (ebook)

Published by Da Capo Press
A Member of the Perseus Books Group
www.dacapopress.com

Da Capo Press books are available at special discounts for bulk purchases in the U.S. by corporations, institutions, and other organizations. For more information, please contact the Special Markets Department at the Perseus Books Group, 2300 Chestnut Street, Suite 200, Philadelphia, PA, 19103, or call (800) 810-4145, ext. 5000, or e-mail special.markets@perseusbooks.com.

10 9 8 7 6 5 4 3 2 1

To Bingo,
You're a potatohead and I know you'll never read this book.
That's okay, I read you all the good parts
out loud while I was writing it.
Thanks for being there.
I love you.
You'd think I'd dedicate this book to Mother.
Mother is dead and doesn't give a shit.
I am not a man of faith but I have faith in that.
Of all the things you can't take with you,
Hopefully ego is the first to be left behind.

Contents

Foreword

"The greatest tragedy in mankind's entire history may be the hijacking of morality by religion."

---Sir Arthur C. Clarke (Writer).

"The superior man understands what is right, the inferior man understands what will sell."

---Confucius (Philosopher).

"Life has become immeasurably better since I have been forced to stop taking it seriously."

---Hunter S. Thompson (Writer).

"Don't worry, don't be afraid, ever, because this is just a ride."
---Bill Hicks (Comedian).

"I'm not going to censor myself to comfort your ignorance."

---Jon Stewart (Comedian).

"Human decency is not derived from religion. It precedes it."

---Christopher Hitchens (Writer).

"Spare no man the fire should he make his ignorance yours."

---Richard "Tude" Wells (Moonshiner).

"Life is like animal porn. It's not for everyone."

---Doug Stanhope (Drunk).

Dear Reader,

    He's a depraved reluctant visionary and debauched accidental guru who wears old suits that were likely once some dead fucker's Saturday night prowling outfit - he's a man of the people who says what must be said for no one else will - total honesty - consequence be damned - no fluffy outside no creamy inside - you get what you get and deal with it - he is our savior - for here in this life where the only guarantee is the ceasing of breath and a healthy death tax for our loved ones he is the one man who dares to plunge the cold dagger of truth deep into the collective brain-dead psyche of our species for the ultimate benefit of all humankind and certainly not since my dearest friend and mentor Hunter have I known an individual with such a profoundly strong sense of moral justice - it makes me sick so I suppose I must ultimately admit that I do not like this man I speak of I fucking love him.

Him being Doug Stanhope.

Johnny Depp
Los Angeles, CA.
19th February, 2016

Preface

AFTER THIRTY-SOME YEARS OF RUTHLESS DRINKING, IT'S MORE THAN probable that I've fucked up a few details. Perhaps it was a year before or after, the wrong town, a different hole. But I've made every attempt to fact-check every story, and I thank all of you who took my relentless calls and emails to make this book as accurate as possible. I'm sure some of you never expected to hear from me again, some probably didn't want to at all. Regardless, I couldn't have done it without you.

A lot of the people involved have grown into responsible adults with families and respectable professions. For that reason, I may have had to tone down a story or two on your behalf. Even if I wanted to smear you publicly, the lawyers wouldn't have it. For that same reason, almost every goddamned name in this book has been changed. If you are reading about yourself and that's not your name, it's not because I got it wrong. They made me change it. I actually tried interchanging names: Molly Brown becomes Sally Jones and vice versa. You'd still be mentioned, just as the wrong person. They didn't buy it.

If the story is graphic and true and wrong and I could STILL use your real name, that is because you are fucking blessed to have nothing to hide, are proud of your scars, and have nothing to lose. There's still a few of us out here and I'm wealthy for still having you in my life.

1

Mother's Last Gasp

ON THURSDAY, I GOT A CALL FROM ONE OF MOTHER'S CAREGIVERS. "I'm here with your Mother. I think you should come over so you two can talk." She spoke like a mortician from a 1950s horror movie. Since I can't remember her name, I'll call her Morticia.

I knew this meant Mother was going to kill herself. There was no need to be mawkishly sentimental. I'd been here waiting for the call. I'm not the "Sit down. There's something I have to tell you" type of guy. I freak out at traffic or figuring out gadgets. I punch dashboards and smash laptops. When serious shit happens, I'm generally rational and grounded.

"Is it time?" I asked.

"Yes, she's ready to go."

"Now . . . as in today?"

"Yes."

In the background, Mother wheezed out "I've had enough" with no less theater.

We'd had enough false flags of a Mother suicide over the years that there wasn't any immediate panic. In fact, there was no panic at all. At this point, she was in terminal care. So much had happened over the last short period—midnight ambulance rides and helicopter medevacs—that we were happy to have her go, for her own sake. She had no reason to be alive.

Of course, at the forefront of my mind was the suspicion that this was another Mother ruse. There was enough history to consider she might be doing this just for attention.

Emphysema is not a disease you can see. It's a horrific, suffocating way to die, drowning in your own fluids like being endlessly waterboarded. But you can't tell how bad just by looking at a person. Mother wasn't a waifish cancer patient with her eyes bulging out. Not cirrhosis-yellow or covered in the sores of an AIDS patient. So although diagnosed terminal, and no doubt withered, there was no way of knowing how much she's embellishing for effect. Mother wasn't above using her own impending death as currency for patronage. I had lost all tolerance for her scheming years ago and now it wasn't necessary. She was dying and I would be there for her in whatever way she allowed me. I left my girlfriend Bingo at the house to make a short recon drive to Mother's place.

You could almost hear gothic church bells toll as you opened the door to her tiny apartment and into the rubble. Morticia had a way of making things overly dramatic and hokey, probably in her own self-interest. Mother was in bed. Inside her 300 square feet of filth, cat shit, and clutter she was now piled with an ER unit's worth of medical equipment. Morticia was playing her role of Sister Helen Prejean, head tilted in earnest sincerity. Mother was sat up, leaning forward as if to vomit up an alien, eyes closed but very alert.

"I can't fucking take this anymore." Even with the raspy smoker's death voice, she could affect the tone of a crying child. "I'm sorry."

There's nothing to be sorry about, Ma. You've taken this for more years than I ever would. And it's all your fault.

Morticia left and Mother and I fell into a calm calculated discussion of what happens next. Even though we were alone, for legal reasons we still spoke in silly, roundabout hypotheticals like one of us might be wearing a wire. "Well, if someone were going to end their own life in a situation like this, they would probably want . . . " She knew that I couldn't "know," much less "assist."

She'd spoken to a doctor that she trusted. Establishing that mother was under hospice care, the doctor intimated that hospice was essentially a suicide machine and that if she were in that much pain, hospice wouldn't assist but she would have adequate medication to make the decision herself. It was offered up that thirty morphine tablets of her dosage would be more than sufficient. She had nearly ninety. Should she decide to do this, she wouldn't have to go out like Kurt Cobain, not that you'd notice the mess.

I called her caregivers to make arrangements for transporting Mother and her machines over to my house. Hospice had agreed to deliver a hospital bed that we could put in my living room. Mother was a hoarder, and since she'd become unable to clean up after herself, her apartment was vulgar. I'd long since given up on trying to convince her not to live like that, but I certainly wasn't going to see her die in that.

I went home and told Bingo that Mother was on her way and that, indeed, this seemed to be the end of the line. We looked at each other comically and shrugged in the way Butch and Sundance did before they jumped off the cliff. How it goes from here, who fucking knows? If you ask me to plan a wedding, I would at least know the basics of hiring caterers and renting a hall. Regardless of how okay we are with the concepts of death and suicide, I didn't know even the first steps of how to prepare. So we talked about hiring a birthday clown just for the pure satisfaction of watching him flounder. They don't have any birthday clowns in Bisbee, AZ. Too bad. That was my only idea on short notice.

Mother's clunky white linen hospital apparatus looked completely out of context with the carnival colors of the interior of our house. We dolled it up with multicolored, polka dot throw blankets. Festive. She was wheeled as far as she could be and the few steps to her bed took an eternity. There she began to build her nest. A tray next to her bed was quickly filled with different pill bottles, a travel mug, kleenex, and, of course, her cigarettes and ashtray for when she'd occasionally turn off her oxygen and smoke. I mentioned—not as a joke—that at least she may as well go ahead and start drinking again. You can't take those AA chips with you.

"Two and a half years of sobriety down the drain? Fuck it!" It was the first time she smiled since she'd made her decision. I went to the liquor store and bought mini-bottles of Ketel One and Kahlua—she was always a Black Russian drinker—to leave on her stand with her pills. I had plenty of large bottles. This was just symbolic and it brightened up her nightstand.

I'd called my friend Betty—once lovingly and accurately described as the Edith Bunker of Bisbee—to hire her as a nurse for Mother. I can co-host your launch into eternity without a blink, but no way I can deal with piss bags and shitting in bedpans. Mother's run-on sentences and complaining are hard enough but the idea of holding up her deflated ass-cheek while she forces out a mushy yogurt turd . . . no.

Betty was more than willing, almost like she was happy we thought of her for the opportunity. She lived just two blocks away so she could be on call. She didn't even want to get paid. We helped her with her long-shot, failed run for Mayor of Bisbee, but that held no candle to dealing with Mother, and there was no way I wasn't going to pay someone for a job that miserable.

Mother didn't take to Betty, sniping and snapping at her both behind her back and straight to her face. Fucking ruthless. This sweet lady who kindly agreed to wipe Mother's ass and change her Foley bag as a favor for a friend was now getting berated at every gentle turn. It was embarrassing and entirely consistent with the woman that I'd now realized her to have been for the last several years of her life. No point in reprimanding her now.

I don't know if I apologized to Betty verbally at the time but I know I must have done it with my eyes. To her immense credit, Betty never missed a beat, was never flustered or frustrated by the verbal abuse, like a veterinarian with a snarling puppy, taking no offense where I would have wanted to say, "Go fuck yourself," and hosed her down in the driveway like a messy baby.

Mother, of course, arrived with cats. There were only two left at this point, down from many. Georgia was a decrepit seventeen-year-old, half-blind, matted with nicotine and her own filth, stinky dreadlocks hanging from her belly like stalactites. The other cat was a new arrival, a stray that wasn't so much rescued as ensnared, dragnet-style, and incarcerated. There's no such thing as a free lunch, kitty. My house was more minimum security compared to the SuperMax of Mother's apartment. The new cat lasted one night at my house before beating feet at the first opportunity of an open door and heading for the Mexican border. Mother was in no place to be accounting for cats much less petting them. Thinking they were there was good enough for her.

What Mother was more concerned with was all of her shit back in her apartment. And it was all shit. She was a hoarder before there was a word for it. Once, it had been at least somewhat clean and organized, if only by her own sense of organization, but as her health deteriorated, it had become squalid. It crawled with spiders and houseflies, the floor littered with plates of cat food, her own food rotting in the refrigerator. Now she was at my place and she was terrified that I was going to go back there and raze the joint.

She'd implore Bingo not to allow me to touch her things. "He's just gonna want to throw stuff away and you can't let him," and then she'd identify different items that had to be kept.

"A lot of that shit is worth a lot of money."

No, Ma. Just because you spent a lot of money on it doesn't mean it's worth anything. And you can't hoard from the grave.

As soon as she was settled in, I set down terms. If you are indeed going to kill yourself, you can't do it on Sunday or Monday because that's football. I was not kidding. If you have the freedom to decide when you are going to die, it would be downright rude to knowingly do it while your host has other events planned. And no loud parties.

I turned on whatever shitty television she wanted to watch and tried to go about my day like nothing was different. I'm not much of a collector but the one I do have is a full wall of stolen clocks. One from the Man Show production office, one from the Girls Gone Wild tour bus, the Hammersmith Apollo backstage clock, and so on.

And they were all on the wall behind the television facing Mother. It never occurred to me what subtle implications that could have had until years later.

All day Friday Mother drifted in and out of sleep, waking up to have me refill her 32-ounce travel mug with diet soda, eating very little if at all. Soft things like cottage cheese or yogurt. She was down to 79 pounds. She'd lived with back pain for years and complained about it in every lucid moment. She complained about her now-hardened breast implants, which on someone of that weight were like bowling balls on a skeleton. She'd had at least three sets in her life and now hugging her was like hugging your grandpa with a boner in his sweatpants. It was obvious from her short, gurgling breaths that her body was struggling to continue. She was sixty-three years old and she was a fucking mess.

That being said, when Saturday morning came around and there'd been no more intimation of suicide, we started to think we'd just wait the whole thing out. Obviously I couldn't send her back to that toxic studio apartment, and in the unlikely event that she did last more than two weeks, that would be great to fuck with my manager, Brian Hennigan. He'd be coming to stay in two weeks, and he doesn't have the spine for this kinda shit.

Saturday afternoon, Tamar Halpern showed up at the house. Tamar had directed Mother in a few independent films back in Los Angeles and happened to be in Tucson. (You'll know more about all these people and places later. For now, shush up. Mother's dying.) Tamar had called Mother to say she'd planned to drive down to visit. She had no idea the condition Mother was in and I felt bad for her. Hey, I'm going to pop in for coffee and next thing you know you're visiting someone on their deathbed. Still, Mother was thrilled to see her. Tamar was one of the only guests Mother ever had in the three years she'd been in Bisbee, and their reminiscing definitely perked Mother up. It wasn't long before Mother launched into her customary, over-the-top aggressive bids of hospitality, pushing Tamar to stay the night.

"C'mon, it'll be like a sleepover. It'll be fun." Yes, Ma. It'd be a fucking blast. Bingo and I wing-manned it so Tamar didn't get cornered and detained like Mother's cats. We had some cocktails during Mother's unconscious periods and later all four of us watched *Bad Santa*, a favorite movie of Mother's and mine, together. Movies were a great way of avoiding talking, or more often, of listening to Mother. When it was over, Mother was out cold and Tamar snuck out. When Mother woke up, she asked where Tamar had gone as though she'd expected her to be there in her footie-pajamas for the big sleepover. I told her she'd left but sent her love. Mother shrugged it off and went back to sleep.

By now Bingo and I were mentally exhausted from three days of spinning plates with caretakers, Betty, hospice, Tamar, and, of course, Mother. Bingo and I split a bar of Xanax, twice what we'd normally take to sleep. Bingo laid down on the couch in the living room with Mother while I went into my office to catch up on whatever emails or Myspace or whatever the fuck was taking care of business back then.

Somewhere around 10:30 that night, Mother yelled for me with a weak scream: "Doug!" with the same demanding tone she'd had since moving from LA. I gave an abrupt "What?" She doesn't hear me and calls again, "DOUG!"

I went to the living room, irritated: "WHAT?!"

She was lying on her side, facing away from me.

"It's time for my pills and my drink!"

Hey, how about you don't say it like an asshole? I grabbed the diet soda and her travel mug.

"No," she said, still turned away from me. "My OTHER drink and pills."

It took a few seconds to sink in what she meant and I felt like a dick for being short with her.

Not knowing exactly what to say, I simply asked her if she was sure.

"Yes," she said, scrambling for breath.

I shook Bingo awake. "It's time."

"Time for what?"

"It's TIME."

"Oh, shit."

I started to move in three different directions, like a fireman looking for a pole that isn't there. Next I did the first thing anyone should do in this situation.

Cocktails!

Mother was always a Black Russian drinker in her early days before AA, but tonight she asked me to make them White Russians— her thinking being that the milk would coat her stomach for the pills. Amazing she didn't want to take them with chicken soup. I poured cocktails for the three of us while she took her arranged medication. We talked for a while to make sure she knew what she was doing. I didn't want this to be an impulse-buy panic decision. She was keen on pulling the "I don't want to be a burden" card—which, indeed, she'd proven to be in her later life but not because she was dying. She was just a general pain in the ass. I knew that wasn't what she was referring to. I also had to make a conscious effort to not talk to her in coddling tones, as one tends to do when talking to someone this frail. You're an adult, Ma. In fact, you are still my mother, making you the authority figure here. So if you say you're ready, I'm not gonna argue. I'm just gonna look the other way. Hypothetically.

With all the theoretical qualifiers and caveats out of the way, it was indeed "time."

Mother took what for her would constitute a deep breath and began swallowing morphine. I want to say she took them with her cocktails, but seeing as she ended up taking all of it, I think that much booze would have killed her before the morphine had a chance. Regardless, it was a long process taking that many pills, and we were cocktailing the entire time. She became more relaxed as it went on and eventually we were having what someone might call "fun." Betty stopped by to check on things, decided it looked like it was a time for family, and left, saying she'd come back later.

I called my brother Jeff and told him what was up. He was aware that this day was coming. Many years prior my brother and I had made a gentlemen's agreement that when the time came when our parents were in their last days, that he'd be responsible for Dad and I'd take Mother. Jeff lived near Dad and I got along better with Mother, far better than he did. I always had. And even though Dad was eighteen years older, factoring in their lifestyles, it was pretty even odds on who would go first.

Shortly after we'd made that arrangement, Dad was diagnosed with colon cancer. It went through him pretty quick—he wasn't a fighter and was pretty content in that he'd lived a full life. But while he was going through surgeries my brother would torture me with phone calls.

(Whispering from the hospital room) "Guess what I'm doing? I just had to wipe off Dad's ass after he shit himself!"

"Stop calling this number!" Click!

Ring!

"I just had to pick up Dad's dick and put it in a bedpan."

"Okay! You get the house! Leave me alone!"

Now I was calling him to let him chat with Mother while she was dozing off into the dirt. Enjoy that for awkward. As with me, she kept looking for validation that she hadn't been a bad mother. He lied and assured her she'd been a fine mother. I went the other way. A bad mother, you ask? Hell yes, you were a bad mother! How else would you raise a child to one day tend bar while you were about to croak! Another round? Me too!

No doubt she'd groomed me with this sense of humor from the beginning. Her Friars Club send-off was just the culmination.

Once she'd finished the unpleasant project of getting all of her pills down her tentative throat, there was nothing left to do but wait and make jokes. She remained lucid for quite a while, ordering more White Russians like it was a Christmas party. I'd bring her drink back, lean in, and fuck with her.

"Hey, Ma! Wait! They found a cure!" and she'd laugh like someone coming out of a nitrous oxide haze, lifting her middle finger towards me.

"Ma, when you go through that white light—see if there's any way you can make the Saints cover 8 points at Oakland tomorrow. That'll be our sign of the afterlife."

She'd occasionally have us crank down her oxygen so she could have a cigarette. Bingo and I had quit for ten months at that point but had schemed since Mother got here to share one last cigarette with her. Considering the prevailing circumstances, it couldn't really count against us. We'd even bummed non-menthols from someone in anticipation. There is no better cigarette than the one you break down and smoke after a long period of abstinence, and this situation removed any guilt from it.

Now that we were all in our pints and in this situation together, we were doing whatever we could to make this fun and funny and comfortable for her. When I was a little kid, she'd always make me rub her feet. I bet she could remember the exact day when I decided it was gross and stopped doing it. But these were extenuating circumstances so Bingo and I each took a foot and massaged it. We went through the litany of old fun stories, the same ones that she'd been repeating since they happened to us as kids, only now I had to act like they were brand new and still hilarious. It was like pretending to be on ecstasy without the wanting-to-fuck-her part.

Mother was always funny on some level. Her Achilles heel was that any time she got a big laugh, she'd always repeat the punch line ad nauseam until it wasn't funny anymore. As she drank what was sure to be her last one, I said, "Wow, Ma, you're really hammering down those cocktails!"

And Mother, barely alert but perfectly intoned in a campy British accent, said, "There's times to be dainty and there's time to be a pig!"

Bingo and I fell out laughing. I could see Mother trying her best to follow it up and ruin it. I stopped her before she could.

"No! Don't say anything else! Those are perfect last words!"

And they were.

Mother lay there in a smiling half coma while Bingo and I put on music. We cried a bit and sang louder than Mother probably would have liked but she was in no state to complain.

I have no idea how long this went on. When my father was dying at my brother's house, I remember putting a mirror under his nose to see if he was in fact still breathing, and I'm pretty sure we did that with Mother as well. At some point, thankfully, Betty came back over, joining what seemed to be a party in progress and confirmed that she was still breathing. Betty was unaware of what was happening exactly, but she knew me well enough that seeing us in full swing with my dying mother wasn't curious at all.

I guess I'd expected that this whole thing would take thirty minutes—this based on absolutely no factual information whatsoever. Now it's been hours and Bingo and I are fighting lots of cocktails and a double-dose of Xanax to keep our eyes open. Finally, after Mother has been unresponsive for far too long, we collapsed on the couch next to her. She drank me under the table to the end.

I woke up and there were people in the house. As a drunk, I'm used to the first several moments of waking up being a cavalcade of confused memories trying to shape themselves like a game of Tetris. It was 6:30 or so and Betty was there, engaged in some sort of activity. There were two men there who at first I thought were paramedics but turned out to be from the mortuary. Waking up in a Xanax-and-vodka haze after just a few hours sleep, my mind was racing to work out the details of exactly what was going on.

I got up to see Mother laying on her back with her mouth gaping open, just like Dad's had been. When I touched her face, cold saliva that had puddled in her mouth spilled over my fingers.

Betty had shown up after we'd fallen down, stayed while we slept, and made the appropriate phone calls when Mother no longer showed vital signs. She told us later that when the mortuary people showed up, they came through the back door and first spotted Bingo, sprawled out across the sofa, and assumed she was the corpse. As they went to move her, Betty stepped in and pointed them the six feet away to the obvious hospital bed with the old dead lady in it. She said they were mortified at their own gaffe. We still think it's hilarious.

I don't remember anything after this. I know the Saints not only covered the 8 points, they won the game, 34–3, confirming that

Mother was in a better place now. And by that I mean that she wasn't all dead and drooling in a hospital bed in my living room while I was trying to watch football.

This is a love story.

2

Not Your
Average Mother

THE MAJORITY OF MY EARLIEST MEMORIES ARE BLURRED OR DELETED
but there's no forgetting the image of your mother jerking off the
family dog. It wasn't even really the family dog. It was a step-dog,
and we didn't like it. I was around twelve years old, standing at
the top of the stairs at our new house in Paxton, Massachusetts,
watching Mother lean down and go from a friendly belly-scratch to
a two-fingered tug job that neither me or the dog was expecting. She
justified it by simply saying, "Well, they like it."

I'm sure I found it awkwardly amusing because I was twelve
and dog dicks are funny. Touching a dog's dick is gross, and your
mother touching a dog's dick is far grosser and gross equals hilarious. I don't remember the dog needing any counseling afterwards. I
assume that's why you never see PETA protesting a Tijuana donkey
show. So long as the donkey is pitching and not catching, it's hard
to cry abuse. The dog belonged to my stepfather du jour, John Kirk,
from whom my mother Bonnie took her name. My brother Jeff and I
called her Ma but would eventually refer to her as Mother, usually in
the same grim tone that Seinfeld called Newman. Or sometimes as
"MOTHER!!!" when the situation warranted, like when she's jerking off the cat in front of your friends and you're no longer twelve,
you're a full-blown adult and your friend is comedian Ralphie May.

13

Or when she's telling your girlfriend's parent's—unsolicited—about jerking off her cats. You know. Situations like that.

"What??? They like it!" she'd still say.

It's tough to pinpoint exactly when Mother started going weird. We grew up in a house on 20 Rich St in Worcester, Mass in a middle-class neighborhood with a side yard big enough to play kickball in. Over the blueberry bushes is an automatic home run. That's how I've glossed up the memory. Mother was evidently quite the drunk until she divorced my father when I was six or seven, but I have no memory of her being sloppy or out of hand. I heard the story early on that after my birth, a neighbor up the street, Rita Herbst, congratulated my mother and asked about me, the new baby. My mother told her that I was the ugliest baby she'd ever seen. The neighbor tried to laugh it off. Mother insisted that she was serious. "No, Rita, he's really fucking ugly! He's got this blotchy skin and weird shocks of hair that go in every direction!" Having a lifetime with her to judge by, I can fairly accurately chalk this up to Mother's insuppressible honesty, not any kind of drunkenness. I laughed when I heard it and I laugh about it now, remembering her telling it. To this day, I've never heard a mother saying—demanding even—that her newborn was frighteningly ugly.

I do remember Jeff and I making lots of plans and preparations to run away from home, including tents, survival gear, and a collapsible fire ladder to escape from our second-story bedroom, so it couldn't have all been summer days and lemonade. But that may have been just as much about us being shitty kids as from any lack of parenting. I had the proclivity to be an unruly little prick from the beginning. Strange early memories of taking a turd out of the toilet and putting it under my dad's pillow and then blaming it on Jeff, two years older and not nearly as adorable a liar. Another memory of putting one of my mother's sewing needles upright in the fabric right where she sat on the couch, and pleading my innocence when she impaled herself upon it. I swore I had no idea how that happened. I couldn't have been older than four or five. That's not a product of an alcoholic household. That's just straight-up fucking evil.

I was clever as well. I remember crawling into their bed on a Saturday morning during cartoons to ask for money to go to the store to get cereal. Junk cereal is what I wanted, of course, and to upend me they said that I had to read the ingredients, and that sugar could not be one of the first two. I came back with whatever Count Chocula or Peanut Butter Cap'n Crunch I'd wanted, and then feigned ignorance to the fact that not only was corn syrup actually sugar, but that it was not two separate ingredients, corn and syrup. Plausible deniability. I should have been a fucking lawyer.

More remarkable here is the fact that, in 1972, there was absolutely nothing odd about a five-year-old child hoofing it down to the supermarket all by himself to buy his own groceries. The idea of that, with the added image of the kid reading the side of the box for nutritional information, slays me. It's weird that I picture the five-year-old me wearing reading glasses at the end of my nose in that image.

Mother divorced my father right around the time she quit drinking and joined AA. He always said that the only reason she wanted a divorce was because it had become a fashionable thing to do, and she would later confirm this. My dad, Russell Stanhope, was Mother's high school biology teacher and married her when he was thirty-six and she was eighteen, or so went the story. Digging through old letters for this book, I now know that they were already a couple when he was thirty-five and she was seventeen, and still his student. Today, this would make him a sex offender and a felon. That may have clouded my perception that, in reality, he was the kindest, most gentle person I have ever known. If you look through your own family tree, you won't have to go far back to find what we call pedophiles now. Your great-grandfather that came home from the war at twenty-two and married your fourteen-year-old great-grandmother. Today that war hero would have his head stoved in on the prison yard. Be careful of how you react to buzzwords. If I were now to be informed that a sex offender were moving into my neighborhood, part of me would think of my father and consider that he or she would be a fantastic role model. My father was anything but a predator. He was like a more lighthearted, less involved version of Richie

Cunningham's dad in "Happy Days." I wouldn't be surprised if my brother and I represented the only two times he'd gotten laid in his life.

———

INITIALLY WE STAYED WITH DAD AFTER THE DIVORCE, A TASK HE WASN'T very well-suited to handle. As much of a rotten kid as I was, at least Mother had some sense of discipline. She could be scary as fuck. One winter she took our two huge toy chests and threw them out of our second-story bedroom window because we didn't clean our room. Jeff and I were always drawn to pyromania and I remember my brother nearly burning down the garage (with me stuck in back of it) while setting dead leaves on fire. Mother took him inside, lit a match, blew it out, and pressed it to his fingertip while it was still hot. She wanted him to know what fire felt like. It sounds cruel but you could argue her point. It certainly didn't kill our love of setting shit on fire, but it did instill the fact that we should never get caught by Mother.

Dad was a complete soft touch. He was too aloof to catch you doing anything even right under his nose, and if he did catch you, he was all Mr. Rogers. "C'mon now, guy," was his disciplinary catchphrase.

"C'mon now guy. You know better than to stand on the roof hitting Whiffle balls full of lighter fluid and burning toilet paper into the street with a bat."

"Sorry, Dad."

And that would be it.

Jeff and I ran amok. Dad had moved into the parsonage of the church—a house set aside for the minister—that had been unoccupied and, for the most part, we stayed with him. Now, not only were we unsupervised most of the time, we also had free run of an entire usually-empty church to use as a playground. While I know they had joint custody, I don't remember much custody at all. The parsonage and 20 Rich were walking distance, and it seemed like we drifted at will between the two. We were monsters. I wasn't big enough to be a bully but I did what a lot of weak kids did. I found someone weaker and paid it downward. On our tiny street that kid was John Schafer. John was two years younger than me and dumb as an onion. We'd send him to people's doors in the neighborhood, saying that if he rang the doorbell and sang a song, they'd give him a bag of candy. Time and again, he'd belt out "Twinkle Twinkle" and then stand there in painful silence, only to have the door eventually closed in his face. We'd get him to blow us behind the garage. We didn't even know what it meant exactly. He'd just blow on our dicks and then we'd make fun of him for doing it. Mother came home to us once with John Schafer on a stool in a noose with the rope swung over a branch. She had to have known that there were discipline issues.

———————

MAURA WAS MY FIRST LITTLE GIRLFRIEND AND LIVED JUST UP THE STREET from Dad's new digs at the church. There was a small field—giant in my eyes back then—behind the parsonage that we were cutting through when Maura stopped and told me to kiss her. I did so but no differently than you would your grandpa. "No. Kiss me like Captain Kirk." And then she taught me how to French kiss. So I kissed her like I would my grandpa, only now with my tongue sticking out.

I don't know why I was hyper-sexual so young. No, I wasn't molested, and I'm pretty sure Maura wasn't either. But we knew what fucking was and we knew we weren't supposed to do it but we tried to all the time in that church. It didn't feel like anything. Nine years old is way before load-blowing years. It just felt like great mischief, like whipping snowballs at cars. It was a fun summer. I don't know how nine-year-olds break up, but I know that Maura wasn't my girlfriend anymore after we moved to Paxton. She would still call me occasionally and I remember her telling me that she had a new boyfriend named Bart and his dick was "waaay bigger" than mine. I remembered Bart because the teachers all called him by his full name, Bartholomew. I was jealous that nobody teased him about that stupid name since he was athletic and good-looking. And now I knew he had a bigger dick and that's not something you should be depressed about as a ten-year-old.

Years later, when I finally played in my hometown of Worcester at the sadly legendary Aku Aku Chinese Restaurant and Comedy Club, a girl named Susan Joy approached me at the bar and asked if I remembered her. She was someone we knew from Dad's church and I had a vague recollection of her.

"Guess who I'm here with? Do you remember Maura?"

No fucking way! I couldn't believe it and would have bet that all those memories had been white-washed from her brain, but I'd have been wrong.

Within the first three sentences of talking to Maura, she said, "Do you remember we fucked when we were little kids???"

"Yes! Yes I do! I can't believe you remember! I got you to put your mouth on my dick and then peed! You started screaming at me and chasing me, so I ran out to where my Dad was so you couldn't say anything!"

Oh, happy days!

We laughed and talked for a little while, short recaps of what we had done with our lives. When she mentioned she was married now, I immediately assumed her husband was somewhere at the venue and told her to grab him and I'd buy us drinks.

"Oh, he's not at this show. Are you kidding? He's mad that I'm even here. He's afraid we have 'unfinished business.'"

Seriously? Your husband is jealous? We were nine god-damned years old! And now we're pushing forty and he's at home, pissed off? "Mr Big Shot comedian coming back home to take what's his!" I've been the insecure boyfriend before, pacing, staring at the clock, and every time my girl doesn't answer the phone I'm picturing her fucking some other guy. But that was as an adult. With an adult girl-friend. If you picture two nine-year-olds fucking, and the first emotion that springs up is jealousy, something is very wrong with you.

God help him if he ever finds out about Bart and his huge ten-year-old dick.

I HAVE NO IDEA WHAT I WOULD SAY AS A PARENT IF I FOUND OUT my kid was trying to have sex at nine years old. I know I would probably laugh. At least he's not trying to burn down the house. That's pretty much how Mother handled things. She could be vicious if it was warranted, but if it was funny, right or wrong, she'd fucking laugh. That was always paramount with Mother, no matter how fucked up other things might be. Humor was right there with it. Comedy albums—Bill Cosby and Bob Newhart—played quite a bit. I remember being tiny and repeating Cosby's "Little Tiny Hairs" routine to my father while he was shaving. I could do a mean Edith Bunker impression as a kid. Carol Burnett was a staple on Saturday nights though I notoriously always fell asleep before it started. Farts and belches were applauded. Just stop setting shit on fire.

Well that wasn't about to happen. Burning shit and smashing beer bottles were endless free fun for kids who couldn't afford a Big Wheel. But like they say, it's all fun and games until your brother Jeff burns his face off with gasoline.

Dad was in charge of us over at 20 Rich when we decided to take a GI Joe on his final mission. Across the street was a vacant wooded lot where we could burn shit with nobody seeing. Jeff filled a paper cup with gasoline from the can used to fill the lawnmower. GI Joe was outgunned. Before they could even drape a flag over GI Joe's molten coffin, Jeff thought to throw a lit match into the cup of gas, which then created a tower of flame far larger than expected. Jeff panicked and stomped on the whole thing to put it out, triggering an enormous fireball engulfing him in burning gasoline until he doused himself out in the dirt.

"Don't tell Dad! Don't tell Dad!" was all he could say. I told him I was going to go get cold water—at this point like getting JFK a Tylenol for his exit wound—and I ran and told Dad.

It was bad. Jeff was hospitalized for eight days with second- and third-degree burns, and spent weeks after having to smear silvadene, a silver-colored topical ointment that helps heal burns and also makes you look like a hideous freak on a schoolyard where you are already unpopular, on his face. He still doesn't like to talk about it and he'll be pissed that it's in the book.

Mother went apeshit with the GI Joe incident. She was furious with my father for not being there, even though he was 50 yards away on a sunny afternoon. He couldn't have stopped it without having us tethered to leashes. She wasn't there either and I'm sure she was directing most of her anger at herself towards my dad.

She'd made their divorce far uglier than it needed to be. There was no way to be mad at my father. He was always agreeable and non-confrontational, almost to a fault. If the blueberries came in well, it was a good summer. He liked bird-watching and kept interesting insects on a pin board. He'd press leaves in wax paper and label them. He taught at Nature Training School where we went to summer camp. My father's primary state was contentedness. He wasn't cold and unemotional. He was warm and unemotional. His relationships were partnerships based on achieving shared harmony. Passion was alien and uncomfortable. Mother would convince me that he just swallowed his true feelings, that he was unhealthy emotionally. It was far too long before I realized that she was just being an asshole who couldn't accept that someone was actually at ease with themselves.

We wouldn't be with Dad much longer. Mother had met John Kirk in AA, and now we'd be moving to Paxton. It was only about 5 miles north of Worcester but it was going to be a completely different and painfully shitty existence for the next three years. John Kirk was a fat ogre of a man who looked like a clammy Donald Pleasence. He played the "when I marry your mother, I'm buying the whole package" card with such thin sincerity that he may well have been beating us while he was saying it. He worked for John Hancock Insurance and brought all the joy and humor of risk assessment and comprehensive liability into the home. He was an ugly dullard and, thankfully, is now dead. Jeff and I weren't thrilled with the move.

3

Paxton: Square Peg in a Sphincter-Shaped Hole

JOHN HAD BOUGHT AN EERIE HOUSE RIGHT IN THE TOWN SQUARE on the common. Paxton is a very wealthy town of about four thousand high-dollar assholes, and our monstrosity was right in the center. The ugliest house in the most visible spot. I'm always grateful to have herpes on my dick rather than on my lip. Pants cover up your dick. This fever blister was weeping square in the middle of Paxton's cherubic face. The house was big but it was a peeled-paint ghastly eyesore, a fixer-upper that never got fixed up. They'd stripped the wallpaper off when we first moved in and never got around to putting anything up in its place, leaving walls of awful horsehair plaster with antiquated fire-hazard electrical fittings. John Kirk was clearly living beyond his means. In Worcester, we'd always referred to the poor kids as "skids," and now we were them. My brother and I wore Star Wars t-shirts and Toughskin jeans or thrift store double knit pants while all the Paxton kids wore Izod polos and Levi's corduroys. For leisure, those kids would go on ski trips or attend tennis camp instead of smashing bottles and burning action figures. We were metaphoric turds in a punch bowl. If I'd been given the chance of literally shitting in their punch bowl, it wouldn't have been a metaphor.

MOTHER WAS CONSUMED IN AA AND WE SPENT MANY A WEEKEND night sitting in the back of the room doing homework. They'd tried giving us the responsibility of staying home by ourselves, but I ruined that in no time by daring my brother to dare me to ride my bicycle naked around Paxton Common. Just my terry cloth bathrobe blowing in the wind behind me, little beans and weenie afloat as I stood up and peddled around the town square. A cop knocked at the door shortly afterwards. Whoever called neglected to mention that it was a little kid. The cop thought it was some grown man exposing himself to traffic. Having no parents at home, I was told that I had to tell my parents what I'd done and that he'd be coming back to make sure. I can't remember if he did return or if I just ratted myself out. Either way, it would be one of countless antics that my Mother would have to act angry about but eventually had to shake her head and laugh at the absurdity. She tried to explain to me: "Some things are funny to talk about doing but you don't actually do them." What fun is it to just "say" I rode my bike through the town square naked? I get your point, Ma. But sometimes it's only funny if you actually do it. Either way, we were screwed now and spending Friday nights sitting in smoky AA meetings.

AA wasn't all bad. You had to stand up, hold hands, and say the Lord's Prayer and the Serenity Prayer but other than that, it wasn't like church at all. People came from every kind of fucked-up background and they'd all take turns telling these amazing stories. Puking and fighting and jail and waking up in weird places. Amazing stories, and the unbelievable part was that they all laughed at them! It was rarely sad unless it had just happened. Once the bail was posted and the wound had turned into scar tissue, it was all show-and-tell. They'd always wrap it up as some cautionary tale, with AA being the hero at the end, but for the most part they sounded like they were bragging, and the laughs and nods of recognition fueled them. Some members even seemed to be a draw. Sometimes Mother would give us a heads-up on the way to a meeting. "John the Indian is going to speak tonight. He's really good. You're gonna love him." It was like AA had headliners. Someone once said that the only difference between sitting at a bar and sitting in an AA meeting is that in the bar you get the stories as they happen rather than after the fact. I was too young to get the bar experience yet, but the meetings were enough to keep me enraptured.

Our world was full of these people now. They were all bruised to some extent but they flaunted their scars. They swore and they smoked and told you about real shit. Half of 'em were probably full of shit but that didn't matter at the time. They were exciting. Our house would fill up with them on holidays in place of relatives and Mother would always laugh about our "one big, fucked-up family!"

Of course, hearing everyone else's confessional AA stories meant you'd eventually have to hear Mother's, and although they might pale in comparison to prison stints or violent altercations, they still came from your mother. And she had a few. She'd been a bartender in her drinking days at the William Paul House, an upscale restaurant in nearby Holden, Mass. She told a story about getting drunk after work and fucking one of the cooks in her car. She said his dick was so small that she didn't realize until she got home that she'd had a tampon in the whole time. I guess I should have been creeped out by this or at least upset that she'd been cheating on my Dad at the time, but I just remember laughing along with everybody else.

Mother loved getting the laughs, especially from me. Looking back at that period of time, I see how much it meant to her for me to think she was funny, to think that she was cool. I'm sure the stigma of the label "alcoholic" meant the same thing as "bad parent" in her head. If she could win me over with tales of banging thimble-dick line cooks in the front seat of her Vega wagon, she was happy to work blue.

Some nights it would just be the three of us, me, her, and my brother, sitting at the dining room table in this creaking old dark house trying to entertain each other. We'd play Boggle or Yahtzee and it was open season to hurl abuse and obscenities at each other. It was fun to be allowed to call your mother a "fuck-nut" without repercussions. She called me "chicken-shit," and she called Jeff "chicken-shit's older brother." We started watching *Monty Python's Flying Circus* on PBS, mostly because we heard there were boobs on it, but eventually the comedy stuck and all three of us had memorized bits and would repeat them in terrible British accents. She'd take us to movies like *Network* and *Kentucky Fried Movie*, the R-rating and adult content never a concern. My humor graduated from *Crack'd* and *Mad* magazine to *National Lampoon* and *Hustler*. Mother usually had *Hustler* magazine, which she didn't bother trying to hide under the bed. I couldn't wait to read the "Bits & Pieces" section for the "Most Tasteless Cartoon of the Month." My favorite showed a graphically drawn dead dog in the street with a kid talking to a cop. "That can't be my dog, officer," says the kid. "Sparky doesn't have guts coming out of his mouth." I had a Larry Flynt sense of humor in a *Better Homes & Gardens* community and it would manifest itself at my peril as I was about to bring it to school.

I LOOK BACK AT THE THREE YEARS I WENT TO PAXTON CENTER School with a fear like Oliver Twist in the workhouse. Teachers treated me as if I were a special needs student. Students treated me like I had shit in my pants on purpose. I don't know if I acted like a mental patient because they treated me like one or vice versa, but I fell balls-deep into my role. I remember stacking my textbooks on the desk and slamming my forehead down on them as hard as was possible as a regular gag only because it didn't hurt. I thought it was a nifty trick. Yes, I just said "nifty." Maybe I have CTE. I was sent to the principal once for farting. "Douglas was passing wind in class," was all the note said, and there wasn't really anything the principal could say. It is, of course, a natural function and I couldn't be punished any more for that than I could be for having to take a leak. The note didn't explain that I was purposely waiting for any silent moments before pulling up off the seat just enough to get maximum torque and bounce for volume, repeatedly throughout the class. Regardless, it was the first time I'd heard the expression "passing wind," and that was probably all I learned in school that day.

The only teacher I remember ever "getting" me was a French teacher named Gertrude Healy, who was a lot more tolerant of my monkey business. I remember delivering some well-timed heckle that actually landed, and after the laughs Mrs. Healy said, "I can see you some day, Douglas, writing for Saturday Night Live." That was quite a compliment back then as it was still the late 70s, when SNL was funny. Mrs. Healy went on to flunk me for not one but two years in a row, but I'd never forget the one time some adult outside of Mother got the joke.

Most teachers generally found me more disturbing than simply disruptive. All of my outbursts derived from a wit too foul or dark. All of my doodles were sinister in theme. I'd trace my hand on paper like any kid does only I'd trace a few of my fingers at an angle on a different part of the page. Then I'd fill in the details of a very realistic, horrific drawing of a hand with severed digits laying in a pool of blood. I honestly thought people would see this as a very clever spin on an old staple.

A random piece of homework I found makes a good example. I assume it was one where you had to use a word in a sentence.

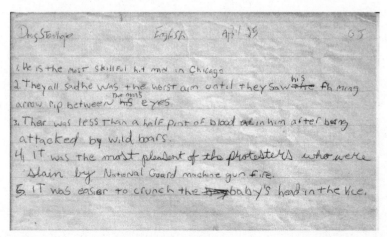

Even I was taken aback finding this gem but then some of it made sense. Dead baby jokes were all the rage in 1979! Didn't these people have their finger on the pulse? They did not. I'd seen Michael O'Donoghue on SNL doing his impression of talk show host Mike Douglas as if he had stainless steel needles plunged into his eyes. The gag lay mostly in the elaborate setup. The impression itself was nothing but a man shrieking and writhing in agony. It killed on SNL, and it killed me. It didn't kill when I repeated it in school. Instead, all my morbid shenanigans led the school to strongly recommend to my mother that I see the school psychologist. Mother wasn't pleased but she still tended to side with me for the most part because this was the same kinda shit we laughed about at the dinner table. Mother would never hesitate to lift a cheek off the seat at home and tear the air with a fart like a lawnmower starting. All of our humor was vulgar or absurd. It was encouraged. Mother would have looked at my drawing of a gruesome severed hand for what it was—very creative. Did they notice the details of the bone and the veins? That's a kid with some rudimentary understanding of the human body. And at such a young age! So Mother read the letter from school, shrunk against the wall, and put her hands up in the air in cartoonish, comical defeat, and said, "Douglas, we're trying to fit into a new town here and this is what you do???" I laughed at her laughing and she'd repeat that joke like a catchphrase for the rest of our time in Paxton.

The school shrink was a fucking idiot and talked to me like I was a retarded version of the *Exorcist* kid. I went through a battery of tests as part of my Chapter 766 psych evaluation, including lofty titles like "The Bender Visual Motor Gestalt" and Rorschach tests. I took none of the tests seriously and I'd undermine them all. I was asked to draw a picture of my family at home. I drew John Kirk fucking Mother doggie-style (something I'd actually walked in on once and still shudder to recall) while drawing Jeff killing a cat with a knife as I was hanging myself. Hilarious.

The assessments came back saying the tests "indicated Douglas to be experiencing some serious problems centering on issues of sexuality, violence, and death," which led to further evaluation, and that in those further evaluations there was "indication of serious problems as a reaction to severe environmental trauma" and "extreme sensitivity to his small size with part of the misbehavior at school as an attempt to compensate."

This made me irate because they were the ones that kept telling me I had an issue with my size. Like I was a dwarf or something. I was just smaller than the rest of the kids. I had no issue whatsoever with my size. If anything, I liked being small. It played right in with my puppy-dog eyes when I was trying to act innocent, which I did quite a bit. The more they suggested I had an issue with my size, the more it pissed me off, leading the assessment to conclude, "Much of Douglas's anger directed towards school personnel is misplaced."

AAAAAAAAAAAARRRRRRGH! My anger at you was placed with perfect pinpoint accuracy, you simpleton fucks! If you wrote, "He seems to think this shit is funny but I guess I just don't get it," you'd have a spot-on diagnosis. But you were prudish, uptight elitists trying to raise preppie snobs into captains of industry, and I had no interest in that world.

That funny business of fucking with my psychological screening only fast-tracked me to weekly sessions with a family counselor as well as extra scrutiny and weekly progress reports from all of my classes. A big target on my little tiny, itsy-bitsy back.

The counselor was back in Worcester, which was a pain in the ass drive and pissed my brother off because it fucked with his after-school drama class, one of a few safe havens he'd found from constantly being shit upon. But once we were there, we'd light up the room. It was our own theater. The counselor was an old, hunched ball of flesh named Ahron Ahronian. He was fidgety and easily spooked, with no sense of humor whatsoever. Jeff and I now did Mother the same way we did her loudly in the grocery store aisles: "Mother, are we going to have to have our beatings tonight?" Mother would bust up while the guy went spastic, slapping at his notepad. "Wait, what's this about 'beatings,' you say?" and Mother would have to try to explain that this was just our sense of humor, all the while Jeff and I sitting stone-faced. We'd make references to doing drugs or drinking alcohol, only to make Mother go back to square one with explana-tions. It was soon clear that this was achieving nothing but burned hours, and eventually this letter came in the mail from the Worcester Youth Guidance Center.

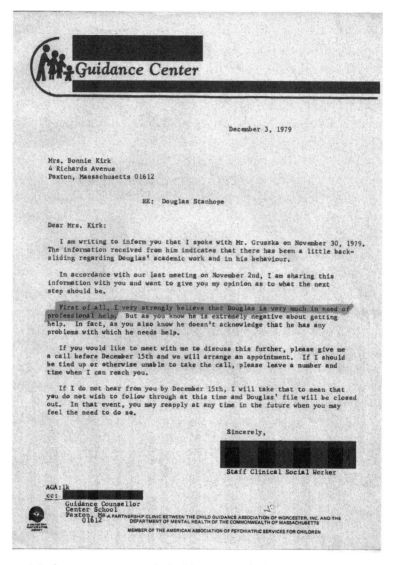

Mother never responded. Close your fucking file, dunce cap. Mother knew that it was all wasted time trying to explain that a twisted sense of funny wasn't a mental deficiency or desperate cry for help. The letter was disregarded completely until years later when I'd include it in my promotional package as an up-and-coming stand-up comedian with the sentence about being "strongly in need of professional help" highlighted.

Turns out that their initial concerns of me "centering on issues of sexuality, violence, and death" would turn out to be the cornerstones for a very successful comedy career. This is the first distinct memory of my mother ever having to firmly stand up for me. I'm sure she felt as much pressure or more in a town where she was boxing outside her weight, a newly sober woman in an affluent, pretentious hamlet. She could have easily caved and played their game. But Mother saw my humor and creativity. She celebrated it at home. I was fortunate enough to have a parent who could see that and allow me the freedom to follow my own path and be my own person, no matter how disturbing it might be to the powers that be. A lot of parents will argue for their kid to get starting positions in sports or demand higher grades. Not so many will defend you for having a morbid and profane sense of humor. Teachers—the vast majority—are there to train you to produce in the appropriate cubicle. They are not concerned with anything outside of that literal box. You can only wonder how many beautiful minds had their creativity, or even genius, stifled or beaten out of them by these glorified, middle-minded classroom babysitters of the public school system. If Benjamin Franklin were a student today, I bet they'd have him under a seventy-two-hour watch in a mental ward as a danger to himself or others. Who but a severely troubled youth would be so disturbed as to be flying a kite in a lightning storm?

At school, I still had to have weekly meetings with the guidance counselor Charles Gruszka to go over my progress reports from each class. He always creeped me out and it always felt demeaning. In a weekly progress update letter to my mother dated November 9, 1979, he writes, "I spoke to Douglas very severely in class because of disrespectful comments and drawings concerning me and Mr. Prince (gym teacher). Several references to homosexuality, mental illness, etc. Told him quite plainly it was unacceptable, I will not tolerate it, and if it happens again he will take his class separately at an after-school time. Wanted him to get the message, his behavior was totally unacceptable."

I don't know what the comments and drawings of Mr. Prince and Mr. Gruszka involved, but I notice that while he deemed them to be "unacceptable," he never said they were inaccurate.

My reports for the most part were good even when they shouldn't have been. I had an English teacher named Mrs. Davidson who also happened to be on my paper route so I knew where she lived. I should now apologize to the people that were on that route for the infrequency of the deliveries. Papers were dropped in a bundle in front of my house at about 5:30 in the morning, and if it were too cold or too snowy or if I was just too tired, I'd chuck the papers down the sewer, wait, and then call the dispatcher to say the papers never showed up before heading to school.

Mrs. Davidson was 60ish, bunch-bellied, and rat-eyed with a meanness that was almost certainly rooted in a palpable fear. I'm sure she was horrified just having me in her class, much less now having to do weekly audits of my grades and decorum. She was always trying to catch you doing something wrong, and I usually was. One day, doodling, I drew a picture of her house with the street number on the door just like I'd memorized it from my route. I drew sticks of dynamite under the stairs with wires running to a plunger. Then I wrote out gibberish as some sort of coded instruction. On the opposite page in my notebook, I wrote in large print at the top, "CODE," and then under it, "9 = A, $ = B," etc. before tearing the rest of the page away. Then I just waited for her to do her prison-guard rounds to catch me doodling.

When she found me not doing my assigned work, she snatched my notebook and brought it to her desk. I saw her face blanch as she realized what I'd drawn.

She walked back to me carefully, leaned in close to me, and said with almost tearful terror, "I Know What You're Doing!" I was sure that I was in serious shit now and waited for the blowback. But nothing ever happened. Turns out, rather than ratting on me, she actually must have thought I was really going to blow up her house and gave me nothing but positive progress reports from then on. I think about this now any time I hear a news story of some foiled plot by a student to blow up or shoot up a school. I wonder how many of them were just bored and misunderstood kids fucking around and finding an outlet in a fantasy that was really just a goof. If I had done that as a school kid today, it could have easily been national news, with armor-clad police in military vehicles crawling across a locked-down campus and a bomb squad searching the teacher's house with a robot; Mrs. Davidson trembling at a press conference and me being marched off in an orange jumpsuit. Because I thought it was funny.

JEFF WASN'T FARING ANY BETTER IN PAXTON, PROBABLY MUCH WORSE. He didn't have the evil class clown persona to hide behind. He was just a geek with a scarred face. They were cruel to him in ways I'll never know. I still load guns in my head when I remember this story. It's straight out of a John Hughes movie. One of the upper-crust kids in his class was having a house party that was basically an open-invite to the class. For some reason—probably a girl he had a crush on, women being the primary reason for every bad choice a man makes in life—Jeff mustered up just enough self-confidence to actually show up. He rode his bike the twenty minutes up the long hill to the outskirts of town to the party. Initially everyone ignored him, which he was used to, but at some point a few of the popular guys started being overly friendly with him. He realized then that they were all drinking. They asked him if he'd do the guys a favor and go buy cigars for everybody. Jeff was so eager to be accepted he would have bought guns and drugs for them. They even offered to let him use one of their own bikes, it being a three-speed to his one-speed, so he'd have an easier time getting back up the inordinate incline. The ride probably took him thirty-five minutes round-trip but it was a small price to pay just to be included finally. Jeff got back, out of breath, and everybody avoided him like used toilet tissue. They wouldn't make eye contact. He couldn't understand. And then he found his own bike, smashed like it had been demolished in a garbage truck. Every part that could be broken, was. The spokes smashed out, the seat torn off. The wheels bent and dangling. He didn't know what to do. It was late at night now. He walked what was left of the bike to the street. He couldn't carry it all the way home on foot but he was too afraid of John Kirk to call for a ride. He stood there in blind terror on the side of the road until one kid who'd been picked up by his parents saw him and felt enough sympathy to offer a ride home. I know your names and I hope your kids grow up to be better human beings. I don't know how many times I've been drunk on Facebook and had to stop myself from telling them what human bags of garbage they were at that age.

Jeff and I even played football in our last year in Paxton, foolishly thinking that might help raise our status as losers and outcasts. It didn't change a thing except to terrify Mother for our safety. First of all, my team stunk. We were tied with Holden as the worst in the league. I played tight end on offense and only made one catch all season. It was an incredible "Bad News Bears" catch that I made with my eyes closed with three defenders swallowing me. I was as shocked to come up with the football as everyone else. This was ESPN highlight reel shit. At my earliest opportunity I ran to Mother on the sideline for exuberant congratulations. She hadn't been paying attention and missed it. She'd been talking. She was too nervous to watch, thinking I was going to get hurt, regardless of the pads and helmet weighing more than I did. I was crestfallen.

Football wasn't nearly as cool as playing soccer in Paxton. One day I said to another geek-act kid at school that soccer was for fags. He ratted me out to some soccer players, one of who confronted me at recess. I denied ever saying it. He pushed me down anyway. And then he walked away. That was it. I was unfamiliar with soccer. I didn't know that a simple fall should have sent me into the writhing agony of a career-ending injury. Fag.

Thankfully, Mother's marriage was quickly tanking as Jeff and I were becoming more and more ostracized at school. The three of us started to feel like the whole fucking scene was a common enemy bringing us together. Soon, we were no longer trying to fit into this new town. This town had gotten old fast, and we were getting the fuck out.

I wasn't leaving anything behind in Paxton. No friends, nobody I cared to keep in touch with, no happy memories. The only girl-friend I had had there was short-lived, although it did lead to my second pre-jizz days of prepubescent sex. I remember one time she read a book during it. I wouldn't get better at it in my later years either. That all ended when I caught my brother in my bedroom finger-banging her. I don't remember being all too hurt about it, but then again, I was too young to cum so sex really had no value save for you weren't supposed to do it. There's a t-shirt slogan for the boys section of Wal-Mart: "Too young to come, too young to care."

Mother's breakup wasn't so easy. It was high drama. She was fran-tic. As the marriage dissolved, she'd discovered that John Kirk had bought a handgun. Tough-guy friends of hers from AA were being called. One of them filed off the firing pin. Mother didn't know if he was going to do something crazy. My brother and I were terrified. It wasn't until long after, I'd figure out that it was all just run-of-the-mill, psycho-chick breakup drama. Although I don't hold any blame against my father for his parenting skills, it would have been nice if he could have sat me on his knee during this high-anxiety freak-out period and said, "Listen, son, your mother is just a raving psycho right now. Most ladies have to do this kind of thing during a breakup just to exonerate themselves from any guilt feelings or sharing of blame. You remember when she did this to me, and I'm the nicest guy on the planet. Just ride it out a little while and it will all be fine again once she's fucking some car dealer."

The problem with Dad was that he didn't have that knowledge to extend. He'd probably gotten laid as often as I had, and I was twelve. Maybe I should have sat him on my knee.

4

Actually, You Can Go Home Again

JEFF AND I WERE NOW LIVING BACK AT DAD'S HOUSE AT 20 RICH ST. with Mother in an apartment just a couple miles away. I was back in a school where my antics were considered more class clown than sociopath although still perverted. My poor father got us in the equivalent of a "Spring Break" period of our lives, taking full advantage of being a single parent with no discipline skills.

The night before Thanksgiving in 1980, I got drunk and smoked cigarettes for the first time. Our neighbor Kerry Hanley and my brother would regularly go out drinking with the other dregs of that teenage wasteland behind Tatnuck Elementary School located near the house. That night they'd made a big deal out of inviting me and I was privileged and proud. They asked what I wanted to drink and I asked for Riunite red wine. It was advertised on TV and I figured it would taste like how it looked, like fruit punch. They fucked up and got me white wine but I wasn't complaining. I was behind Tatnuck, getting drunk with the older kids, and I felt like I was being made by the Mob. Later, in the alley behind the hardware store, someone gave me a Marlboro Red and the first drag gave me the spins so bad I had to lean against the wall to stay standing. My first drunk was also the first time I got into trouble drunk. After I finished my bottle of wine, I was completely fucked up and sitting in Holiday Pizza with my brother and some other kids. At another table I recognized the mother and brother of a girl I went to school with, Kelly Coyne. I thought it would be funny to start a loud and entirely false conversation about fucking Kelly Coyne in the back of a van, as though I had no idea that her kinfolk were right there within earshot. Well, evidently they knew who I was, too, and when I got back home, as I was trying to make a stealth entrance past my dad and his holiday company to my room, he stopped me to say that he'd just gotten a phone call from the irate mother of my classmate. I told him as I swayed that it was all a mistake, that I'd said something else that was misunderstood.

"Okay then, guy. Get some sleep."

CHRIS O'CONNER WAS MY NEW BEST FRIEND AND WE'D PROVE TO each to be the kid that the other kid's parents forbade us from hanging around. He was a boozer as well, and together we were all brands of vagrant, vandal and delinquent. He—and myself for that matter— are the reason I'm terrified of kids today, knowing the kind of truly monstrous amounts of senseless destruction we'd caused and havoc we created just because we were bored. Setting dumpsters on fire. Putting roadkill in the ice cream freezer at the corner store. Throwing stuff at cars—snowballs in season, anything else the rest of the time—was always a go-to time killer, but we'd been chased enough and almost caught that we needed a safer target. So we'd make what we called "crap-frappes," containing a little bit of every single thing in the refrigerator: milk, eggs, vinegar, ketchup, Cheerios, leftovers, mustard, pudding, dog shit if we could find it . . . everything. It was put into a gallon-size storage bag and then taken down to the bus stop. The great thing about the bus stop is that we figured the driver couldn't strand a bus load of passengers in order to chase us. So we could walk out in broad daylight, wait for the bus to stop and the gear to back up before walking out casually in front of it and smashing the bag-o-shit all over the windshield before laughing and strolling off into the day. Now I sit in fear that every kid I see that age is going to move in next door to me.

It wasn't that hard getting booze back then. It may have been hard drinking it at first. I hated beer so much I had to mix it with cranberry juice the first few times I drank it just to get it down. Procuring it wasn't that much of an issue. If you couldn't find someone's older brother or sister to do it, you could just hang out in front of the liquor store and ask strangers. Someone would eventually say yes. It was referred to as "tapping" and the store was state-run and called a "package store" or "packy" for short. "Weah goin down to the packy to tap for bee-ahs," in the proper Massachusetts accent. This would be funny years later when I first played the UK and found out that "Paki" is a derogatory term for Pakistanis and held as contemptible as the word "nigger" is here. I can imagine how often a Brit would cringe on a Saturday night in Worcester.

We lived a quarter-mile away from Cook's Pond, where we kept a canoe chained up to a tree. Cook's had several small islands, the largest of which had a cinderblock building where The Tatnuck Island Club held its monthly meetings and events. It was a private men's club of which my father was a member and, at one point, president. Once a month they'd get together for a clambake or ice fishing, whatever the season made possible. The other islands were as small as a campsite. We'd tap beers and then a bunch of us would canoe load after load of people to a small island, build a huge fire, and then get hammered. It was flawless because if the cops ever came, there's no way to get to you without a boat. I don't know if they ever got called but if they did, they got to the shore and said, fuck it.

My dad never knew when I was drunk because he never drank. Early on in their marriage, my mother tried to force him to drink with her. They sat down at the dining room table, and after his first glass of wine he got up and said he was going to bed because he felt dizzy. "That's the fucking point, Russell!"

He'd walk in on me vomiting up Peppermint Schnapp's, unable to walk straight, and say, "Hey guy . . . looks like you caught a bit of the bug!" That bug was gonna be going around for quite a while.

I was also developing all the personality traits of a serial killer. Like Jeffrey Dahmer, I'd also dug up my old cat George's bones where we'd buried him in the blueberry bushes years before. I boiled and bleached them and then tried to reconstruct him dinosaur-style. I can imagine Aharon Aharonian's face if he'd heard that story in a counseling session. They'd have had me on Thorazine making paper hats. Fuck you, sir. That was the mind of a curious and inventive child.

One year there was a plague of Gypsy Moth caterpillars so thick that you couldn't find an empty inch between them on the trees and the houses. Local news showed footage of cars struggling to get up a steep hill, the road like ice from caterpillar guts. That summer, I'd run a Nazi-styled Gypsy Moth death camp where caterpillars were to die in any variety of ghastly fashions. When you set a gallon-size plastic milk jug aflame, it will start dripping small balls of flaming plastic with a "vvvvip" sound. When it really gets raging, masses of these fireballs are falling down at once like napalm. Caterpillars would be rounded up en masse and placed inside the walls of a cinder block laying on its side. The milk jug would get lit, and then they'd die by the dozens like the firebombing of Dresden, until it was just a cake of molten plastic and dead insects. Some would get frozen in the freezer, with subsequent attempts to reanimate them and do it again. Others would get soaked in water, placed across the base of an electric plug, and then the ends inserted into an outlet.

But the BB gun would be our favorite. It had been in hiding like a murder weapon since our days back in Paxton. Back then, we'd been on the porch roof plinking potshots at the restaurant sign across the street one afternoon when we decided we'd better knock it off before Mother and John came home. Mindlessly and without looking, Jeff pointed it downward and pulled the trigger to empty the last chambered BB. It struck a passing car's driver's window and shattered like a waterfall. We ran inside as the brakes screeched and went downstairs to the couch, put on the TV, and sat there shaking as the cops eventually showed up out front to take a report. We peeked through the blinds as we got our stories straight but the cops never came to our door. Later, a neighbor kid who'd walked by the scene said the lady driving assumed someone threw a rock through her window but didn't know who. We thought we'd killed someone.

Now back at 20 Rich St. we had short memories and a new supply of BBs. Aerosol cans would explode quite spectacularly when shot with flaming paper towels wrapped around them. Necco wafers made great targets as they'd shatter like skeet clays. Sadly, it wasn't just inanimate objects that got shot. Dad worked for the school department and had to leave for work before we left for school. Many mornings, he'd wake us up and we'd assure him that we were getting ready. As soon as he left, I'd go downstairs, litter the side yard with torn-up white bread and go back to sleep. When we woke up, there would be plenty of birds and squirrels having breakfast in the yard as targets. Any creature smaller or uglier than a kitten was prey. Like any animal lover, we had distinct, cute-based boundaries on what was okay to murder. No member of PETA ever caught crab-lice and, instead of killing them, tried to relocate them to a better home. But we killed some shit that we shouldn't have.

A toad in a microwave.

Firecrackers in fishes' mouths.

I'm glad the small-animal torture period of my serial killer profile was short-lived. I didn't even want to put it in the book for fear that some kid—or adult even—would ever think that was okay. It haunts me to this day and I could never donate enough money to animal cruelty foundations to make up for it. I was a rotten shit-bag as a kid, and although I find a lot of the stories amusing, fucking with animals is unforgivable. I feel as guilty now as I should have then and I always will.

Jeff and I lived like absolute pigs. We were back in our old upstairs bedroom with side-by-side twin beds. We had an antique wooden checkerboard that my great-grandfather had handmade that rested between the frames as a mutual nightstand. At night, we'd generally bring up a glass of milk or orange juice, in the morning maybe a bowl of cereal. But we'd never bring the dishes back downstairs to the sink. Eventually, half-drank glasses and unfinished plates would start to curdle and rot to the point that we couldn't sleep due to the heinous stench. Even then we wouldn't take them downstairs. Instead, we'd spray them down with Right Guard aerosol deodorant or just set a book over the tops of the worst offenders. We'd do this until Dad would ask why there were no dishes left in the kitchen.

We had a couple of great years with Dad, running roughshod and destroying the neighborhood, and then he went and fucked it up by getting remarried.

Not only were we going to have a stepmother in the house, but she had a daughter a year or two younger than me and they were immediately unpleasant. Gail, my stepmom, had some science background and was a humorless bore. The daughter, Carla, looked like a buoyant, milk-fed Kathy Griffin who sang opera, affected an Old English Ren-fest accent, and was a snob without the credentials. They didn't like us, Jeff and I hated them, and Dad didn't seem to notice.

It became evident that we were going to be in a Flander's Field standoff, fighting for yards of ground in manipulating Dad's favor without thoroughly cock-blocking him. He was still our father and we had to cater to him to some extent. He was happy for fuck sake, and he actually scored a lady. He wasn't in love. He later told me he never had been in his life, that he didn't understand what it meant. But he was fulfilled and we couldn't fuck him over completely yet, we couldn't let these greenhorns take what was rightfully ours.

It'd be three more tumultuous years until I was eighteen and the battle was over and I could walk free.

———

I ended up spending more time with Mother. We were becoming a lot closer and allies now that the burden of responsibility was more or less off her shoulders. She treated me like her buddy, almost like an equal in that she was running pretty rogue herself. We'd drink coffee and talk shit about people like a couple of gossipy fussbudgets. We'd smoke cigarettes and tell dirty jokes. My friends found her outrageous the way she'd swear and talk about sex and still rip these awe-inspiring chainsaw farts that could have lost her the security deposit. A dream parent for a *Beavis and Butthead* kinda kid. But as crass as she was, she was always educational in the process. She'd make jokes about fucking but also make clear the importance of safe sex and avoiding pregnancy. She just did it in a way that made you laugh. She was rigid about proper manners, if only her own sense of them. She wouldn't hesitate to smack me for chewing with my mouth open. I appreciate that she did. To this day, nothing disgusts me more than seeing and hearing someone's food while they eat. Mother stressed the importance of honesty but also treated you with an acceptance that never made you feel like you needed to lie to her. She was always genuine even when she was completely wrong, and oftentimes I mistook her honesty for wisdom. AA still loomed large in the picture, and now that she was single she surrounded herself with an amazingly colorful, if sometimes unsavory, cast of characters. Most of them trying to bone her, quite a few succeeding. They all had tales to tell, glorified sagas from the gutters of addiction, perfected by years of repeating them in a circle in church basements. AA probably exalted alcohol to some extent in my eyes, but it also raised my appreciation of a good story.

Holidays with Mother were still a mishmash of wayward AA stragglers with nowhere else to go, and those were usually the ones that were the most fucked-up and exciting. Mother didn't have much, but she shared what she had and you knew that it was fantastic. She and I exchanged Christmas stockings every year, usually with gifts that were vice-related. Table lighters and ashtrays and scratch tickets and coffee mugs. Not the kind of presents that young teenagers should give, much less receive, but they were wonderful years. I never had or never would see her that joyous again. The problem with getting attached to fucked-up AA people is that AA rarely works and those people eventually die or go back to the bar. But it was fun in the short run.

Mother was working any and every kind of job she could get to make ends meet. She had business cards made that said "Jill Of All Trades" that she was very proud of. They should have been subtitled "Mistress of None." She'd been a surgical technician after high school until she had Jeff. After she divorced my father, she was a waitress. I have no idea why she didn't go back to her professional, high-paying position but later experience would make me guess she just sucked at it.

She got some jobs now bartending. Generally they all ended when someone proved to be too much of a "fucking cunt" to work with or some other series of problems with the boss or customers. It was always someone else and I always believed her. She was bartending briefly at the Sole Proprietor restaurant, fairly upscale dining with a lounge, when her AA dogma got in the way. Turns out that anyone who had more than a couple of drinks would begin to get a Scientology-recruitment level talking-to by Mother about alcoholism. She was warned more than once but explained to her boss in undignified terms that she was just "telling them the fucking truth."

She ended up getting knocked down to working graveyard shift at a filthy truck stop out on Route 20, Uncle Will's, or as it was more fittingly known, Uncle Swill's. Glamorous! But it did afford her the opportunity to fuck a lot of truckers. I'd met a few of our "uncles"— she used that jokingly—from AA and they weren't too much different than my trucker uncles. One of them became serious—he was both AA *and* a trucker. Double bonus! His name was David Hatch but everyone called him P.O.W., due to his time as a prisoner of war in Vietnam. He looked like UFC legend Randy Couture, only older and fatter but badass nonetheless. His arms were covered in Special Forces/Green Beret and POW/MIA tattoos. He was everything that my father and stepfather were not. He was tough and funny and the whole Vietnam thing made him kinda cool in a scary way. Sometimes he'd talk about it. One story from being a prisoner was particularly gruesome and once I heard it, I couldn't ever see him without it coming into my head. He trembled and welled up with tears when he'd talk about his time there. The stories gave me goosebumps. I couldn't wait to repeat them to my friends. Mother was in love again and I completely approved.

This relationship led to Mother going to truck-driving school at Andover Tractor-Trailer school. People were aghast. Driving eighteen-wheelers wasn't something ladies do, certainly not something a mother does, and I am sure that spurred her on even more to do it. In a couple of months she was licensed and on the road with P.O.W., driving all over the country. They'd bring me home silly truck stop gift shop stuff. A "Turd Bird," which was a hunk of cow shit with glued-on eyes and a beak with pipe-cleaner legs attached to the base. A tit mug—a ceramic coffee mug shaped like a tit where you drank through the nipple. Shit and tits? I'm fifteen and I have the coolest mother in the world! At one point she called from a pay phone to say they were hauling nuclear warheads between air force bases in the southwest. I bragged to my Home Economics teacher about it. She laughed at me like I was describing an invisible friend and said in whatever teacher-friendly verbiage that I was full of shit. I told Mother that on her next call and, soon enough, my teacher was getting postcards from all over the country. You teach me to make cupcakes. Mother will teach you to eat crow.

School was becoming less and less important to me. I was constantly getting suspended for fucking off or being late or sometimes not showing up at all. That always killed me, the idea of being told you can't go to school as punishment for not going to school. Perfect.

I missed the class trip to an amusement park when I broke my jaw or, more accurately, when my brother broke my jaw for me. We were fucking around and he put me in a headlock standing up and squeezed until I passed out. He assumed I was faking it—faking it was always my go-to defense—and he let me go, unconscious and face-first onto the concrete floor. I had to have my jaw wired for weeks. No solid food, and worse, no way to brush the insides of your teeth. Yech. Mother brought me from the hospital to Friendly's Ice Cream where all I could order was a milkshake—the Friendly Fribble.

"Chocolate Fribble," I ordered through clenched teeth, "hold the onions." It broke Mother into hysterics far beyond its value and it was the joke she annoyingly retold more often than any other for the rest of her life. But any time I could make her laugh hard was a solid victory.

The threat of puking on a roller coaster with my jaw wired shut banned me from the class trip. I can see where it made sense. Other things I was sent home for didn't make sense at all. I was sent home by a gym teacher once for wearing a t-shirt Mother had brought home for me from the road. It was for an alleged bar and it said "Liquor Up Front, Poker in the Rear!" It's hackneyed now but was hilarious to me at the time. I remember arguing very calmly and concisely that, due to the spelling, it could only be considered offensive if the reader decided to interpret it in that fashion, therefore HE was the one with a dirty mind. The teacher conceded that I was perhaps correct but sent me home to change clothes nonetheless. At home, I'd found an audaciously gaudy polyester pantsuit in loud multicolored swirls of my stepmother's in the laundry. I decided to wear that to school the next day with a Flava-Flav style clock around my neck. I lasted about two periods before I was sent home again. I argued that there was no dress code and this couldn't be considered offensive by any means like the t-shirt had been deemed so—what? I am being sent home as a matter of your own personal taste? I was told that I was a distraction and this time, when they sent me home, they called my father. The next day was the last day of school so suspending me was moot. They decided that a proper punishment was to make me wear a coat and tie on the last day, which backfired when everyone thought I was doing this as yet another goof and found it funnier still. And that was the end of Chandler Junior High School for me. I had already been beaten out for the title of class clown in the yearbook, and that's all I really wanted out of that school anyway. A girl on the student committee of whoever does that shit told me that she'd been one of the vote counters and she was sure that I'd won. She said that the powers that be on the faculty had changed the results. Maybe that's why I am so into conspiracy theories. I don't remember who got my title but they will go to the grave knowing it was an Inside Job.

The next year would be on to Doherty High School and I don't remember much of anything except that it had a smoking area for students outside during breaks, very strange to imagine now. I mostly remember rarely showing up. In our system, you went to Chandler Junior through ninth grade, and Doherty High 10–12. I showed up occasionally half-way through tenth and quit the day I turned six-teen, the minimum age when they allowed it. My dad wasn't all that happy about it. Seeing as how he worked for the school department, it probably looked bad but he deferred to Mother who allowed it on the condition I got my GED and that I look for a job.

I have always contended that quitting school was one of the best decisions I've made in my life. There was nothing there that inter-ested me. I couldn't pay attention when I tried my hardest. I proba-bly have some form of dyslexia. Writing this book has made me sure of it. But even if I had been solidly diagnosed with that in school, it wouldn't have made it any less boring. School was just mundane and pointless, and it started far too early. It's always baffled me that if everyone hates getting up early, why we set the hours that way. Why can't it be noon–8 instead of 9–5? If school started at 11 a.m. instead of 7 a.m. maybe I'd have a useless diploma instead of a worthless GED. If I had to take my GED test today I would fail miserably because nothing that I was forced to know in school ever came up in real life. I was disinterested in class and was generally terrified on the schoolyard. There was no payoff in a diploma and no allure in any occupation that would require one. I was about to get a jump-start on real life. The problem was that I was only sixteen years old.

WHAT I REALLY WANTED TO DO WAS GET THE FUCK OUT OF Worcester. P.O.W. was driving a truck for Dart Transit out of Shakopee, MN, and let me go on runs with him as a "lumper," getting out at the loading docks and unloading shit into the warehouse. P.O.W. would kill the miles with war stories, the "how to kill a guy with a credit card" kinda stuff, explaining the term "Columbian necktie," and whatnot. I learned CB radio lingo and could fuck with other truck drivers just like making prank phone calls. I don't think I've ever slept better in my life than in the bunk of a moving eighteen-wheeler, including one LAX-to-Heathrow trip on Virgin Atlantic First Class on a full bar of Xanax. Sleeping that well made getting out into a freezing trailer at six in the morning to hump boxes that much more debilitating. I remember a cold morning in Grand Rapids where I had to unload like 30,000 pounds of Cocoa Krispies before breakfast, one case at a time. Trucking was fun for a while, but like a kid with progeria syndrome, it got old quick.

Back in Worcester, P.O.W. had talked to his mother in New Jersey who told him she was going to be renting out a room in her house to help bring in some desperately needed money. Mother and he knew I wanted to get out of Dad's house and thought it would be a great idea for me to move down there. His mother was a yellow/gray corpse color of indeterminate age who looked like that new lady they just hired here at the corner store across from the baseball field. How's that for a reference you don't get? She lived in Maywood, NJ outside of Hoboken in a creaky, dark Victorian house full of lots of old-people shit. Afghan throws over the backs of wooden rocking chairs. This was a horror movie set. His mother—I haven't a clue what her name was—slept no more than four hours a night, and the rest of her time she spent literally rocking in a chair or looming over you to make sure you didn't do anything against the house rules. The house rules were "don't do anything." If you stirred a cup of coffee with a spoon, that spoon shouldn't hit a countertop for even a second. It should be washed and put away immediately, and you were an ingrate if you didn't know that on your own. I needed to find a job quick and I did, at the Maywood IGA grocery store stocking shelves.

It was shit money but it gave me somewhere to be. The store was owned by an Italian father and son who seemed Mob-affiliated. Not the well-dressed, kill-people-in-the-basement type of mobster. More like the connected type that makes pasta and launders money for the cool mobsters. Like that kind. They were nice enough and paid in cash and ignored my poor work ethic for almost a month before I was fired for eating more from the shelves than I was stocking. I left New Jersey but not with my tail between my legs. Oh, no. You can't fail at leaving New Jersey. Bruce Springsteen failed by staying. Loser.

So now I was back at Dad's house with a stepmother who hated me and a stepsister that I was constantly fighting with and my Dad trying his best to keep everything smooth. He knew I didn't want to be there and I knew everything would be easier once I was gone, but I was still sixteen. So for the next year and a half, we'd just have to sit there and stare at our watches until I turned eighteen and could beat feet somewhere else.

The other problem I had was that all of my friends were still in school so I didn't have anyone to hang around with during the day. Even my brother was leaving now. He'd joined the Marine Corps on the delayed-entry program. This is where they sign you up at seventeen, so that when you turn eighteen and can actually smell freedom to the point where it's real, it's too late. You're fucked. Sure enough, in the year between first signing the papers to actually getting his head shaved, he'd gotten in a band, had a couple different girlfriends, and was almost popular. He knew there were ways to get out of it but didn't want to look like a coward. He'd looked like that his whole life, he thought. So he sucked it up and headed to Parris Island for boot camp. Thirteen weeks later, I took the Greyhound bus with his then-fiancee Jodi twenty-eight hours to South Carolina to watch him graduate. I really looked up to him at this point in my life. We went through a lot of shit together where it seemed like we were outnumbered and outgunned and we only had each other to count on. Now he was going to be a Marine and I was truly proud of him. The night before the ceremony in the hotel, I saw an opportunity, a moment of beer-induced weakness that I took advantage of, and I fucked his fiancée.

Ooh-rah!

It wasn't just payback for finger-fucking my girlfriend back in Paxton. Shit was getting very incestuous around now. I'd started dating Jeff's most recent ex-girlfriend, Christine. She was gorgeous, artsy, and kind of punk-rockerish and very intelligent, all very rare qualities in even the far reaches of our social circles. How the fuck, then, would she wind up with Jeff or me? Oh, that's right. She was eighteen and already had two children, dropping her stock down to Stanhope levels. I'm guessing a lot of people will think teenage mothers are normal. It certainly wasn't where we grew up. So when Christine dumped my brother, he started going out with his best friend Jeff Brown's recent ex, Jodi, and they got engaged, much to Jeff Brown's annoyance. Then I started dating Christine, and after that ended, I banged Jodi while Jeff was in boot camp. In the end, all parties involved were part of Jeff and Jodi's wedding party.

It's not important to the rest of the story. It's just funny that we never had any clue that we were white trash.

So now I was alone. I went to Job Corps for a very short time. Job Corps is like reform school that you sign up for voluntarily where they teach you a skill and pay you basically prison wages while you try not to get killed by the serious dregs of troubled youth that surround you. Hardcore deviant criminal element. Fuck that, I can learn to master culinary arts on my own. I left in a hurry but started hanging out with a couple kids I'd met there since they were dropouts as well. One of them was Keith Kingsbury.

Keith Kingsbury was that last person in the world that you'd want your wayward teenage son to start hanging out with unsupervised at your house with nothing but idle time. Keith really was a bad seed of the kind I hadn't known before. Chris O'Conner was a delinquent but Keith had a rap sheet. He was always getting arrested, usually for petty shit. He'd always have warrants for unpaid tickets—speeding, no insurance, suspended license, expired tags. Yet he'd still be speeding with no license or tags, now with active warrants. He'd get pulled over again and go to jail again. And not pay the fine again. So long as it was him going to jail and not me, I thought it was funny.

We landed jobs at a 24-hour diner in downtown Worcester working the graveyard shift, Keith cooking and me waiting the counter. The place was right across the street from the only gay bar in town, so at last call the place was transformed into a gay diner. I might be ugly now but when I was seventeen I looked thirteen and was cute as a fucking bug. Parachute pants were all the rage and I soon realized what any hot chick in the service industry knows, that tight pants scored big tips. Sometimes the folks at the gay bar would send someone over just to see if I was wearing my parachute pants to decide if they'd even come in at all. It didn't matter to me what sexuality they were; I relished the adulation. I even dressed in drag to work on Halloween. There was a middle-aged couple—swingers—who came in regularly and flirted with me to no end. Her name was Cookie and she always threatened, "We're gonna take you home with us one of these nights!" and I always played along, knowing that my shift not ending until 7 a.m. was my easy excuse. Act interested, get the tips, have an out. It was like tittie-dancing.

The owner of the place was a guy named Simeone Braio, who went by Simi, a boozy, old, hardened hustler who also turned out to be gay, which shocked us since he was a hard-ass who looked like Nick Nolte's DUI mugshot. I was always comfortable with gay people, not a popular attitude in lowbrow Worcester. Some of Mother's best AA friends were flaming. They were fun and never a threat. But Simi was a revelation, the first guy I'd known to be gay that you bought as a legitimate tough guy.

When the glut of post-last call queens moved out, the wee hours at the diner were left mostly to transients and stumblebums. Lots of homeless. There was one guy who'd come in, order coffee, and then go to sleep with his head in his arms right on the counter. I'd wake him up and tell him he couldn't sleep there, over and over, and he'd just end up falling back asleep. Finally, I walked into the kitchen one night and grabbed an 8-quart metal cooking pot along with a metal soup ladle. With a small audience of patrons and Keith watching in anticipation, I leaned the pot at an angle just over his sleeping head and then proceeded to wail away on the bottom of it with the ladle. He shot up like he was inside John Bonham's drum kit. Not long after, a reporter from the Worcester *Telegram & Gazette* came in doing a story on Worcester after hours and talked to me about what it was like working overnight downtown. I repeated the soup-pot story, it being one of my favorites and it got printed. I couldn't understand why Simi went through the fucking roof. It was wicked funny! I couldn't wrap my head around why stories of homeless people not only sleeping in the diner but also being abused could be bad for a new business. It didn't matter. Mother bought every copy of the *T & G* she could get her hands on.

At the same time I was working graveyard shift at the diner, Mother started going to massage school just down the street. Truck driving had lasted as long as most of her other ventures and now she was going to Bancroft School for Massage on a loan from my grandmother. It was a loan she wouldn't have to pay back, as Grammie had recently died of lung cancer. We'd have to go see her in the hospital, most of the time with Mother in the hospital room visiting while Jeff and I smoked cigarettes in the hallway. Yes, you could smoke in schools AND hospitals. Those were wonderful days.

Grammie was always someone Jeff and I had to endure rather than enjoy. We looked forward to her greeting cards on birthdays or Christmas and shook them out without reading them to see how much money fell out. But spending time with her was arduous, even for Mother. Mother had been an only child whose father died at forty-two. As a child and through her adulthood, Mother could never live up to her own mother's expectations. Her accomplishments were always passive-aggressively torn down, every compliment was backhanded. After Mother died, I found a letter she wrote to Grammie on January 7, 1963. Mother was seventeen and in high school while working in a nursing home. Evidently they'd had a tiff.

January 7, 1963

Dear Momsey,

I'm sorry I acted like such a stinker. I hope this is all caused by my being all worn out, 'cause if it isn't, I'll go nuts living with myself for the rest of my life.

I didn't mean to make you feel unwanted when I said I wanted to go to the doctors by myself, but when I overheard you telling Rose that you 'had to take Bonnie to' to the doctor's', I felt like a two-year old. That's why I said it.

I want you to go with me tomorrow, but may I ask one favor? Please let me talk to him myself. I do feel that I am old enough to tell him my own symptoms. (I don't mean to be sarcastic by that, either.) Sometimes you have a tendency to exaggerate and mix up information. Then I have to tell it over again and I don't like to do that 'cause it might seem to make you out a liar, and that isn't true. Do you see what I mean? Another thing is, I haven't told you all the things I feel are wrong with me because I don't want you to worry. I just want to sit by myself and tell him about all my little aches and pains. O.K.?

I hope that when I get rested up and get some of these tensions to leave, we can do things together. I hate being mean to you and I don't do it on purpose. It's just that by the time I get home, I'm fed up with people in general and little things get on my nerves. Sometimes at work I get so mad at people I could reach out and strangle them, but I have to live with them and I can't. You know that I'm not the type to yell at people or tell someone off, and with being tired and run-down and tense, and having to put up with little irritants, I get so keyed up that I take it out on you. I hope that after a little time, I can calm down and take life a little easier.

Mom, Russ thinks that once I quit work I should join the Y or something. He thinks that I'll get into a rut if I just go to school and do homework and stay around the house. But I'm scared stiff at the though of meeting other people and being rejected. I've never gotten along with people, and I feel like a sore thumb around them.

Even in school, I hate to walk down the corridor. I can just feel people staring at me and saying, "Boy, is she ever a fink." Sometimes I'd rather die than walk through them. I just feel that people would be happier if I weren't around. I think I am a regular oddball. I feel so stupid around other kids I could just die. That's one of the reasons I hate to leave work. I at least know that the people, especially the patients, like having me around.

Maybe someday I'll adjust.

So will I see you tomorrow? I really want you to come. I'm awfully sorry.

Lots of love,

Bonnie

I know that feeling, Ma. I used to walk down the hallways of Paxton Center School so afraid, feeling that I was walking funny. That everybody was staring at me. That everybody was making fun of me. The more aware of it I became, the more I seemed unable to control my legs. I wanted to die too, Ma. But I knew you had my back.

My mother was always overly-conscious to make sure she let me be my own person. Or forced me to be my own person. She would never even order for me in a restaurant. I'd go hungry before she'd ever tell the waiter what I wanted for myself. I understand that now. She was deeply affected by her own upbringing to the end and was deliberate not to hobble her own children that way.

When Grammie finally kicked the bucket, all we cared about was when we got our inheritance, which Jeff and I coined "Grandma's Dead Money," never not laughing when we said it. It seemed like an eternity before it showed up and we're pretty sure Mother grifted us out of a lot of it beforehand. Mother had been made power-of-attorney while Grammie was still alive to take care of her bills, and using some presumptive arithmetic after seeing how little we eventually received, we figured Mother had moved the lion's share into her own bank account before Grammie died.

Mother's massage classes started shortly after I'd leave work in the morning from the diner and it worked out where I could be used as a test dummy in class and get free massages. It was an unbelievable perk as I always left work with my back in agony. I've had the hunched spine of a defeated man since I was old enough to care when a girl pointed it out. My seahorse posture was made for drinking over a dive bar, looking through the bottom of my glass, long before I was old enough to be served there. Working for a living only seemed to aggravate it.

One morning I was at her school, covered on a slab, on my back like a naked cadaver when the class started. After a brief tutorial from the instructor, one of the class members started going up and down my leg. I immediately threw wood like it was going to leave me and stick into the ceiling. I'm seventeen and some girl is rubbing her hands up my lubricated inner thigh. What could possibly go wrong??? I was mortified. I'm laying in front of a class of twenty or so people, one of them being my MOTHER while sporting a no-nonsense boner through a thin white sheet. All I could do was pretend to be asleep. This is a rare instance of something I could call a "traumatic" experience in my youth, in that I have never to this day been able to enjoy a "legitimate" massage without fear of inadvertently getting an obvious hard-on. I'd rather go to any yank-house out by the airport where they expect to give you a hand job at the end and leave you wanting more.

We also suspected that a lot of the transferred dead money was going to buying P.O.W. his own big rig. I don't know if that ever came to be as they were having trouble. He'd gone off the wagon. Mother got him into rehab. He was going to be in it for thirty days, and during that time he said I could use his old Chevy Luv pickup. He warned me that it leaked oil, as much as 2 quarts a day. I was just happy to have a ride. I could, with some training from friends, probably figure out something as foreign to me as "checking the oil." And I did. I checked the oil relentlessly, terrified that if I didn't, the whole thing would explode. I was always afraid of shit exploding. Mother and I even shared an irrational fear of balloons. I checked that fucking oil twice a day, and for days and days it never registered as low. Trusting P.O.W.'s estimate of two quarts a day, I eventually assumed that the dipstick was broken. With my below-sea-level mechanical skills and trust in P.O.W., what else could I think? So I started putting in two quarts of oil a day regardless of the dipstick. Before long I noticed the truck was getting extremely sluggish. Soon, when I would floor the gas at a green light, plumes of thick, white exhaust smoke would fill the intersection—so thick that traffic behind me would come to a standstill. Eventually, I asked Keith to look at it. He knew cars. He opened up the hood and saw there was so much oil in it, it had filled the carburetor and was spilling into the air filter. I learned a valuable lesson that day. The lesson was that you could have Batmobile options like massive smoke-screens at the touch of a gas pedal for the price of just 2 quarts of oil a day.

We drove around fumigating traffic every day until P.O.W. got out of rehab.

I can't remember if it was the Chevy Luv or one of the many other fleeting hunk-of-shit cars I owned, but I do recall driving into the lot of Sunnyside Ford in the middle of the night in Holden. I don't know if Keith was behind the wheel or if it was me, but we proceeded to reverse at high speeds into the sides of brand new cars demolition derby-style before disappearing into the night. They had insurance so nobody really was affected was our rationalization. We wouldn't do this to some poor prick who had to get up on a winter morning for work and deal with this shit. We were good people. And we believed that. I just had to Google the dealership right now to remember the name. Since it was up on my screen anyway, I figured I'd call and apologize. I could imagine the owner's eyebrows furrow in confusion as I stumbled through an explanation. Eventually, I just told him I'd just send a copy of the book when it's done and hung up.

Usually it was always Keith that got arrested. I got away with everything. For a while. I scored a job at Honey Farms, a convenience store right in Tatnuck Square by Dad's house at 20 Rich St., where I'd work the register and after a short training period, was left to work by myself. A huge blunder on their part. It wasn't that my friends and I would simply steal, we'd try to see *how much* we could steal and then break our record the next time. And not just cigarettes—which we took by the cartons for ourselves or just gave away to friends who'd come in—we'd leave with food, soda, snacks, diapers for Christine's kids, kitchen supplies that we did or didn't need just for volume. A few years earlier I used to hang out at Honey Farms generally causing trouble and being a pain in the ass to the clerk who was the older brother of a kid I went to school with.

One day he told me I had to leave and I refused. He chased me up and down the aisles until he caught up with me and tripped me while holding my arms behind my back. I went down on my chin and it opened up like a baby's vagina. Mother closed it up with a butterfly stitch. She knew she could have sued the shit out of them, but she also knew it was my fault for being a fuckhead. I assumed my massive theft was a small price to pay in comparison to what we could have sued them for.

There were no cameras but the store had a separate back entrance where security could come in secretly and watch you through a one-way mirror. I never believed they actually did. I assumed I would have been able to hear them come in. The night I found out I was wrong, the security guy got quite a show. Not only had I been stealing from the register by not ringing up purchases and giving away the store to any friend that showed up, but Keith had come by and we went at the place like it was the L.A. riots. We'd dump 2-liter bottles of 7-Up down the sink, refill them with water, and put them back on the shelves. We played football with loaves of bread. At the end of my shift, just before I locked up, Honey Farms security came in through the front. He'd seen the whole show from behind the one-way mirror. He didn't have to say one word. I immediately knew I was screwed. I had to write out a statement, a confession, and sign it. Although I did my best to minimize it, it still looked fucking awful. I was charged with petty larceny. Fortunately, I only admitted to stealing $35 in cash so it wasn't a felony. I wasn't arrested but had to go to court so it made the local paper in the courthouse records section. My parents weren't thrilled.

Not long afterwards, Keith was pulled over just at the foot of Rich Street for yet another traffic stop. I was in the passenger seat. Of course, he had an outstanding warrant and was arrested. I'd been told to wait across the street while they called the paddy wagon. Keith didn't like cops and hated getting arrested, and let the cop know that in no uncertain terms. Screams came from the back of the paddy wagon.

"Fuck you, you fucking pig motherfucker! Take off that badge and gun and see how fucking tough you are, you fucking faggot! Your mother sucks cocks in hell!"

Meanwhile, I am literally down on the sidewalk, rolling in laughter. I couldn't believe anyone would have the balls to talk like that to a cop.

The cop walked over to me, jumped on top of me with his knee in my back, and said, "You think it's funny? You're under arrest for disturbing the peace," and next thing Keith and I are on our way to the Worcester city jail. It was mostly empty save for Keith and me in our own cells. We didn't get strip-searched, just made to empty our pockets and sit in our cells until my friend Stan Cohen bailed us out within an hour or so.

When my court date arrived, I pleaded not guilty because I was not fucking guilty of anything but laughing. Cops should be held to the same standards as the citizens they are sworn to protect. If he were not a cop, and just tackled and shackled me for nothing but laughing on a sidewalk, I would have been well within my rights to shoot him in the fucking face to get away. In fact, I'd be hailed as a hero for doing so. The headline would read: "Quick-thinking Youth Evades Kidnapper With Swift Shot To Face, Keeps Laughing." I didn't have this argument when I went to court, which was probably a good thing. But I had everything that I was going to say ready, and when I took the stand I forgot most of it. What I remembered was hard to hear because my voice was shaking like I was in front of a firing squad. I sputtered out, "I know it's probably wrong to laugh when someone is telling a cop about specific acts his mother is committing in hell but I don't think that's any reason to ruin a perfectly spotless record." The judge asked the prosecutor about my record. The prosecutor brought up the Honey Farms larceny charge. I hadn't considered that since I wasn't actually arrested that time and just had to pay a fine. The gavel came down.

"Guilty."

Still, after twenty-five years of speaking in public professionally, my voice still quivers when I have to speak in front of authority figures. Interviewers always ask if I ever die on stage. I don't count the times when I've fallen apart merely speaking at local city council meetings or trying to talk my way out of a ticket. Those times, I die on my ass every time.

I was just given another small fine but it made me even edgier to get the fuck out of Worcester. Until then I kept getting into trouble.

That summer, Dad and Gail had gone off for a week's vacation to Prince Edward Island. We immediately threw a massive party that filled the house with local miscreants and eventually led to fights spilling across the neighbors' lawns. We'd also realized that Gail's Toyota Corolla wagon had a faulty ignition switch that you could start just by turning with a butter knife. Joyrides abounded! In the morning we cleaned up, putting all the empty Coors bottles back into the cases (they were returnables worth a nickel each back at the packie). We stood proud in the kitchen when the stack of cases reached just inches from the ceiling.

That weekend, I took an overnight trip with Mother up to York Beach in Maine. On the way back the next day, we happened to pass Dad and Gail on the highway also heading home. Oh fuck! The cases of beer were still in the kitchen. I told Mother and we drove like hell to beat them back to the house, an iffy proposition seeing as how often Mother had to stop to pee. We didn't make it. Not only did dad and Gail walk in to find our monument in the middle of an otherwise spotless kitchen, they had church friends there to meet them. I can't imagine what my father could have come up with to excuse it. Gail had written down the mileage on her car before she left. She wasn't stupid.

In the meantime, I had several jobs that didn't check your references. I worked overnight making donuts with Weird Joe Vancelette, another Job Corp flunk-out. I washed dishes for a while. I was a security guard at a warehouse for a few days where I looked so young and so ridiculous in the uniform that at one point someone said to me, "Excuse me, miss?" I tried to fake a slip-n-fall scam but couldn't even fall down correctly, so I quit.

Two jobs lasted less than ninety minutes. One was stuffing circulars into newspapers on a conveyor belt. "I'll be right back. I have to go to the bathroom."

Another was mopping up after shows at the Centrum, the major concert arena downtown. "I'll be right back. I have to go to the bathroom."

Keith started there with me at the Centrum and we walked out the back, taking the mop and bucket with us. We had walked out in the middle of a shift one night from the gay diner a while before. Now we wanted our jobs back and brought Simi the mop and bucket as a peace offering. How could he say no?

The shortest job, though, was still to come.

———

ONE FATEFUL NIGHT, KEITH AND I WERE AT THE DINER AFTER hours just fucking around and eating for free on a night off when Cookie and her husband came in. She was on me like body armor, grabbing my dick through my pants and nuzzling up in my neck, "Why don't you come home with us tonight?" I didn't have the excuse of having to work and, on paper, she certainly wasn't anything you'd ever want to poon. She looked like the fat neighbor kid's mother from the movie *Better Off Dead*. If you got that reference, you should put this book down and high-five yourself. For the rest, think heavyset, bouffant hairdo, overly made-up lunch-lady in her forties. But then again, I'm seventeen and she is twisting my cock through my pants, which is a strong sales technique. So I became "Doug Stanhope—Male Prostitute!"

I thought I was slick as Gypsy Moth caterpillar guts. "So, are you going to make it worth my while?"

"Oh, absolutely!" still grabbing my dick.

"You'd better go check with your husband."

Meanwhile, I'd run back to Keith and updated him. "You're never gonna believe this! Cookie is gonna pay me to fuck her!" Even back then I knew the value of a good story. If I could come back and tell that a woman paid me to fuck her, then I was a king. Nobody besides Keith had to know she was a hideous beast. My fatal mistake was in never naming a price and getting it up front, something I'd learn later from getting prostitutes. For some reason I had five hundred bucks in my head. I have no idea why. It seemed like the number someone would pay you to fuck them. I should have said it out loud. We left and drove to their house out in the sticks of one of the neighboring towns. Maybe Holden, maybe Rutland. Upper-middle class. The whole time I'm playing it like I'm some experienced gigolo while I'm really shitting my pants.

They gave me a beer and then we were in their bedroom where they took off their clothes. Thank God it was dimly lit. I don't know if I was naked then but I knew I didn't know what the fuck to do next.

"Um . . . I don't do guys," as though I've done this a thousand times and have my regular rules. "That's okay, sweetheart. My husband can go first and you can watch."

He piled on top of her and grunted it out, probably even more repulsive than walking in on my mother and stepfather. I just stood in the doorway like I was witnessing a murder. Any attempts at appearing like a seasoned pro were torpedoed. I couldn't have appeared more awkward if I'd been openly crying, which I'm sure I wanted to do. He finished before his heart exploded, and now it was my turn. The great thing about being a teenager is you could get a boner naked in an ice storm whether you wanted one or not. That's how boners work at that age. Random, unannounced, and sometimes inappropriately timed. There must have been unsolicited teenage boners in concentration camps. It had to happen. Think about that. Statistical probability. This time, ready wood worked in my favor. I got on top of Cookie—my imaginary price would have doubled if she were on top—and gave a few strokes but my dick kept slipping out.

"Hang on," she said, "it's probably just a little messy." She went to the toilet and queefed out a towel-full of her husband's seed and then plopped back down on the bed in position. I should have leapt out a window. I mounted her and was done in under a minute. I'm sure I apologized for my barely-legal faux pas and they said we could wait a while and try again. Instead, I just went to bed on the couch. Needless to say, the morning was uncomfortable.

The husband had to drive me back to Worcester in near silence. I was on my way home and so far there had been no mention of payment, aside from an early, tenuous promise of Cookie making it "worth my while," which, for all I know now, could have meant the privilege of boning her. I was now petrified at the thought of going back to Keith and having to admit I did this for free.

Finally, he cut the tension and said, "So, did you have a good time?"

My voice croaked. "Ah . . . well. I was kinda expecting some financial compensation?" unable to keep the question mark out of the end of my sentence.

"Ah, yes." he said in a fatherly tone. "My wife likes to live in a fantasy world sometimes. How much were you expecting?" That $500 figure dropped like penny stocks.

"Um . . . fifty dollars?"

"I can give you thirty."

"That's fine."

So long as I got paid a dollar, the story stood. I was officially, if only technically, a paid male escort. I could put that on my resume next to petty larcenist and high school dropout.

I WAS ABOUT TO TURN EIGHTEEN AND A FREE MAN. DAD AND Gail had had enough of me. Carla was contemptible. I watched her slap my father in some fit of pompous frustration. It was like seeing someone kick a kitten. I punched her right in her fat fucking greasy, pimpled face. I never felt bad about it. I was raised to never hit a woman but it was instinctual that you never hit my dad. I hate her to this day. She continued to live with my father even after her mother eventually left him. He was a pushover and claimed to like the company. He should have just got a dog.

I'm not sure when I decided that I wanted to move to Hollywood to be an actor. I know I'd taken an acting class and done a play that had advertised auditions in the newspaper but I don't remember having any strong passion for the art. I liked the attention. It was more of a pipe-dream of being famous and the prestige of being one of the few people that ever seemed to leave that shithole town. I know that I was at least talking about it at Christmas just before I turned eighteen, as I found this inscribed on a greeting card from me to Mother:

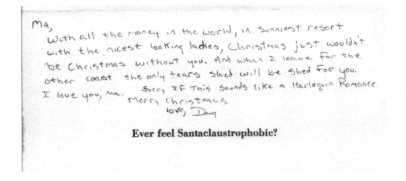

MA,
With all the money in the world, in sunniest resort with the nicest looking ladies, Christmas just wouldn't be Christmas without you. And when I leave for the other coast the only tears shed will be shed for you.
I love you, Ma. Sorry if this sounds like a Harlequin Romance.
Merry Christmas,
love, Doug

Ever feel Santaclaustrophobic?

Exactly three months later I turned eighteen. My father, maybe unsure if I really had planned on leaving, left me this letter.

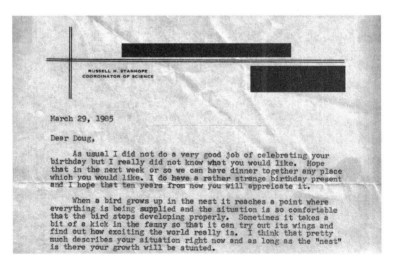

RUSSELL H. STANHOPE
COORDINATOR OF SCIENCE

March 29, 1985

Dear Doug,

As usual I did not do a very good job of celebrating your birthday but I really did not know what you would like. Hope that in the next week or so we can have dinner together any place which you would like. I do have a rather strange birthday present and I hope that ten years from now you will appreicate it.

When a bird grows up in the nest it reaches a point where everything is being supplied and the situation is so comfortable that the bird stops developing properly. Sometimes it takes a bit of a kick in the fanny so that it can try out its wings and find out how exciting the world really is. I think that pretty much describes your situation right now and as long as the "nest" is there your growth will be stunted.

Your presents will include

On April 8 you will have the final $130 from your bonds to take to court. Also, any money that I have given you for the truck, concert tickets and whatever will be written off so that you and I are free and clear. Your appointment for the eye examination will be paid plus the cost of glasses or contacts as you may decide. On April 13 you will get $100 in cash from Gail and I as a birthday present. When you get your own place we will try and help out with the furnishings, including the frig if you need it, dishes, chairs and similar materials. The bed and bureau of course are yours. Finally you will have free room and board through Saturday, April 13.

Starting this weekend we will be moving things around getting ready for the plumber and heating contractor. You will have a bed available for you - but no overnight guests - on either the basement or first floor levels through April 13. You will have your new place ready for the night of April 13. I shall take off the extra car insurance as of April 15

There are many training opportunities available if you decide to take advantage of them and I will always be available to help and advise.

Happy Birthday with many, many more to come.

Love

I still choke up reading that because I know how hard it was to write it, how much carping he had to take from his wife to put his foot down. Not to mention the shit we put him through to bring it to that point. There was an ocean of reasons I deserved to be kicked out of the "nest." It didn't matter. I was leaving anyway. Though it would be a while before the full amount of Grandma's "Dead Money" came through, the stock portion from Cincinnati Milacron, where my grandfather had worked, was released to us and I cashed it in post-haste. No need for the fridge and the dishes, Pop. I'm going to Hollywood.

5

Hollywood: Scams, Queers, Scamming Queers and Queering Scams

I TOOK THE AMTRAK FROM WORCESTER TO LOS ANGELES IN APRIL of 1985 with 450 bucks in my pocket and no plan whatsoever. I didn't need a plan. "Rules don't apply to me" was a phrase I was fond of saying any time I got away with something I shouldn't have. In those years of blissful ignorance, rules usually don't apply. Caution comes only after grand miscalculation. Until you fuck up profoundly in life, you can skip through minefields like it's *The Sound of Music*.

I figured the train was a great way to see the country, and it was. I hadn't seen bupkis past New Jersey save for the few trips in the truck across the frozen wasteland of the upper Midwest. I still love the train to this day but now I get a sleeping car for anything longer than a few hours and doze almost as soundly as in P.O.W.'s truck bed. Sleeping in a chair for three and a half days is a lot easier when you're eighteen. The first train went from Worcester to Chicago, and even though I still looked like a thirteen-year-old, I got the bartender to serve me beer. The bar car was usually empty so I think he was just happy to have company. The second train, from Chicago to Los Angeles, wasn't so easy. That bartender initially refused to serve me but I had forty-three hours to badger him and, at some point, break him down—with the stipulation that I get out at a stop in Albuquerque and try to find him weed. I remember just standing in the train station looking around like there might just be a guy that looked like a pot dealer, whatever that looked like. There wasn't. But the bartender admired my fortitude and served me anyway, making it a hell of a lot easier to sleep curled up in a ball in a vaguely reclining seat. It was good to be small.

By the time I got out at Union Station in downtown LA, I'd been on the train so long that my equilibrium was shattered. For the first day it still felt like my body was swaying. I checked in to the closest cheap hotel I could find. It had a name like The Grand and was anything but, and cost about $35, which was a lot for someone with only 450 bucks to start a life. I was happy just to be getting off the street. I had no idea that downtown L.A. wasn't Hollywood and it hadn't begun to be gentrified yet. It was all skid row and frightening, to say the least. I found a coffee shop and a newspaper, thinking maybe they had ads in the classifieds for actors. And guess what? They did! I could also make thousands part-time from home stuffing envelopes! My future was bright!

The first scam I fell for was from an ad for Hollywood Theatrical Studios, an acting school that sold itself as an "earn while you learn" program of acting class as well as placement. I took the bus from downtown to Hollywood and was soon relieved as the decay of downtown turned into some of the palm trees I'd been expecting. The owner of the school, Maurice Kosloff, was an old movie producer who had a few movie posters from the 1940s framed behind his desk with his name in small print at the bottom. He'd put you on camera to gauge your level of talent, allegedly to see how much "training" you'd need. The real angle was making enough small talk to gauge how much money they could siphon out of you. Don't worry, he'd tell you. They were going to send you out on acting jobs while you were in training so you'd just make that money back. Well, heck yes, sign me up!

I had a cousin who was an actor in L.A. named Grant Forsberg. He lived in a nice apartment in Beverly Hills with his hot soap opera actress girlfriend Deborah Goodrich. He was seven years older than me, and although he was one of only three cousins I knew, I still didn't know him all that well. I was dead-set against leeching off of him. It would have felt like cheating. But I did make contact and stayed a couple nights on their couch while I looked for a place of my own. Short on cash, I moved into an incredibly seedy weekly-rental rooming house called the St. Francis (now the Gershwin) at Western and Hollywood. It was somewhere around $45 a week and absolutely terrifying. The front desk was surrounded in thick, discolored plexiglass and you had to talk to them through a small hole. I remember coming in one night while some dude was randomly beating the shit out of a homeless guy in the entrance for seemingly no reason. He wasn't yelling or anything. He seemed bored, like he was just doing it as a workout. The guy behind the plexiglass didn't even look up. Each floor had a pay phone and people would quarrel over it like it was prison. I remember calling Mother collect on that phone more than once, scared shitless, telling her that everything was fine.

Mother was in the process of getting the fuck out of Massachusetts herself. She'd graduated massage school and was moving down to Florida to start up her own massage business. She'd worked briefly in Worcester for a chiropractor before the move. In her things, I found a reference letter he'd written for her. Obviously in jest but indicative of the relationships she'd foster.

Mother, at her best, made those kinds of relationships. She brought the best of the wicked out of people. She made people at ease with being raunchy, even led them into it. Now she was bringing that vulgar charm to Florida (see opposite page).

She'd had another breakup with P.O.W. and was heading out, kicking it blind like I was. Thanks to AA, she had new friends immediately in Florida and was traveling all over the state: Daytona Beach, Key West, gay bars, tittie bars, comedy shows like it was her own nonstop bachelorette party. She really didn't need to drink to have a good time. Being away from all the gloom and baggage of

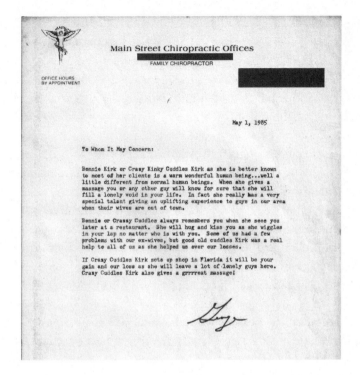

Massachusetts was enough. We were both out on our own, on great adventures for the first time in our lives, and we racked up some healthy phone bills—hers—keeping each other updated.

I wasn't getting any of these earn-while-you-learn acting gigs that they told me about, but at least I was meeting people at the school. Some good, some not as much, all of us suckers. Joe Miller was a kid from Kansas who, except for the bleached-yellow hair, looked every bit like a kid named Joe Miller from Kansas. He was about my age, freckled and with a corn-pone accent that hid—from me and only me it seemed—that he was a raging homosexual. He stayed with me at the St. Francis a few nights with our eye on getting a regular apartment. Joe had stories—big stories. He told me about how he'd been taken away from his family as a child as part of a government experiment because of his paranormal abilities. Mother always had a predilection for psychics and had taken me to some as a teenager. While I was not fully sold, I wasn't by any means the cranky skeptic I am now. While Joe Miller's story was so implausible, I still wanted to believe it. Joe had a car and, as our money dwindled, I proposed we drive to Las Vegas and use his psychic powers to take down the house. If his story were all fiction, I figured he'd find an excuse. But he was fully on board, heightening my fantasies of coming back stinking rich.

Halfway to Vegas, we stopped at a rest area when the car overheated. Joe put his stupid face over the radiator and took the cap off. His telekinetic powers must have been so strong that he was immediately awash in boiling water. He ran around screaming in circles and rolled like there were actual flames. It burned the fuck out of him but he still didn't want to turn back. We made it as far as the casinos at the state line but with my baby face and his now-giant red blobs of water-blisters, we were shooed out of every casino within minutes. We never had the chance to test his supernatural talents. It was a long and dejected drive back to L.A.

Days after, Joe came to my room and, with great theatrics, told me he'd been so broke he'd had to go out and hustle men on Santa Monica Blvd., a regular haunt for gay prostitutes. He said that most of the time he didn't even have to do anything. He'd just give them a sob story and they'd give him money. Regardless, I was frightened at how quickly someone could slip so far down that they'd have to turn to that. I was clueless that this hadn't been much of a stretch for Joe Miller. At some point we were too broke even for the St. Francis and had to sleep in his car for a few nights. That's when he finally made an advance on me in a sad, pensive way—like Phillip Seymour Hoffman in *Boogie Nights*. I wasn't offended but I was somewhat dumbstruck at my own naïveté. Later, I told my cousin Grant about it. Grant, who had met him, saw that he was so obviously gay that he considered maybe I was trying to hide that we were secretly a couple. I had no idea and it would happen again. In fact, this whole chapter gets really, really gay.

Joe and I stopped hanging out. His bullshit stories had gotten thicker and thicker. Having a gay, telekinetic roommate isn't a big deal until you're living in a car. He drifted into full-time gay hustling and I drifted literally into the background. By now I had signed up with a few casting companies for work in movies as an extra. If you ever saw such blockbusters such as *Hamburger: The Motion Picture* or the TV movie-of-the-week *Tough Love*, with Lee Remick and Bruce Dern, that was me walking around way in the background for a second. Lee Remick said hi to me at the craft service table. I couldn't wait to call Mother to tell her about my first brush with fame. (If I hadn't been so slipshod in deleting Mother's hoard postmortem, I'll bet there was a VHS or three of *Tough Love* in there, queued up to the second I walked by.)

———————

BACKSTAGE WEST WAS THE ACTORS' RAG THAT WOULD LIST AUDITIONS and casting information and it was always littered with ads for tele-marketing positions promising boatloads of money. So one day I put on the only suit I'd brought and went down to for an interview. The place was a gutted apartment on the second floor over the shops on La Cienega Blvd. across from a car wash. Everyone was bedraggled, sitting at highway salvage desks, yelling into phones. I noticed the manager had a water-bong on his desk. I guess I didn't really need to wear the suit. In fact, I probably looked like a little tiny narc at first glance.

The scam was selling toner. You had a lead on an index card for a small business along with the type of copying machine and the name of the person in charge of purchasing.

The pitch went like this:

"Yes, Barbara? Hi, this is Doug calling on the Xerox. How's the copier working for you?"

You don't say you are calling *from* Xerox. You insinuate it.

"The reason for the call is we just had a price increase for the toner and developer you use for the machine. Now normally we give you a thirty-day notification in the event of a price increase. We didn't get that notice out to you in time so what I did is set aside two cases of each at the OLD price and that's going to put into effect a price-freeze for the next six months so you'll still be paying at the old price. I'm really sorry that we didn't get that notification out. I'll get these two cases out right away. Do want that C.O.D. or on a thirty-day open billing?"

Theory being that a lot of these purchasers really have no idea what they pay since it isn't their own money, they just write the check. We'd send out inferior product at several times the regular price and nobody was the wiser. Until someone did wise up and by that time the phone room had packed up and moved across town with a different name.

The job gave you a $100 bonus just for showing up on time. The day started at five a.m. calling East Coast businesses, and with the sad sack drunks and drug addicts that worked there, getting them in on time was always a problem. At this point, Grant had gotten me a rental car for a while—I was too young to rent it myself—from Ugly Duckling Rent-A-Car. It was an early '80s Chrysler Cordoba and it was a boat with plenty of room in the back seat to sleep. Mornings were still dreadful but I could just park it in front of work and the boss would bang on the window on his way into the office to wake me up. I never missed my bonus. My first week I made $435, by far the biggest paycheck of my life. Before that it had been $180 for fifty-some hours of washing dishes. Now I was flush without the backache and out the door by eleven a.m. Plus now I could call Mother—or anyone for that matter—for free.

The paychecks were great but there was a problem. I soon found out that generally only for the first few of the checks would they actually have the money in the bank to cover. So when pay-day came, it was a gumball rally to be first to the nearest bank to cash it. If you were too late and there were insufficient funds, then you had to endure the process of finding a check-cashing place that didn't have this company on file as deadbeats. Those pre-Internet days where everything was done on index cards in a Rolodex were golden when it came to scamming the system.

I was there for less than a month before they shut down and fled but there were plenty more in town, and if one shut down, you'd have a job at another by the end of the day. Some were really shaky, some almost felt corporate. One had it down to such a science that you could only call people with certain first names—names that were generally of young people. You could call Tim but not Walter. Walter is an old person who has all the time in the world to track you down over a $250 dollar bad beat. Tim was a young man with shit to do. And if Tim had any objections while you were pitching him, you were then told to call him Timothy to psychologically bring him back to being scolded by his mother. Crafty motherfuckers. I worked for another that sold some kind of vacation scam. I remember a tall, older black salesman with a booming deep voice named Bill Brown who told a hilarious tale about a phone room that tried to screw him on his check. He saw the double-cross coming and showed up at the office on payday with a shotgun. He laid it across the boss's desk.

"You going hunting this weekend, Bill?" he allegedly asked.

"That all depends on you" went the story.

His story went on hysterically with him imagining having to chase the boss around the office had it come to that: "Dontchoo run for that door or my shotgun's gonna go crazy! Clack-clack POOM-WA!" For those of you who know my act, the "clack-clack POOM-WA" shotgun quote from my "School Shooters" bit was lifted directly from Bill Brown in that Hollywood phone room fifteen years earlier.

I had enough cash now to get my first basement apartment on Whitley near Franklin just north of Hollywood Blvd. Technically it wasn't an apartment because there were restrictions in L.A. against renting basements due to earthquakes. So it was rented as an "artist's studio." I don't know why an artist wouldn't get crushed to death any more than a resident in an earthquake but for 250 bucks a month, I wasn't asking a lot of questions. It was a single room, maybe 200 square feet, with a mattress and box spring on the floor. It didn't have sheets and I probably never bought any. I lived like a pig when I had sheets at home and didn't ever use 'em. I wasn't wasting good beer money on 'em now.

I hung around Hollywood Blvd. quite a bit. If you are unaware, Hollywood Blvd. is a filthy fucking place. It is now and it was then. Deviants and criminals, runaways and riffraff, tourists stepping over sleeping homeless to take a picture of some dead guy's star on the sidewalk. I wandered around wide-eyed and oblivious. Besides, some of those riffraff were chicks. But the chicks weren't the ones looking at me.

————————

ONE EARLY AFTERNOON ON MY WAY HOME FROM WORK, A GUY THAT looked like John Candy stopped me on Hollywood and Fairfax and said, "Excuse me . . . do you speak English?" which I found hilarious, my first time immersed in a place where so many people didn't speak English. He asked where I was from. Since I lived alone, without any real friends, I was exuberant to talk to anybody. He told me he'd show me around the city. We bought a 12-pack and started driving through the Hollywood Hills. He showed me the hill where the opening scene from M*A*S*H was filmed. I loved M*A*S*H! He was a really cool guy, and funny, too. The afternoon got to evening and I was getting pretty drunk and agreed to go to his place. After more beers there, he said I should spend the night, which was no problem for me. I was a lightweight and could fall asleep right there on the couch that minute. John Candy guy says I should just sleep in the bed with him. Plenty of room. Hey, no problem. I get into the bed and he stops me and says, "Hey now . . . we don't keep our pants on in this bed." Still, I have no clue. Maybe just manners I'm unaware of like taking your shoes off at the door. It wasn't until he suggested I take off my underwear that it dawned on me. Is everyone gay in this town and I just don't know it? Am I just a complete moron? He wasn't very happy when I told him that I wasn't gay and wanted no part of it, and he wasn't very cool or funny anymore as he drove me back to Hollywood Blvd. I guess I can see that getting that close to what he assumed was a sure thing, I'd be pretty pissed off as well.

I GOT A MAIL AND ANSWERING SERVICE ON HOLLYWOOD BLVD. so I had a phone number where you could leave messages. This was before even voicemail. You left a message with a nice lady and when I called in or stopped by, the nice lady would give it to me. Quaint. One day I got a message from Kerry Hanley, my neighbor from Rich St., informing me that her older sister MaryAnne was coming to L.A. and wanted to stay with me. MaryAnne was a punk rock chick who had a band named the Mumbling Skulls. When I had dug up my dead cat George and bleached his bones, I found out about her band and I gave her George's skull. Now she was coming to visit. Unfortunately, she showed up with her drunk, stinking boy-friend and their dog and her "visit" didn't seem to have a departure date.

It was her sister Kerry that got me drunk for the first time, and now MaryAnne was going to upgrade me to mushrooms. I had never done any drug except for smoking pot, which had never worked for me. I had no intention of doing drugs. In fact, I was so naive about drugs that I thought mushrooms was a slang term for LSD. A little peer pressure and the knowledge that it was, in fact, an actual mushroom—"It's *natural!*"—were enough to persuade me. In comparison to later experiences, it was a pretty mild trip, but at that point I had never laughed so hard in my life. We dressed up the dog in my suit and walked him up and down Hollywood Blvd. All the freaks came alive. Some Jesus cult street-theater group was perform-ing these insanely, if inadvertently hilarious, street theater scenes in full costume. The devil dancing, spinning a ribbon around a young girl, taking her into bondage and the like, acting out the scenes from their pamphlets. I watched in a trance for what seemed hours, liter-ally drooling I was laughing so hard. Mushrooms were a good thing. To this day, I'd say of the Top Ten nights of my life, probably seven or eight were hallucinogen-related. And a few of those nights were day-into-night-into-day again.

MaryAnne was old enough to buy beer, which made life easier, but her boyfriend drank most of it and would get into violent screaming fights with her to the point I thought I'd get evicted if I didn't ask them to leave. I had a girlfriend now as well. Two semi-homeless people and a dog in a single room kinda killed the romance. For all the trepidation I felt in telling them they had to go, they took it all in stride. It wouldn't be until later that I knew it was just part of life for them back then. Crash on someone's floor until they throw you out. Then find another floor. Punk rock.

I have no idea where I met this new girlfriend. She lived over the hill in North Hollywood and she went by "Dragon." I have no idea anymore what her real name was but I know she'd take the bus over the hills into Hollywood and fuck me. I'd bought a moped—the kind with actual pedals to barely assist on inclines but not nearly enough to conquer the Hollywood Hills. She'd come down and fuck me and then I'd drive/peddle her to the last bus stop on Highland before the freeway started back over the hill. Most every night when I turned around afterward to go home, there were prostitutes in front of one of the motels there down from the Hollywood Bowl, and one always catcalled me when I rode by.

"C'mon baby," in a loud whisper, "I'll suck yo dick for **free**!" and I might have considered it if it hadn't been for just having banged Dragon. I'd had my first prostitute on Sunset back when I had the rental car. She blew me for $20 and I remember being amazed at how she'd secretly put the rubber on me by rolling it down with her mouth. These offers were now coming for free but my chamber was always empty on those occasions. And besides, how are you supposed to get a blow job on a moped?

I also started hanging out with another guy from the acting school named Julio, who went by Jules. He was about twenty-six, a Cuban from Miami and a psychopath who wanted to be Scarface. He drove a Porsche 914, or what they call a "poor-man's Porsche," and we'd drive down Sunset to Malibu beach at—without exaggeration— speeds that rivaled any movie car chase I'd seen. He was absolutely insane, passing in between cars, making three lanes where there were only two, passing into oncoming traffic around corners, darting back into his own lane just before a head-on collision. There was a movie that had just come out a year before called *Against All Odds* where Jeff Bridges and James Woods have a similar car race on the same winding part of Sunset. I assume Jules was always trying to recreate it and did a damn fine job.

————————

JULES MOVED INTO MY STUDIO APARTMENT FOR A WHILE BUT IT wasn't big enough for two people. We found another place that was bigger and, of course, more expensive in a building just across from the Scientology Celebrity Center on Bronson. I hated to call Mother for money but I needed it to be able to cover my share of first month's rent and the security deposit. It was no problem. She still had "Dead Money" left. Mostly, I just wanted to call and tell her all these stories. I had some friends that I'd send occasional postcards to back home, but they were all waiting for me to be famous and I didn't want to let them down with the truth. Mother was always the first one I'd call when something fun, scary, or weird happened. The more fucked up it was, the more she ate it up. She'd still give me advice—usually "wear a rubber" or "put castor oil on it"—but nothing preachy like a parent.

Mother and I were both out on our own now, trying to make it in new, strange places with only each other to share it with. I'd tell her about my near-death experiences in Jules's Porsche, mushrooms on Hollywood Blvd., and stories of predatory homosexuals. She'd tell me about her going to the beach to feed Alka-Seltzer to the seagulls to see if they'd really explode. Sadly, that's only urban legend, but I was impressed that she actually went as far as to bust the myth.

Mother was acting now too in local dinner theater so we were all the more on a similar path. Only I wasn't acting at all. Nobody who fell for the "earn-while-you-learn" program at Hollywood Theatrical Studios did anything but pay. Mother was actually getting parts. Her relationship with P.O.W. was off and on. She'd been dating other guys. I got one of them to buy one of the vacation rackets I was selling. I told him that it was an outright rip-off but that if he'd just wait a few days until I got paid commission on it, he could call his credit card company and cancel it. He did it happily. He had to. He was fucking my mother. And I was scamming the scammers.

Jules wasn't working and he was constantly broke. The phone rooms I'd been in most recently weren't paying off and we were about to move into a new apartment that we weren't going to be able to afford at this rate. You can only call home so many times.

We had a gap of a couple days between when I had to be out of my old apartment and into the new one. We found a cheap motel to stay in for the duration. We had just checked in when I realized:

"Jules! This is that motel where that hooker was always trying to blow me for free!"

That night I'd start making rounds, walking out front where she'd usually be. Finally, she showed up and I asked her if her offer still stood. She told me to call her room at a certain time. When I called, I asked her if she had a friend for Jules. She said she did. She sent her friend down to our room while I went upstairs to hers. It immediately felt wrong. It was pitch black in the room, blacker than she was. She obviously had guests over that she'd shuffled into the bathroom when I showed up and it sounded like a poker room. She took down my pants and told me to lay on the bed. I lay down and she started blowing me. I reached down to grab her tit and she pushed my hand away. The bathroom party kept getting louder. She got up on top of me and pushed my dick inside of her, hand over her clit. I went to grab her ass but again she pushed my hand back down. Then she leaned down to kiss me and had a five o'clock shadow like my Dad. All the air went out of the room. My body went rigid and my dick went limp, trading places at the exact same time. Even my dick was creeped out, and my dick wouldn't usually care if it was stuck in the side of a grapefruit.

I muttered through some garbled excuse about not being able to concentrate because of the noise in the bathroom and barely had my pants yanked back up before I was out the door. I went back to our room and told Jules in a panic, "I think that was a guy!"

"Well, whoever she sent down here was obviously a guy and I slammed the fucking door in his face."

Thanks for the heads-up, Jules. I was only a kid for chrissakes. I took a shower hot enough to burn hair off my body. I walked down to the supermarket and tapped people to buy me beer. I walked back with a six-pack of Coors tall-boys and sat by the pool, pounding them. "I just fucked a dude" was all that went through my head. Years later, as a comedian, I'd have a violent confrontation with a transvestite prostitute who'd been in the act of blowing when she picked my pocket and I turned that story into comedy gold on stage. I wasn't embarrassed either because that time I knew it was probably a guy and just didn't care. In Hollywood, I was just a simpleton and I got straight-up hoodwinked. It was probably a while before I told Mother that story. To date, I have only been with three black women, and two of them were dudes. I'm not saying that most black women are dudes. I'm just sayin' is all.

Two days later we were in our new apartment. Everything was starting to go weird, and not in the fun way. We didn't have any money. We started to work out scams. I remember Joe Miller's grift about laying sob stories on gay suitors and getting money without having to do anything. Jules was dubious. I went to a gay bar/restaurant next to where the Laugh Factory is now (and maybe was then). I waited to get propositioned, which didn't take long. I told him a long story about how I came out to be an actor and now could barely find money to eat. He told me that he'd give me a hundred bucks to come back to his place. I told him that I wasn't really gay and didn't know if I could go through with it. I looked like a frightened child, and really, I was. He said that I should come back with him and talk and that he'd give me $100 regardless. I'm sure he was really a decent person with a good heart even if he was a dupe soliciting young boys in bars. He took me to his house in the hills and we talked. I embellished more of my downtrodden situation, told him about my imaginary girlfriend back home that I was supposed to bring out and marry yet now could barely afford to call. I could always cry on command back then and used it mostly as a parlor trick to amuse my friends. I don't know if I did it that night but with my story I probably had him close to tears. He still did halfheartedly ask me if I'd consider having sex with him—he is a dude after all—but had no problem when I said no, gave me a hundred-dollar bill, and drove me back home. It was the best and only acting I'd ever do in Los Angeles.

Jules shit a sandwich when I walked through the door with a crisp hundred-dollar bill in my hand. He didn't think I'd get anywhere with my stupid idea. Now we had what we thought was going to be an easy scam and we'd never have to work again. We sat up planning more strategies and eventually we over-thought it with a ridiculous plan. We'd go back to the bar—and as I write this, I realize how stupid it was that we'd use the same bar where I just conned a guy using a different story a few nights before. What an *Ocean's 11* duo we were! It's not like there was a lack of different gay bars in West Hollywood. The plan was that he'd try to sell that I was new to town and trying to get into gay porn. He'd act as my manager. If nothing else, we'd easily get these "fags" to buy us dinner. We sat in a rounded booth and I'm fucked if I remember how exactly we got two guys—allegedly in the industry—to our table to hear our poorly-rehearsed bullshit story, but they listened. I remember one of them asking me how big my package was. I told him 7 inches, scared that if I lied any bigger that he'd call my bluff and ask me to show it. We ordered steak dinners and drinks. They had cocktails and we talked for a while. We'd had foolish notions of getting someone to give us money up front for me doing gay porn. The last time, I'd got an easy hundred just for putting on a sad face. This should have been a cakewalk. At some point the two gentlemen said that we should give them a call sometime, wrote down a phone number, and left.

Jules and I, forks in hand, steaks in faces, stared at each other. What the fuck were we going to do now? We didn't have money to pay for this meal. We looked around the room trying to find anyone that looked like an easy mark. Nothing.

"Okay. You go to the bathroom. I'll order another drink so it doesn't look like we're leaving. Then I'll go start the car and you meet me out there." All that planning, all that preposterous backstory and absurd expectation just to end up pulling a basic chew-and-screw on a restaurant. We were defeated and embarrassed and Jules blamed me.

Everything after that started to spin out of control. Jules and another friend from the acting school, Chicago George, came into the apartment one morning in a frenzied state while I was just waking up. At first he wouldn't tell me what was going on. They were just racing around, closing blinds and talking in whispers. Later, when Jules left, George told me that on their way home from wherever, Jules had told George to slow down and pull up next to a woman walking down the sidewalk. George thought Jules must know her. As they came up beside her, Jules screamed at him to hit the gas just as he reached out and grabbed her purse. They sped off, pulling the woman over in their wake. Now they were freaking out as to whether anyone had taken down their license plate.

This was all too much for me. Con art was one thing—I actually looked at it like an art form even when I sucked at it. Strong-arm robbery was something altogether different. I started to think about leaving. I'd been there less than six months and nothing ever made sense, everything was always some fucked story. It had been funny at first but there was never any normal to balance it out. It was all *Midnight Cowboy*. I became terrified of Jules after the robbery. I tried to distance myself from him, and the more I did, the more menacing he became. Everything he said seemed like veiled threats, or so I read them that way. He was excessively paranoid and my own paranoia fed off of it.

I remember the breaking point. Yet another acting "student" of Hollywood Theatrical Studios was an older—fortyish?—black guy named Anton who talked like a gentle, punch-drunk ex-boxer. The story we heard is that he was left an inheritance, moved to L.A. to follow his dream, and left his money in the capable hands of Maurice Kosloff for safekeeping. We all guessed how that would turn out. But Anton was the sweetest, most genial if imbecilic guy I'd met my whole time in Los Angeles. In my loneliest days at the basement apartment, he'd occasionally come over and share a six-pack in the evening and he'd always have a huge smile on his face. He was like a big black Lenny from *Of Mice and Men*, like my pacifist bodyguard.

I hadn't seen him in a couple of months. Jules and I had given up on Maurice's bullshit a while ago. I walked into the Asian restaurant on the corner of Hollywood and Bronson by Jules's and my apartment one afternoon when it was all going poorly, and Anton was sitting in there by himself. At this point, I was in such a state of disarray, so confused and anxious that there couldn't be a better sight for beaten eyes. I called out his name and sat down with him. He looked up at me expressionless, stared for a minute, said nothing, and then looked back down. I didn't know if somehow I'd made him angry at some point and was unaware of it. He couldn't have possibly forgotten me in that short amount of time.

I asked him how he'd been doing, if he still went to class. He ignored me. I was stupefied. Anton started yelling to the waiter in what I assumed to be Chinese, followed by the same order in English. "(Gibberish, gibberish) Bring me another Coke!" Then he went on to ramble about how he was in the Israeli mafia and that a hit had just been put out on my policeman uncle, Ron Stanhope. I have no such uncle but was too dumbstruck to bother correcting him. He continued to talk nonsense in an intimidating tone, topping it off by slowly and deliberately drawing a straight-razor out of his pocket, using it to cut pieces of chicken in his plate. I was Robert De Niro talking to Christopher Walken at the end of *The Deer Hunter*. Anton got up abruptly, paid his bill, and left. The confused waiter asked me what language he'd been speaking when he was yelling at them. I didn't know what he was saying even when he was speaking in English. Today I know that Anton was most certainly suffering from severe mental illness. But at that moment I could only think that Los Angeles had caused it. Kosloff exploited his simple hopes, ran off with his windfall, and left him a bumbling madman. I walked out speechless onto the sidewalk. I didn't even go back to the apartment before going to a pay phone and asking my mother to fly me home to her.

———

MOTHER BOUGHT ME A TICKET TO ORLANDO, THE CLOSEST AIRPORT to her new place in Crystal River, Florida. Having flown millions of miles, I am now keenly aware that Tampa is actually a lot closer, but in those days neither of us were professionals. I'd never even been on a plane before. It didn't matter. I was getting the fuck out. As I planned my escape, Jules was getting even more spooky. It may have all been in my head but if it's in your head, that is your reality. Rent was about to be due. I had it by this point but saw no purpose in giving it to Jules when I could just bail. I didn't have much stuff and the shit I had was ready to grab and go on my back, the same way I got to L.A. The day before my flight, I had it planned to where I could just go to my cousin Grant's place, stay the night, and fly out in the morning. As soon as Jules left the house, I was gone and safe in Beverly Hills.

Grant went out that night and I sat in the apartment counting the hours and drinking his beer. Jules must have come home and seen that my room was empty by now. He was going to be pissed. It didn't matter because in the morning I'd be . . .

Knock Knock Knock at the door!

Oh fuck! Jules knows where Grant lives! I opened the little ornate security window that allows you to look out. It was Jules, demanding his rent money.

This is where I pulled the last brilliant move of my Los Angeles experience. I told him through the peephole that it wasn't that I didn't have the rent, it was that I didn't trust him anymore. I offered him a few examples of how he was becoming unstable.

See what a genius I was? Instead of ignoring the knock on the door, I answered it through a peep-window and told the violent, irrational guy on the other side that he was unstable! But that wasn't enough! To prove to him that I wasn't just fleeing to avoid paying the rent, I took the rent money out of my pocket and waved it in front of the window! This made perfect sense to me somehow because, if nothing else, the door was locked so I had nothing to worry . . .

BAM!

He kicked the doorjamb apart on his first try, beat the shit out of me, took my money, beat me up some more, and then left. He hit me so hard that my vision was too blurred to focus on the dial pad to call 911. I had to do it by memory of the keys. I was taken by ambulance to the hospital for a quick diagnostic, let out to go back to a horrified Grant and Deborah with their home torn apart, and then to make my flight to Florida and my reunion with Mother.

6

Deathbed City, Florida

I WAS PRETTY BANGED UP WHEN I SHOWED UP AT MOTHER'S. JULES had been arrested before I even got on the plane. I'd get calls for the next few days from the LAPD regarding my ability to come back to L.A. to testify. I told them that they'd have to pay my airfare. Eventually, they called to say they were going to consider it a civil matter as it concerned rent money, and they dropped the charges. Sounded more like home-invasion robbery and assault and battery to me but I guess the cost of a plane ticket dropped it down to a Judge Judy matter. Cheap pricks. At least he spent a bunch of time locked up until then.

Crystal River, Florida was a dead, one-story highway town on US 19 north of Tampa. Sawgrass, strip malls, rednecks, and dying people. I bet it hasn't changed. Mother was renting a three-bedroom ranch-style house at the end of a dead-end street. I didn't know why she needed three bedrooms living alone but they all seemed to have stuff in them. It was the beginning of her hoard and that hoard would include cats. A lot of cats. She introduced me to them like they were my siblings. When I got through meeting her cats, she started showing me pictures of her cats. A lot of pictures of cats. Gosh, did her cats do funny things.

"Look at this one, it's Peter sitting up like a person! And here's Margaret licking Alice's head!"

Yeesh.

It was still great to be there. It was safe. Like a convalescent home at the butt of a dead-end road. Of course, Mother had ground rules. If I was going to stay I had to get a job and pay rent. Clean up after yourself, help with chores. Normal shit.

She was still in the process of getting a Florida massage license and was slowly getting leads of potential clientele, mostly people she'd met in her local theater group, a few AA folk but she wasn't nearly as active in it as she had been in Worcester. She'd traded drinking for AA and now AA for acting. And as a fellow actor, no less her favorite son, she was eager to show me off. She was scheduled for the lead in the next play called *The Folks Next Door* and there was a part I'd be perfect for, playing her son, of course. Since I was this Hollywood actor kid, I was a shoe-in but still had to audition since other people already had. I showed up one afternoon with all the confidence in the world until I went on the stage, opened my mouth, and proceeded to suck copious, toxic amounts of shit. My voice warbled and whispered. It sounded like it was struggling from under-inflated lungs and warbled. I couldn't remember my lines. I couldn't make eye contact. I was *Napolean Dynamite*. I fucking stunk. I mean embarrassingly stunk, and it reflected like a funhouse mirror in the eyes of everyone present including Mother—after she'd made such a production over me being in Hollywood chasing my acting dream. Testifying-in-court kind of stink. If you've ever had the honor of publically sucking on a grand scale, you know that the worst part is how you're treated afterwards. People avoid you like you're carrying head lice or, if cornered, try to spin an illusive positive angle, as though you are somehow unaware that you just ruthlessly embarrassed yourself. I've had friends with terminal cancer who've talked about getting similar reactions. I had acting cancer. The big time had eluded me even on the small scale.

I got a job part-time as a dishwasher at a steakhouse but most of my time was fucking off, hanging around with Ma smoking cigarettes and cracking jokes. Mother had gone to Florida's east coast with some friends and seen a comedian named Jay Hickman at a tittie bar. She'd bought his cassette tape after the show and we listened to it until we knew it by heart. When her friends came around, she'd make me do Jay Hickman bits for them. She could have just played the tape but she preferred my version. Anything comedy we consumed like starved hogs and quoted back to each other. Or we created ourselves.

I became a Reverend of the Church of Gospel Ministry through a classified ad in the back of a National Enquirer. It suggested a $5 donation that I did not include but they sent me my credential regardless. So then I got my brother Jeff his own Reverend title as well. I had a typewriter and started writing to Jeff, now stationed in Okinawa and trying his best to get thrown out of the Marine Corps. Going AWOL for days, drinking heavily, and failing piss tests. I called the letters the Reverend Doug Newsletters. They were mostly semi-fictional and grotesque accounts of Life with Mother and my first stabs at writing comedy. He was called into the company CO once and asked to sit down and explain why he'd been sent a now-confiscated letter with the return address "Adolph Hitler Fan Club." My bad.

Somewhere I'd stumbled upon Paladin Press, who published all sorts of subversive books, mostly about guns, combat, and survival. I got books on revenge like George Hayduke's *Get Even: The Complete Book of Dirty Tricks*, as well as books about scams, spy techniques, and changing your identity. I was mostly interested in books and information about getting a fake ID. Mother would collect these books and literature from the mail and was sure she was going to be put on some watch list, long before watch lists became trendy to fear.

There was detailed information on changing your identity— going to a courthouse, finding someone who died as an infant that would be roughly your age (or the age you wanted to be), getting the birth certificate, and then getting a social security number as that person. It was all too much work. I wasn't on the lam or faking my own death. I just wanted to be able to buy beer.

Eventually, I found a place where you could buy a simple kit that had blank, vaguely official-looking (for that time period) ID that you typed your own information onto, added a photo, and then laminated with an iron. It wouldn't fool a cop but it got past the loose eye of the girl at the Stop & Plop. I was now Doug Reed from Blair, Nebraska and I was almost twenty-two years old. Mother wasn't exactly what you'd call "happy" that I was now buying beer at the corner store but she thought I was clever as shit. Where my father would say, "C'mon now, guy," Mother would say, "You're a hot shit!"

Mother's co-star in her play, Bruce, was also someone she was dating (randomly getting boned by). He was a real estate agent and told me I should go to real estate school. He said I could come to work with him if I got my license. He had to. He was fucking my mother. I aced the six-week course at the Sun School of Real Estate and left knowing absolutely nothing about selling real estate. All I learned was that if someone mispronounces a word, that word will come out of their mouth a thousand more times. It's "similar," nice teacher lady, not "simular." Fucking hayseed. I didn't bother trying to take Bruce up on his job offer.

I wasn't going to be an actor or a real estate tycoon. I wasn't even good at dishwashing. That's what I was doing on January 12, 1986 when the underdog New England Patriots played the Miami Dolphins for the AFC championship. I bet the cook twenty bucks that the Pats would win. We got scoring updates from the waitstaff when they came into the kitchen. I celebrated when the Patriots won but the fat-fuck cook didn't have the twenty. We settled out of court on a thick chunk of prime rib. I wasn't even good at gambling—even when I won.

Within a week, I left to go back to Worcester.

I can't remember Mother being exactly sad to see me go, though she always was. She had to know there was nothing for me in Crystal River. P.O.W. was back in her life again, even taking over the payments of the Mercury Zephyr that Mother had co-signed for me from a scumbag used car lot. Out with one deadbeat, in with another.

7

Tail Between My Legs

I WAS BACK IN WORCESTER EARLY IN 1986, LIVING IN THE BACK seat of Keith Kingsbury's hunk-of-shit Chevy Malibu. Keith lived up front. It was cold as fuck and several times a night Keith would crank up the engine to get some heat, then invariably fall back asleep. You could smell the fumes coming in from the rusted-out exhaust system. I was aware of potential carbon monoxide poisoning. It was the first time I ever had what could be considered suicidal thoughts. I wasn't depressed that I remember. I just didn't care. I was just really fucking cold. I'm sure I could have stayed with Dad and Gail—we were parked just one street over—but I was too stubborn. I could go over during the day to shower when nobody was there, and would stop in for meals, but I'd still sleep in the car out of spite-pride. I got a job as a collection agent for a few months, wearing a coat and tie and yelling at deadbeats all day, always expecting my own name to come up in a file. All of my co-workers were frail old women but I could make them laugh. The building was as decrepit as the employees, and days under fluorescent bulbs, harassing poor people, took its toll. I went back to making donuts overnight with Weird Joe Vancelette, working the fryer and napping on hard bags of flour in the basement when I could sneak it in.

Mother was back together with P.O.W. in Florida. He'd found out that she had dated her co-star of her new play and wasn't happy about it. She sent a typewritten a letter inside a Valentine's Day card like a gossiping girlfriend. It was written like she was giggling, whispering under a bedsheet:

> David's gone berserk about Bruce and I doing the play, me ending up in-on-the bed and the kissing scenes. He has been nuts since Saturday—hope he comes out of it soon. Not violent, just his mind worried about what-ifs? Jealousy's a wicked thing!!

She went on to tell me about her first massage client and getting involved with Mary Kay Cosmetics:

> Wild living here in Crystal River. I think I'm catching some of what you got sitting at the typewriter. Or maybe because you're the only one I can communicate nutty with who understands. I miss your nuts. Not those.
>
> I love you. I love you. I love you. I love you. I love You. I love you.
>
> Just wanted to see how many times I could fit that into a line.
>
> Destroy this letter. People will think there's something weird between us.
>
> Stay nuts, Hon. But do it legally. Jail's a bitch. So is court.
>
> Love ya. HAPPY VALENTINE'S DAY!!!! WRITE!!!!

There was something weird between us. We got along like best friends. We wrote to each other like lovers.

MY BROTHER WAS NOW STATIONED AT CAMP PENDLETON IN Oceanside, California. I talked Weird Joe Vancelette into taking another stab with me on the West Coast. We flew out, again with no plan whatsoever. Jeff was living on base so he couldn't put us up anywhere but he did write a lot of bad checks at Big Boy's to feed us. We stayed a few nights at a Motel 6 before Jeff found out a friend was going out on some kind of thirty-day sea duty and was willing to let us crash in his 1977 Ford Bronco parked at the Greyhound bus station. It was the third time in a year I'd lived in a car with a roommate. Save for joining the Marines, this was no place for us. We didn't last till the end of the thirty days.

Coming back to Worcester was getting old. Fortunately, I still had my fake ID. My friends and I would drink a shitload of beer that summer. We'd drink scorpion bowls and eat cheese monas at Ken Chin's Chinese restaurant lounge, singing "You're Just Too Good To Be True" or Tom Jones's "Delilah" on the jukebox at the top of our lungs. Jeff Brown had been my brother Jeff's best friend, part of that incestuous wedding party—the guy who lost the bride that I banged to my brother. Let's try not to rehash that. Too confusing. Jeff Brown and I would take excursions to Atlantic City, driving through the night to piss away what little money we had. Atlantic City was and is a bankrupt slum but we loved to gamble. To be clear, we're not talking Michael Jordan/Artie Lange level of gambler. We're talking Lotto, scratch tickets, betting-each-other-five-bucks-on-the-game kind of gamblers. But it was constant and, to us, five bucks *was* Michael Jordan money. So we started talking about moving to Las Vegas. It was utopian drunk talk at first but the more we fantasized, the more we had to make it happen. My brother said he was in as soon as his long-awaited discharge came through. It was on. "Money. Women. Danger!" went our Vegas war cry as the plan became more legitimate.

———

I WENT BACK DOWN TO VISIT MOTHER THAT SEPTEMBER. THE ONLY surviving "Rev Doug" letter came from this trip.

Dear Slob,
    As you know, I've left Massachusetts and returned to Death-bed City. Why, You ask? This is why.
    Hellsville 2; The Reverend's Revenge

Thursday, Sept 11. 2:20 pm. I board the jet from Worcester to Baltimore. I sit in my assigned seat on the right of the plane at the window. The smell of impending doom lay thick in the air. The plane lifted smoothly into the air and soon the No Smoking light went out. Not because the pilot turned it off, mind you, but because I disassembled the overhead compartment and smashed the fucking light bulb. All was well, but that didn't last long. I picked up the refreshment list only to be faced with a decision more difficult than choosing the method in which you will die. The decision was between Miller Lite and Michelob in a can. The only thing more amazing than the limited selection was the fact that these two of the nastiest beers on the market could be listed under "refreshments." A Fleet enema would be more refreshing and have the same after effect. A cold sweat broke on my face as the drink cart wheeled menacingly towards me like a Sherman tank. "Would you care for something to drink?" she says. I order the Michelob. "Anything else I can get you?" she asks. "Yes, something to vomit in," I say. She laughs. She didn't laugh when I choked up Cream of Broccoli soup in her change cup. I got off the plane in Baltimore and immediately went in search of food. I stopped at a portable snack cart in the hallway and asked "What's it, about 34 bucks for a Snickers?" "58 cents," she tells me. Not too outrageous for an airport. So I grab a box of Jujyfruits, assuming they are the same price, "$1.32" she says. "You've gotta be kidding!" I say. "That's what you pay at the movies," she says. "That's why I don't go to movies," I say, and pitch the box back on her cart. I felt like punching a carpet tack through the soft spot in her knee but I figured I'd save my strength for Dismal River. I move on to the regular snack bar where the chili dog looked fairly appetizing. I had to take out a loan in order to pay for the fucking thing and after I consumed it I felt far less than comfortable. The sonofabitch caused internal hemorrhaging and I had to have my stomach pumped. I refused to get discouraged. I still had Charlotte to look forward to.

4:08 pm. I boarded the flight to Charlotte. I sat in my assigned seat on the right of the plane, again at the window. The smell of impending doom lay thick in the air. This flight was no different than the one prior. I gagged down another can of Michelob and again vomited profusely on the stewardess. In the airport at Charlotte I began to think of what lay ahead in Lobotomy Land. I had lots of time to think due to the fact I had a 3-hour layover. The smell of impending doom lay thick in the air. Since there is nothing to do in Charlotte for three hours, I had no choice but to fuck with people to pass the time. I held my carry-on bag tight to my chest, sweated out of my forehead a lot, and looked around all sorts of shifty until a security guy walked by and I jump[ed] and walk[ed] away real quick. It didn't work. I guess I just don't look like a terrorist. So then I'd sit in my seat like I was sound asleep and wait for a kid to walk by with his mom. When his mom wasn't looking I'd leap up, grab the little fucker, pull his hair, twist his ear, smack him in the face, and then jump back in my seat sound asleep so his mom wouldn't believe him when he told her. When that got boring I got up and went around stealing people's luggage and putting it next to some other poor fucker so he'd get blamed. The fun was just beginning when they called my flight to board.

8:45 pm. I board Flight 67 to Orlando. Again I sit on the right at the window. My neck is like fuckin' concrete from looking over my right shoulder to see out the window. This flight was more enjoyable only because it was longer, meaning I could get drunker. I order my Michelob and this asshole steward has the balls to card me. Lucky for him I have my cheesy excuse for a fake I.D. with me. I knew he'd accept it cuz he was a stupid fuck. It could have had some big black guy's picture on it and still he would have said, "OK, Leroy, here's your beer." As if I wasn't upset enough, it seems that this particular beer had endured a bit too much turbulence because when I opened it, it did its best impression of Mt. St. Helens all over my lap. I kept pressing the call button for more beer until I was fully blasted. The alcohol that clouded my brain could not overshadow the smell of impending doom that lay thick in the air.

The humidity was so high in Orlando that I grew gills. I met Mother at baggage claim. She seemed more beautiful than ever before. Her breasts seemed full and supple, with nipples that almost pierced the thin material of her nearly see-through blouse. She stood solid and tall in her knee-high, black leather Gestapo boots, fishnet stockings, and black leather miniskirt. Her tight ass jiggled ever-so-slightly as she walked towards me and embraced me. She brought her riding crop slowly up the inside of my thigh until it lightly tickled my throbster. She slid her 9-inch tongue deep into my esophagus. We were swapping spit for just a brief moment when she stopped abruptly and stepped back. She brought the riding crop to my cheek and turned my head to face her.

"Have you been drinking?" she asks.

"No, ma'am," I replied.

"Then what's that smell?" she returned.

"Impending doom, ma'am," I said.

She sniffed the air again as I picked up my luggage. She forced me down on all fours, sat on my back, and rode me out to the parking garage.

As we pulled up to Mother's new home I saw a modestly small sign reading 'BONNIE KIRK, MASSAGE THERAPIST.'

We parked in the carport, unloaded my bags, and walked to the door. There on the doorstep was Mange, the cat. We stepped over rather than move him. Mother is afraid that his limbs will fall off if she lifts him, not to mention he carries more diseases than the Mayo Clinic has cured. Once inside, a large sign read a little less reserved than the one outside.

"Mistress Bonnie's House of Pain and Sodomy"

I was a little disturbed by this until she reassured me that I would not be charged for her services. But not tonight. I had to get a lot of sleep to prepare for the Armageddon to come. I woke the next morning a little groggy from the trip. Mother had fixed a black coffee enema to get me going. I packed an arsenal of weapons, my bible, and some dental floss and I was on my way to clean up this town once and for all.

But as I walked out I came to the realization that I was doing God's work for him. And why the hell should I have to pay him all that money if I'm not gonna even let him work? So I said fuck it and made a few prayers such as letting Homosassa sink into the marshland and all it's inhabitants be eaten by reptiles. I've already put my time in here. There's a whole starving nation out there. I could be out there waving a fried chicken leg in their face. Which reminds me: I thought of a great hobby for Las Vegas. We hang out in casinos and watch some poor bastard come in with money out the ass, gamble it all away along with his house, personal belongings, shirt off his back, his kid sister, etc.

As soon as he's completely destitute and heading for the door with his head in his hands, we run up, you spit on him and I kick him in the shin. Personally I think it would be funny as a bastard. Oh, shuvitupyerass.

Missing the punky stuff that forms in your tight little pucker,
Rev. Doug
P.S. Tell your lady that I'd pay up to 37 dollars in American currency to toss my nuts up her crapper.

In reality shit wasn't going well for Mother in Florida. P.O.W. had been back around, had even proposed to her earlier in the year. But while he was out on the road trucking, a suspicious letter showed up in the mail, addressed to him from some random address in New Hampshire in a woman's handwriting. Mother, never one to respect someone's privacy, steamed it open. The letter began, "David, how dare you propose to me and then disappear!" It went on to betray a long relationship he'd been having with another woman, covering his time away on both ends by saying he was off driving truck. Mother got in contact with the woman and traded stories. P.O.W.'s bullshit started to fall like dominoes.

Cheating on Mother turned out to be the least of the deceit. The more she probed, the more she found that his entire life story was all bunkum. After connecting with the other woman, Mother called P.O.W.'s mother who I'd lived with in New Jersey and started asking more questions. Turns out she wasn't his mother at all. She laughed at the idea. David was just a kid in the neighborhood that always referred to her lovingly as his mother. A P.O.W.? David hadn't even gone to Vietnam. He'd been kicked out of boot camp for having a heart murmur! And David Hatch wasn't even his real name! His real name was Wendell Fritsch! This is a guy that she'd been with for the better part of six years and now nobody knew who he even was. We were both floored. He'd been Clint fucking Eastwood to me. All those horror stories of his time in a prison camp that I bragged to all my friends about. That "particularly gruesome" prisoner of war story I mentioned? Yes. That was a story about being shackled on his knees with his arms manacled behind him when the prison commander came into his cell and threw his best friend's severed head into his lap, leaving it there for days. Sound familiar?

IT'S A FUCKING SCENE FROM *APOCALYPSE NOW!*

Jesus, did I feel like an asshole! But not nearly as bad as Mother. She was devastated and humiliated, if not just for herself, but for the fact that she'd introduced him into my life and knew that he'd been a role model and a hero to me. If there was a turning point when Mother started down the road of bitter and mean, it may well have been right then. She felt cheated, guilty, stupid, and unbearably alone all at the same time. Three of the four were accurate. I'm the one who should have felt guilty. How the fuck had I never seen *Apocalypse Now?*

In Worcester, I'd started dating a girl named Lisa, a rare friend of my beast stepsister. I probably just asked her out initially to piss off Carla, but Lisa said yes and we were a couple almost immediately. We were in love and ran amok for a couple of months, but it was going to have to be put on hold, as the move to Las Vegas was about to be realized. The long-awaited day of Grandma's "Dead Money" came in to finance the move and I knew if I waited, I'd piss it all away on beer and cheese monas. Lisa was still a senior in high school and wasn't going to be able to join us until she graduated. That worked perfectly because she would be kind of an obstacle on the "women" part of our "Money. Women. Danger!" plan. Late in '86, we flew to San Diego where my brother picked us up in his Alfa Romeo Spyder he'd just purchased, wearing a WWII aviator's cap with goggles. It was a two-seater that the three of us drove in all the way to Vegas, with all our shit, top down, freezing our balls off.

8

Las Vegas: Money. Women. Danger!

Coming into sight of the Las Vegas strip at dusk, I had no doubt that I'd made the right move. The south end of the strip was lousy with cheap motels back then and we grabbed the first one we saw. We were cold and exhausted. My poor brother had to turn around and head straight back for duty the next morning. Jeff Brown and I drank beer and stared at the lights, giggling and high-fiving to the bounty that lay ahead of us. We got up at first light and started the long hump north on the Strip. It was fucking magical. Las Vegas in 1986 was a broke man's paradise. You could find anything cheap or free. You could find Fun Books everywhere, with coupons for everything from free shrimp cocktails to free graveyard-shift breakfasts and free cocktails. We found a cheap weekly rental at the Fun City Motel on Las Vegas Blvd. and Sahara. It had a two-burner counter-top stove where we'd cook 39-cent spaghetti using five-for-$1 ramen noodles covered in 19-cents-a-can tomato sauce, cooked in an aluminum pie plate. We learned quickly that you could drink for free by pretending to play a nickel slot machine. Wait for the waitress to come into sight, drop a nickel in, and spin the wheel while you order your beer. Drop in another nickel when she came back with it.

I'd loiter in front of the motel office and wait for someone to buy a newspaper out of the machine, then casually jam my hand in the door before it shut. Every coin could be the one that made you rich in Vegas, no point in wasting one on the paper looking for a job. Finding a job was a breeze. At that time, boiler-room telemarketing was the second largest industry in Nevada next to gaming, for what reason I do not know, most likely due to lax regulation. The classifieds of the *Las Vegas Review-Journal* were loaded with ads for phone room work just like the ones in LA. I found one that was within walking distance and went down to apply, knowing this time I wouldn't need a suit and tie.

AMERICAN DISTRIBUTING WAS IN A U-SHAPED STRIP MALL ON Industrial Blvd. (now Frank Sinatra Blvd.) just behind the Circus Circus. The manager was a fun drunk-uncle named Al Ferguson, bow-legged in tennis shorts like Hunter S. Thompson, with curly gray hair. I told him about my toner work in L.A. and was hired immediately. It was the Wednesday before Thanksgiving. He stopped me as an afterthought before I walked out the door. "Hey . . . you want one of these?" They'd handed out Thanksgiving hams to the salespeople and had some left over. I walked home beaming with it clutched in my arms like a baby, waiting for vultures. Jeff Brown and I lived on that ham for five days.

Shortly after, Jeff Brown met and moved in with some skank. I found a studio apartment just across the street in what was then the Naked City area of Las Vegas. I worked from 6–11a.m. and then had all the time in the world to do nothing all by myself. I gambled a bit, which I loved, but that didn't last long. I still had my fake ID that worked at most of the shitty dive casinos like Slots-A-Fun but could get heavily scrutinized elsewhere. Even if they didn't accept it, at least they gave it back to me. Until they didn't. Security had thrown me out of Bob Stupak's Vegas World several times, but I kept going back because it was the closest casino to my place and I was lazy. The last time, they brought me into the back room—yeah, I was afraid it was gonna go like that too—but they just went through a state-by-state book of legitimate identification. Seeing that mine was not in there, they took a Polaroid picture of me and told me never to set foot in there again.

I was already lonely, and now I couldn't go anywhere fun (at least until I ordered a new fake ID kit), so I did what anyone would do. I joined AA. Having grown up in AA, I knew that I'd be immediately accepted and have a ready-made circle of new friends. I'd get even more attention for being a "newcomer." I don't know if I really thought I was an alcoholic but I knew I always liked to drink and the dogma of the program was deeply entrenched from the years growing up with Mother's preaching it. I went to a meeting and was welcomed with great fanfare. Like drinkers, nondrinkers don't like to not drink alone. I don't ever remember taking it seriously. I certainly never "worked the steps," nor did I have any good alcoholic stories to share. Even if I embellished my best stories and said I'd been "forced" into prostitution, or "woke up" with a transvestite—I was fucking sober for those stories. I didn't even have alcohol as an excuse, much less as the problem. I quit drinking because I had nobody else to talk to? How boring is that story? I kept my mouth shut but I did find a lot of people there roughly my age and we had a decent group of friends. Nonalcoholic friends but the entire Las Vegas world was so new and foreign to me that not drinking was just something else different.

Pretty soon, Jeff Brown got dumped and came back to live with me in Naked City. The apartment was even smaller than that basement "artist's studio" in L.A., and Jeff had to sleep on a cot. Over a course of nights we heard kittens mewing outside. We eventually went out to investigate and found four newborn kittens at the bottom of a large trash can full of building debris. Now we lived in roughly 175 square feet, with two of us and four kittens I named Lumpy, Mange, Grinch, and Mother. I named that one after Mother. And with all of our stuff and cats piled up in a small place, it was like a microcosm of being at Mother's.

———

JEFF BROWN STARTED WORKING AT AMERICAN DISTRIBUTING AS well. Except for the early morning start, the phone room was a blast. American Distributing operated a different hustle than toner. They sold advertising specialties, or "ad-specs," as was the nomenclature. The industry standard ad-specs pitch—called a "One-in-Four"— worked roughly like this:

"Congratulations! You've been selected to win one of the four major awards in our big promotion! You are now guaranteed to win one of the following: a brand new car, a trip for two to Hawaii, a wide-screen television set, or $1000 in cash! All we ask is that you place a token order for one of our many advertising specialty prod- ucts to show that you are a current customer in good standing."

They'd buy three hundred bucks' or so worth of pens, key-tags, coffee mugs, etc. with their company name printed on them, think- ing the worst they could do was win a thousand dollars. What they did win—in that scenario—would be the Hawaiian vacation, which was really a certificate that allows one person to go for free if the other one pays double. Every company's pitch had a variation and a different boobie-prize. One had a "home sauna" that everybody won. It was pretty much a heavy-duty dry-cleaning bag that you'd get inside of and attach a blow-dryer to. Blow-dryer not included. One I'd heard of was a big-screen TV, meant to sound like you mispro- nounced "big-screen TV," but was, in fact, a large magnifying screen that you put in front of your own shitty television. The legality lay all in the wording.

At American, we had a "no-sale" pitch as our main pitch. The One-in-Four had been burned out and most of the leads you were calling were old order forms drawn from its victims. Once somebody got burned by one of these scams, their name was a valuable com- modity. Once a stooge, always a stooge. So the leads would be sold but not before being copied and sold to every other game in town, who all called them relentlessly with the same "You've won one of these four prizes" bullshit.

The no-sale pitch—which, at American, I ended up extensively rewriting to perfection, and was proud to have stolen by phone rooms across the city—came on like some middle-man, honest broker. "Hey Tim. This is Doug Reed from American Distributing. Listen, a little while ago you got a call from one of our salespeople about winning a big award in a promotion? You turned him down on that, correct?"

Now you hold the phone away from your ear until the person goes hoarse from screaming at you. "These goddamned people call me night and fucking day with this bullsh . . . "

"Hang on, Timothy. Listen to me. I am not a salesman. The reason I'm even calling you today is that I can see you've spent a lot of money in this industry . . . "

"I've spent money and you fucking people have ripped me off so many goddamned times."

"Here's the thing, Timothy. You know as well as I do that there's always some 'boobie-prize' in these promotions. Some piece of junk jewelry or a worthless vacation that everybody gets. The thing is, those 'legitimately' large awards—the new cars and the big cash prizes—they have to go out by law, it's just very rarely. The reason I called you back today, you came up 'legitimately' lucky on this promotion. You were actually selected to get one of the major awards. I know you've spent a lot of money in this industry and now you're in a rare position to walk out ahead of the game. You just have to stick with me on this.

What is the 'legitimately' major award? I can't say. I'm not even supposed to be calling you back. This could jeopardize my own job. I just couldn't see you turn your back on something so against the odds. Just do me a favor. Once I put you out ahead of the game, don't ever buy into any of these promotions again. Because the chances of you hitting this big again are slim and none.

The old-timers would constantly bitch about the boom days of the one-in-four pitch and how much money they used to make before all the other rooms burned it out. But I fucking slayed with this new pitch. The "legitimately big prize" was maybe a microwave oven or a boom box radio/cassette player. They got something, and since we never told them what it was, what could they say? Who's to say in court what's "legitimately big"?

The phone room was loud. You could hear everyone else's pitch but you had what was called a "confidencer" on your mouthpiece, making it like a directional microphone so anything not said directly into the mouthpiece wasn't heard. Chaos could continue without it fucking up your pitch. The offices were glorified cubicles, separated by walls that didn't quite make it to the ceiling. Like a good coke-snorting bar toilet. There were maybe ten or a dozen in a U-shape. Pepper Roach was at the top of the U. He was a former boxer from Boston and brother of Freddie Roach, now famous as the boxing trainer of Manny Pacquiao, then working another phone room across town. Pepper was a fucked-up funny little Irish runt with a flattened nose. He had a tattoo of a rooster in a noose on his calf and never got tired of the joke . . . "See! I got a cock that hangs below my knee!" That's commitment to a joke. He would regularly use a line in his pitch saying, "Lady, I'm going to tell you what I tell my Sunday-school kids at church. Have faith and believe! And I'm gonna tell you the same thing. Because I didn't call you to lie to you." He's belching this into the phone at top volume, standing at his office door with his pants down to his ankles, wagging his cock at the other salespeople.

I was one office away from the other end of the U. Beside me was Tom Konopka. He was just as funny but far more dry and abstract. "Is Bob in? Who's calling? Tell him it's Ima," he'd deadpan like Lurch from the *Addams Family*. "Ima Junebug." To this day, memories of Tom make me laugh. With adjoining offices, there was about a 12-inch gap between the wall and the ceiling. We'd regularly throw things over the gap in the middle of a sale to try to make the other guy laugh. I'd start with some loose change. He'd come back with some empty soda cans. I'd respond by dumping a week's worth of newspapers in a fluttering thump. I remember him once countering with the legs of a stacking chair coming over. It would have never fit but the image made me spit coffee. I was in tears. He was odd and brilliant. He'd always teach me new words.

"Doug. You have a head like an obelisk," I'd hear over the wall as I walked into my cubicle.

"I don't even know what that means."

"Look it up," he'd monotone as a dictionary spilled over the top of the wall, dropping on my floor with a thud.

People would ask me later in interviews who my comedy influences were and I'd parrot the same names every other comic of my generation says: Richard Pryor, Eddie Murphy, etc. But Pepper Roach and Tom Konopka influenced my sense of humor as much as or more than any stand-up comedian. Not to mention Mother.

———

MOTHER STARTED SENDING "CARE PACKAGES" TO ME AT THE OFFICE. They'd be mostly full of thrift store carnage of not-quite-yet vintage, hideous plaid sport coats, which we'd make the hourly-wage new guys wear as "trainee" suits. There was usually some truck stop-grade pornographic magazines of obese women or the like. Near Christmas she sent a stocking. Along with a whoopee cushion and a "Thank God I Farted" keychain, there was a cassette tape with a hand-drawn title, "Classical Gas." I kinda knew what it was gonna be before putting it into the player. Sure enough, it was a series of crudely taped farts—Mother's own. She'd taken the time and care to have her tape recorder ready so that any time she had to fart, she could just pick it up and rip one. When she had a full cassette tape, she drew up a cover and mailed it to the office. I'd play it for people and they'd say, "That's from your Mother???" She was a legend there at American Distributing without ever having set foot in the place.

Let me take a moment to defend flatulence. While I can appreciate and enjoy intelligent humor that makes you think, I never want to become so ensconced in artistry that I no longer laugh at farts. There is nothing even remotely close to how much a powerful, wet, gurgling blast of gas and matter can make me laugh. From the beginning, as a child, they made me weep snot, and have continued to make me fall out every time since. I couldn't name one other comedy source more timeless than farts. Stand-up comedy has the shelf life of mayonnaise in the hot sun. Jokes get old. Movies like *Caddyshack* still hold up fairly well but could never make me spill off a chair with tears running down my face, gasping for breath, like a well-placed, turbulent anal expulsion. Repeatedly, over and over, even when you see 'em coming. Jeff Brown and I commonly ate at the Sahara dinner buffet where I had—to this day—the best spectacle of bowel-wrenching flatulence of my life. The room was full of mostly elderly people, tables tightly packed, and we were seated dead center. It was silent except for the slight tinkling of silverware on plates. I felt my lower intestine chamber up and I knew it had championship prospects. I knew Jeff Brown would have absolutely no appreciation for what was about to happen, which made it way funnier. My chair was the perfect hard plastic for maximum reverberation. I was choking down the belly laugh as I leaned up and into the table, hands on the corners, thoroughly telegraphing my intentions. What came out of me was Hell's Trumpet. A deafening tear echoed off every corner of that muted hall. It lasted at least 6–7 seconds, a veritable eternity of hang-time for nonstop wind. The pitch roared up and down the scales in range. The clarity of sound would have made you feel like you were actually dining inside my colon. People were seated literally a foot behind me. When it concluded, all sound in the dining room had completely evaporated. There was no question that every single person of the hundred or so in there had bore witness to my masterpiece. Jeff Brown was paralyzed with inner fury as the mortified silence turned to widespread murmurs of disgust. I simply stared at my plate as tears flooded my eyes, my nose ran, and I began to drool while convulsing and desperately trying to contain any audible laugh. Jeff would have run for the door had it not been situated so far away. He was genuinely enraged, and still comically fumes to this day when I bring that story up. I laughed just as hard now recounting it here as I did that pleasant afternoon. (And again, during rewrites.) Farts are the funniest things in life, and if you disagree, then you have no soul. End of story.

Meanwhile, back at work I was becoming the top salesman at American as well as class clown. Money was rolling in, Lisa and

my brother were about to come out, her from high school and him
finally out of the Marines.

By the time they arrived in summer, 1987, Jeff Brown and I had
rented a sweet three-bedroom house with an in-ground pool on
Sixth St. at St Louis Ave. I'd picked up a 1984 Dodge Omni from
an auction for four hundred bucks. We bought a huge ten-piece sectional couch from a secondhand furniture place and got a used pool
table for the living room. Party central. Fuck AA, I had real friends
now and wasn't gonna let these new digs go to waste with sobriety.
Mother could stop sending me the chips.

Mother had been putting her life back together after P.O.W. with
the help of self-help books, psychics, and fake titties. Self-help books
were nothing new. She'd been quoting Dr. Wayne Dyer's *Your Erroneous Zones* like scripture since we were kids. Now she was reading
any self-help she could find for twenty-five cents at the thrift store.
Each new one was the end-all secret truth to health, beauty, or spir-
itual enlightenment. Psychics weren't new either. She'd always gone
to them and brought me along quite a bit as a young teenager. It
was harmless and fun but she was taking it very seriously now, being
extremely vulnerable from the breakup. You were with a guy for six
years only to find out he was liar, a manipulator, and a complete
fraud? Who better to help you rebound than a psychic!

With the P.O.W./Wendell Fritsch backstory laid out to chum the
waters, the psychic didn't even bother with a slow burn. She told
Mother right away that the reason for her bad luck was because
someone in a past life had put a curse on her! Haven't you noticed
all the bad luck and loneliness in your life? Now that you mention
it, I have! I have noticed my luck is cyclically bad! I mean, except
when it's good—but yes! A *curse* would explain Everything!

The psychic went straight to work on this, no time to waste. She
instructed Mother to tape hundred-dollar bills to different affected
parts of her body, then sleep with them taped on for specific amounts
of days. Then Mother would bring them back to her so that they
could be burned in a secret ceremonial fire. And when she still found
bad voodoo in Mother's aura after that, a new process of the same

would begin. Mother only admitted this to me a few years later when she'd read in the local newspaper that the woman had been arrested for pulling this scam all over Florida. The way she saw it, the amount of other people who fell for it somehow proved that she wasn't really a gullible sucker. Like Christians or other large-draw religions.

Where mystics grifted her and self-help books only helped the authors, fake titties really did lift her spirits. She got her first pair when I was a teenager, and now, after being part of a class-action lawsuit against the makers of the originals, she had upgraded to a less toxic brand. She flew out to Vegas that September and sported them like heads of wall-mounted game trophies. The great thing about chicks with new tit jobs was their willingness—their desperation— to show them off, whip them out, and even let you cop a feel. If it's your mother, this is the opposite of great, although I remember finding it funny at the time. Who's that lovely woman yanking her tits out in front of my friends? Well, that's my mother, of course!

Straight off the plane in Vegas, all Mother wanted to do was show off her tits and then get straight to the gambling. I wanted to show off my new digs. I was rich, for fuck's sake! At least in my world! I was making 1,000–1,500 bucks a week some weeks! Look, Ma! We have a goddamned waterfall in the fucking living room, for chrissakes! Sure, it came with the rental, was made outta some kind of foam, and was now hideously discolored from us putting food coloring in the water to make it look like it was vomiting blood . . . but still I have a goddamned waterfall and a pool and a pool table! I was sleeping in cars for a year and look at me now!

"That's great. Take me to the slots."

I knew Mother liked to gamble but those experiences were limited to scratch tickets at the coffee table or occasional trips to the horse track. Unlike Vegas, the horses eventually stop running and you have to leave. At the casino, Mother went on a rampage.

"You wanna eat first, Ma?"

"I'm fine. You go ahead, I'll catch up," she said with a thousand-yard stare at the spinning wheels.

Hours would pass and we'd catch up with her again.

"Hey, do you wanna see a show or something?"

"No. Leave me alone. And get me more nickels."

She'd arrived with a guy named Randy. She'd been fucking a lot of dudes since David. She never had a problem finding a guy back then. Or losing one either. Randy was quite a bit younger, thirty-five or so to her forty-two, and sold insurance. You could tell he was of little consequence in her life by the way she interacted—or didn't interact—with him. He was the trophy boyfriend of a third-place finisher, like something to compliment her new tits. He hung back with us while we lost Mother to the slot machines.

"C'mon Ma, it's 7:30 in the morning. Let's go and hit the breakfast buffet."

"I'll meet you there," she'd say, now playing two machines at the same time, absolutely maniacal. It was honestly no different than watching someone glazed over in the midst of a crack binge. This wasn't fun. This was pure hypnotized *need*. We'd go home and then come back for her, all to no avail. If she was in Las Vegas for five days, four of them were spent in front of a slot machine. God knows how many times she went to the ATM or the cashier's cage to withdraw from a credit card. It was kind of a letdown but I figured she deserved it, finally getting out of that dismal town for a minute. The one thing we did get her to do that was the most important thing for me, was getting her to make an appearance at American Distributing. I wanted all the sales people to meet the lady that was sending all these weird clothes, pornography, and recordings of tremendous farts. Hey guys, come meet my mom.

————

JEFF BROWN, LISA, MY BROTHER JEFF, AND I WERE ALL NOW working at American. Not so much nepotism as willing warm bodies. We'd get up at five, pile into the Dodge Omni, grab some breakfast, and hit the phones. The Jeffs were selling and Lisa worked as my secretary, a job that consisted of nothing but dialing the phone and handing it to me when there was a live one on the line. It was all a happy little family except that I was the only one pulling down any real money and so I had to cover everyone's bills. Lisa and I weren't getting along all that well and my brother was constantly trying to fuck her. I think Jeff Brown had started getting into coke, and if he wasn't then, he would be shortly.

At American, I'd become known as the Customer Abuse Department. Customer abuse was strictly prohibited, and, like police abuse, was rampant. And I was the best. New guys would bring leads to me of people who'd been excessively rude and I'd tack them up on my bulletin board for regular punishment.

I'd get them on the phone and start pitching them in a robotic voice until they hung up. Then I'd call back and be talking in the same voice and from the same point in the pitch where they'd just slammed the phone down. This could continue into the next day. As long as it took to get the entire pitch out.

If it was a rude secretary, I'd call and ask to leave a message for the owner.

"Hi, can you leave a message for Bill? Thanks, tell him that Todd called and that I'll be taking the 12:45 flight on Delta to St. Louis, and then connect to flight 791 to Little Rock. I'll be staying at the Days Inn but not the one by the airport. It was sold out so I'll be at the Eunice Park Days Inn, and that's where I'll be meeting with Ted Atkinson and Dave LaBonneret. Got that? Atkinson and LaBonneret. L.a. Capital B, o.n.n.e.r.e.t. And let him know that's regarding the Mudripple account. Now write down—this is important—that tomorrow I leave Little Rock on United Flight 880 back through St Louis and on to Flight 3306 to Tallahassee to have lunch with Bert Bronwinsen . . . " The minutiae in the message would go on and on relentlessly and every part was "very important" until the secretary finally broke down.

"Does he really need to know all this???"

"Well, you and I both know what a stickler Bill Yelvington is for detail!"

"Yelvington? This is Bill *Carter's* office!" as the tears and curse words faded into a click.

The worst guy you could get on the phone is a stroker. He's the guy that has no intention of buying anything but has time to kill to fuck with you. They act completely like they're about to lay down for a sale, ask a lot of excited questions, and keep you on the phone for as long as they can before telling you to go fuck yourself right at the end, right when you were sure you were about to close a monster. It's the most demoralizing thing that can happen to you in the phone room. You were already spending that money in your head.

A stroker would get me fired from American. It was some doctor so I knew he had money and he laid down for me like a whore on clean sheets. I probably tripled whatever order size I'd pitch anyone else. I was going to walk out that office door and put that number on the board like a god. And right at the end, I asked which credit card he'd like to use, and after a full conversation of "sounds great" and "absolutely," he simply said, "Yeaaaah, I'm not interested," and hung up.

I called back: "Hey, I think we got disconnected."

"No, I hung up on you. I'm not interested." Click.

I was livid. I looked over the lead, which was an actual photo-copied order form of a previous rip-off from another company and—lo and behold—his credit card number was on it.

I called him back, and when he answered I just started reading the credit card number into the phone.

"That all sound familiar, jerk-off? That's your fucking Mastercard number, and now every time I see a late-night commercial for Ronco records or Ginsu knives I'm gonna order a thousand of 'em to be sent to your fucking house. How do you feel now, smart-fuck?" and I slammed the phone down.

I was really satisfied with myself and stayed that way for a while until the owner of American, Steve Sisolak, came storming into the sales office. He almost never came into our offices, and unless he was dressed as Santa for the company Christmas party, you really didn't want to run into him. He blew into my office red-faced, shuffled through the leads on my desk until he found the doctor. He shoved

it in my face and yelled, "Did you tell this guy you were going to
order a bunch of shit to his credit card???"

"Yes, but . . . well, Steve, the guy stroked me . . . "

"Pack up your shit. You're fired!"

I fucked up hard. In my rage, I'd forgotten that I'd given the guy
all the company information, the phone number, and my alleged
name. How do you feel now, smart-fuck?

———

I HATED HAVING TO LEAVE AMERICAN. I OWNED THAT ROOM.
Finding another phone room would be easy but I'd be starting from
scratch with a new pitch. On top of that, we were gonna have to
move out of the house since I'd been the only one making money
and now that money was gone. The house wasn't the same sweet
party place it had been when we moved in five short months before. The party had gone on, indeed, but it had never been cleaned
up afterwards. Never. We'd literally gone through every dish in the
house and they now stood like a monument a foot over the top of
the sink. We'd gotten down to eating only frozen dinners to avoid
washing dishes. If you desperately needed a fork you could pull one
out of the sink, but it was like a game of Jenga. The whole pile could
come down on top of you. There was a sandbox out next to the pool
that the cats used as a litter box until that got too full. Then they
started using the closets. There was no way we'd be getting a security
deposit back no matter how hard we cleaned so we didn't bother
cleaning at all. I take that back. Before we left, I thought it would
be funny to chuck all the maggoty dishes into the pool where they
lay like the lost place settings of a white trash Titanic.

I know the sweet-smiled, well-mannered kid I appeared to be
when I rented the place. As trustworthy as they come. And I know
the barbarian I'd become after we actually moved in. I swore I'd never
be a landlord because of it. Jeff Brown and I got a new gig at a boiler
room called Midwest Enterprises, where we found a one-bedroom

apartment in a complex right next door. Lisa and I got the bedroom, Jeff and Jeff Brown slept on chunks of that ten-piece sectional in the living room. Most of our shit was left behind at the house on Sixth St. We didn't have the room. At one point, my brother and I did go back to the Sixth St. house to cherry-pick a few items we'd left behind, and had the unfortunate timing of being there when the owners showed up. We scrambled to get what we needed out and loaded up before they could take in the full extent of the damage. There were holes in the walls, garbage strewn everywhere, countertops layered in chicken bones and maggots.

"What the hell is this? There's shit in this closet!"

Loaded another box and pretended not to hear.

"Jesus Christ! What in God's name happened here?"

I looked into the bedroom that had been my brother's. The landlord was standing over a giant red stain on his new beige carpet where Jeff had spilled a Big Gulp of Hawaiian Punch. It looked like someone had bled out.

"Um . . . I think that was there when we got here."

The landlord's rage began to blister. He couldn't focus on one defacement without finding another. We had to get the fuck out of there immediately. He was rightfully losing control and about to get violent. We crammed what we needed in our arms and made for the car. As we were putting shit in the trunk, we looked up to see the wife wearing rubber gloves holding up a large papier-mache phallus. Halloween had just passed and I'd gone out as a dick-head. Now she's standing in shock, holding the two-foot tall dick-hat up by the neck like it was a dead rat. The husband went apoplectic as we hopped in the car and started it. He was already to the back of the car, screaming and pounding on the back window with the cock-helmet as we sped off, gasping in fear and hysteria.

Later, he would sue us for damages, but by that time I'd be gone and Jeff Brown would have to deal with it.

MIDWEST ENTERPRISES ON MARYLAND PARKWAY WAS THE SAME thing, promotional advertising products, but with a basic one-of-four pitch. Every one-in-four has three big awards and one lofty-sounding hunk of shit, and most of the people you're calling are savvy to it by now. At Midwest, the booby-prize was the "Roman-Greco coin," which was, of course, "priceless." You couldn't give the customer a number on its value as that would be "mis-repping," a far bigger sin than customer abuse. There was a very specific language you had to use. That was the difference between immoral and illegal, and "priceless" kept everyone out of jail. You'd tell them about the four awards and as soon as you got to the coin . . . "Wait a minute . . . what the hell is that?"

At first I thought it was completely unsellable, there was no way to pitch it. But it was all in the way you phrased it. Saying it was "priceless" only got you so far. When they'd get skeptical, I'd just laugh at them under my breath and say, "Bob, let me just say the owner of one of our biggest accounts in Arlington, VA is an avid coin collector so unless you've spent a half a million dollars with us this year, heh heh, well then, I wouldn't get your heart set on that Roman-Greco coin. You with me?" Perfectly legal, gray-area bullshit.

Lisa and my relationship was spiraling down and my brother was falling in love with her. She started taking classes at UNLV and my brother got a job cooking at the Four Kegs Sports Bar just across the parking lot. Jeff Brown started getting into cocaine. I was quickly a hotshot at Midwest and making even more money than at American. I was about to turn twenty-one, sporting a wonderful mullet and needed new places to stick my dick. Midwest was loaded with hot secretaries. I had my out when Jeff Brown told me he'd walked in on my brother banging Lisa. Lisa and I had definitely been on the outs but hadn't technically broken up. So while it wasn't outright treachery, it gave me free reign to plow the fields.

I'd spend the morning on the phone and afternoons across the street at Family Billiards, drinking beer, shooting pool, and playing video poker. I hit a royal flush once and got an official Family Billiards satin baseball jacket. That went sweet with my mullet and I wore it all the time. Probably with acid-wash jeans, possibly pleated. One of the secretaries at Midwest named Dori would hang out and flirt with me. She wasn't hot like the rest—kinda plain but she was ten or eleven years older than me, which really intrigued me for some reason.

One Friday payday, Dori and I were playing pool, getting drunk, and we decided that we should just run off to Tahoe. It sounded like something a cool guy with a pocketful of cash would do, but eventually we got too shit-housed and decided to just get married instead. You can do that in Vegas and nobody tries to stop you. We went to Chapel of the Stars, just down from the Fun City Motel where this whole Las Vegas adventure had started just eighteen months before. I remember the Justice of the Peace, or whatever his title was, being quite irritated by our casual, if not sloppy, attitude. You'd figure he gets this all the time. During the vows, I said the "to love and to cherish" part, but then, after "Til Death Do You Part," I just laughed, waited a beat, and repeated "to love and to cherish."

We stopped by the apartment afterwards, stumbling drunk, so I could tell Lisa and my brother that I was married. I wasn't doing it to be a dick. I was pie-eyed and honestly thought they'd be amused. My brother slammed me against the back of my car, screaming, "What the fuck is wrong with you?" while Lisa stood bawling in the apartment door. It made quite a ruckus. Neighbors peeked through their blinds. I bet they weren't guessing it was a wedding reception. Dori and I decided maybe it was best to stay at her place.

Lisa and Jeff Brown stayed in the apartment until Lisa finished her semester at UNLV and moved home. Jeff Brown hooked up with a clichéd Jewish American Princess who shared his love of blow. My brother and I moved in with Dori, who was sharing a huge single-story house with two other women, Bridey and Pam, along with Pam's two kids.

I called my father to tell him that I'd gotten married. He laughed like it was another one of my jokes he didn't get. When I finally convinced him that I wasn't kidding, he just congratulated me and said, "Well, good luck guy," in the same way you'd say it to someone about to go over Niagara in a barrel.

It didn't take anything to convince Mother. This is the kind of fodder that she expected from me, and she took it like any good drinking buddy would. "Why you little shit!" We flew out to see her as a honeymoon. Probably not as romantic as Dori would have liked but what did I know? They got along fine, Mother being as close in age as Dori and I were. We took some boat trip to an island where there was a petting zoo. I stocked a cooler of beer so it would be fun regardless. That's where I found out goats will wash down kibble with Meister Brau. You gotta do something while chicks are yapping. Mother had started dating a cop named Mike. Fuck knows how they met. Maybe she blew him to get out of a ticket but I never knew her to be much of a speeder. Either way, he was a fun guy to kill time with.

As much as Mother was getting along with Dori, it was almost as if she were trying to railroad me.

"Well, hopefully you can stay faithful to *this* one. You know Doug's cheated on every girlfriend he's had, right?" she said as though she's just mentioning the weather.

And then off my look, "Well it's *true*! You've said it yourself!"

I'd learn this later with drinking, comedy, and life, though I sometimes disregard what I've learned. The fact that something is true doesn't mean that it's admirable, much less necessary to say. I could tell my mother anything but that didn't mean she would keep it confidential. She was a gossip to the marrow and anything she gleaned from you could be used against you. "I'm just being fucking honest." I don't know if this was all blowback from the humiliation she'd faced when Wendell Fritsch's lies and deception came to light, but there was a misplaced vindictiveness to it. The first hints of bitterness. It wasn't just me. Mike was getting it as well.

Deputy Mike was affable, not overly bright but not completely country-dumb, with a decent pull-my-finger sense of humor. He was balding, pudgy . . . you know, a rural southern cop. He loved NASCAR and would volunteer to work security at the local racetrack just to watch the cars run. He liked to fish and would watch it on TV. Okay, maybe he was full-on country-dumb. But not the mean kind. Mother had dated a lot of broken people that she thought she could fix. Mike wasn't broken, he was who he was and saw no reason to change. Mother saw plenty. If he put clothes in the dryer and forgot to turn it on, he was a "moron."

"Jesus, Michael. THINK!" she'd say as though him forgetting something as simple as turning on the dryer was a calculated transgression meant to fuck with her. If he'd drive too close to the car ahead of him she'd be stomping imaginary brakes. Finally, he'd just pull over and let her drive. It was easier just to avoid the histrionics. I was on his side 100 percent.

Mother really enjoyed acting—a lot more than I enjoyed her acting—and was getting lead roles in most of the local plays she auditioned for. As much as I was proud of her, I hated and still hate theater. It's always boring and uncomfortable to watch. I hear people sometimes say the same thing about stand-up, that they feel too nervous for the performer and that they feel too much pressure to respond appropriately. I feel that way watching a play. All my reactions are forced as a courtesy to the actors and I never want to do anything but go outside for a cigarette.

Mother had co-starred in a local production of *The Odd Couple*, obviously in a female version of the role of the drinking, smoking slob Oscar Madison. I didn't get to see it live but don't you worry, Mother captured it all on a shitty VHS recording that would haunt me for years to come. Dori was the first of many girls or friends of mine that was forced to sit through it. At least on VHS you could smoke and drink—heavily—while you watched it. But if it felt long live, it was twice as long on tape, with Mother pausing every few minutes with a director's commentary, usually about someone she hated in the cast. "This cunt fucked up that line so many fucking times I wanted to kill her," and so on. When it was finally over, well . . . it wasn't over at all. Now she'd mine a critique out of you.

"I loved it" wasn't good enough.

"What part did you like the most?"

You scramble for anything you remembered.

"Did you like the part where I said . . . "

"Oh, yeah. That was hilarious."

This didn't happen just watching her video. It was any compliment at all. After we left to go back to Vegas, she'd call. What did Dori say about her? Did she like her? Well, what exactly did she say? How did she say it? And then what did you say? And then what else did she say? Mother fished for compliments with dynamite. If you didn't have anything, you'd have to make something up.

"Did she say, 'Well, that's not your typical mother?'"

At some point in my early teens, some friend had commented on her smoking, swearing, cat-jacking antics, and said, "Well, she sure isn't your typical mother." Mother had kept that as some kind of moniker and she always tried to live up to it, pulling her tits out or ripping farts at the dinner table even when it seemed forced. I could tell she was becoming a bit undone. It didn't matter. I was still highly amused and she was still my best friend.

DORI AND I WENT BACK TO VEGAS AND SETTLED INTO OUR unsettled lives. This was all big silliness to me. Abrupt change and chaos had become the norm and comfortable. Exciting. Ridiculous. Pam, who rented the house, was an upstanding mother of two blonde-haired, goofy kids about the age of the Simpson's kids, whatever that age is. We didn't trash the house like we did with the last one but we probably corrupted the kids as brutally. In harmless ways, no doubt. Excessive profanity. Drunkenness. Photographs started showing up of them posed with cigarettes and beers in their hands, shit that seemed dumb-funny at the time but today would get your kids put into foster care. It was fine to actually smoke in the house. So long as the smoke was only secondhand for the kids.

Dori started raising some red flags with her back story. She talked about her twelve brothers and sisters and how she was her father's favorite. Yet after we got married she didn't call a soul to tell them.

One time she recounted a tale of having been arrested as a dupe in a drug-smuggling sting and extradited from Miami back to California where she stayed for months in an Inyo County jailhouse without being charged. She described it as an Andy Griffith, single-cell jail where they all loved her and treated her like a pet. I was by now a bit more keen on spotting bullshit, and when I pointed out a few inconsistencies, Dori ran into the bedroom, slammed the door, and theatrically started packing until I begged off my doubting her.

Rumors were afloat that Midwest Enterprises was about to go under. They'd run a sales contest and the winner was going to be given a brand new Yugo at the company Christmas party. The day before, I'd crunched the numbers and the manager confirmed that it was indeed mine. I rented a white tuxedo—tails, of course, to go with the mullet, and Dori wore a strapless black evening gown. I was king shit, waiting at my banquet table for my big moment. But just like our customers who were planning on the big award, I got the Roman-Greco coin. Awards went out all night for different achievements but then the announcement was made that, unfortunately, nobody had reached the minimum numbers to win the Yugo. I looked like a giant slapped ass and I was pissed off. I pulled the manager aside and was told that we'd discuss it when we were back at work. I tried to ignore it and enjoy the night but it was ruined. Midwest was about to be ruined as well.

Shortly after the new year, some scandal split up the owners of Midwest Enterprises and the place was turned upside down. One of the owners was opening a new room. Top salespeople were getting calls from both sides to stay or go, with threats of the other side collapsing. The new room was in Pahrump, outside of Las Vegas, and offered big money for me to jump ship. I ended up striking a deal with the people still at Midwest to take the job at the other room as a spy, find out what their pitch was and if they were using leads stolen from Midwest.

This started a brief period of cloak-and-dagger drama. I worked at the other room and brought back any information I could. One night I was drinking at the apartment of Larry, the Midwest manager, and some secretaries when a shady henchman sent by the Pahrump owner broke down the door and confronted Larry with a gun. I hid on a bedroom floor, that close to being caught sleeping with the enemy. It was all overblown nonsense—as overblown as someone crashing through a door with a 9mm can be—but at the time it felt like an intense, clandestine thrill-ride, and I was right in the middle of it. Money. Women. Danger!

No spy movie would be complete without a sexy ingenue, and that came in the form of my coworker at the time, Deena. She was a super-hot redhead that would come on to me at work like a cat in heat. She'd leave erotic musings on my desk of all the things she wanted to do to me along with boudoir photographs of herself in lingerie on a fur rug. They're corny viewed now but beat-off worthy at twenty years old. One night I was going over to Larry's apartment for cocktails with the gang from work while Dori was home deathly ill with the flu. Deena was there, and it didn't take too many cocktails before not only did I have to fuck her, I had to stay the night and fuck her again in the morning.

Mother was right. I cheated on everybody.

When I got home, I was sober and had no excuse for why I never came home to take care of Dori. I must have thought the night before that somehow I'd get away with it, but in the ugly reality of morning, I was fucked. My bullshit was strong on the phone but face to face, I came up empty. So I just told her the truth. And now I know that you never, ever do that again. Dori started packing her bags in a fury, and again, I somehow begged her out of leaving. I told her I'd quit Midwest. I told her we'd move. I told her I'd quit drinking. I told her anything. I wasn't prepared to lose her. In reality, I just wasn't ready to lose period.

Leaving, as it turns out, wasn't a bad idea. I'd been hanging around with another kid from Midwest, just younger than me, named Mikey. Mikey was mop-haired half-Chinese and an adorable stoner who always saw the glass as half-there.

Mikey and I figured we were chumps by working for somebody else at all. There wasn't a single aspect of the business we couldn't do ourselves. If we could get ahold of some leads and some product, we could do our own racket. My brother was more than ready to bail back home so we planned to all head back to Worcester and get into business for ourselves.

We stayed at Midwest for a while longer to steal as many leads as we could, a little at a time so it wouldn't be noticed. We had a yard sale at Pam's house to get rid of as much shit as we could. At the end of the day, we were too lazy to drag all the unsold shit back in so we just left it out with the sign up. That yard sale ran 24/7 for weeks until we left.

In the interim, Mikey was the first person to turn me on to LSD, coming to Pam's house with a few hits one afternoon. I took a hit along with Dori and my brother, and within the initial burn I was completely sold on it. It was mid-afternoon and a bunch of kids were playing basketball with Pam's kids in the driveway. We were just hanging around watching trails of the ball swish through the hoop. We decided to go back in and take another hit. It was paper blotter acid about an eighth of the size of a postage stamp. I'd just put another tab on my tongue and walked back out into the drive-way when I saw the basketball coming at me. I inhaled deeply as a reflex and the blotter stuck to my uvula, making me gag. Gagging didn't dislodge it and finally I puked into my mouth. But I didn't want to spit it out, knowing there was a fresh and precious hit of acid in there. Tears were running down my face and all the kids were staring at me, waiting for me to give back the ball. I tried to swallow it. As you can imagine, there is nothing that will make you puke more dynamically than trying to swallow puke, your own or otherwise. I wretched a huge pile into the street but I wasn't giving up. I threw the ball back to the kids who now watched in grotesque horror as I got on my knees and started picking through the vomit for the acid. I found it, wiped it off into the neck of my beer bottle, and swilled it down. The image of a man rifling through his own sick looking for lost valuables may have been terribly upsetting to young children, but it would go on to be one of the best nights of my life and I strongly recommend it.

LSD was nothing new to Dori and she guided me through it. She couldn't believe I'd never seen *Pink Floyd—The Wall* and had gone out to rent it before the onset of the trip. As cliché as that may be, that soundtrack is still like religion to me. I remember the song "Mother" rubbing my emotions threadbare. I had no doubt, no shame even, that I was a mama's boy. The scene didn't make me feel stupid for being so. It made me miss my Mother.

Mikey was an absolute retarded genius on acid. He was one of those people I'd meet more of throughout the years, a guy who is really extremely bright but comes off as a dunce because he has a hard time communicating. I remember smoking cigarettes that night with my brother, Dori, and Mikey—all fully ablaze now—while Mikey tried to tell the parable of The Scorpion and the Frog. We'd never heard it before and Mikey had us completely engrossed as he stammered and mumbled his way through it, forgetting parts and having to start over. By the end, we were on the edge of our seats.

"And then the frog says, like, 'Why did you sting me?' And, uh, the scorpion says, um . . . 'Just cuz.'"

That's it??? Just cuz??? We waited twenty minutes for that???

And then we're in tears laughing again. A knock at the door at what was probably 8 p.m. but seemed like 3:30 a.m., sent us into a panic. Everyone was too scared to open the door. Finally someone— let's say me—mustered up the courage to open it. It wasn't the cops, as we'd all been scared it would be for no sensible reason. It was just some kid, about fifteen, who, now, as scared as we were, wanted to know how much we wanted for a briefcase in our yard sale. We fell to our knees laughing and finally, when we could talk, bartered a free briefcase if he'd walk to the corner and buy us cigarettes.

Jeff flew back to Worcester. Mikey and I continued to skim leads at Midwest. On my twenty-first birthday, I walked into Family Billiards and showed my favorite bartender my ID. He'd been serving me for months and was initially pissed off but got over it and we drank the night away.

Shortly after, we packed up two cars—one a Mercury Gran Marquis I'd bought from the same auction lot as the Dodge Omni—with all the fragments of life we could fit, including the four cats, and headed for Worcester, barely ahead of the law. The Feds raided Midwest Enterprises not long after and Jeff Brown, among many others, was arrested. They had him on tape telling someone the Roman-Greco coin was worth $20,000. He'd do six months in a halfway house. Light compared to the hard time I was about to do in the car.

9

Worcester:
You Can't Go Home Again
and Again and Again

OUR TWO-CAR CONVOY MADE IT AS FAR AS SALT LAKE CITY WHERE the drivetrain on the Mercury fell out on the freeway. Our good luck was that Bridey had just moved back to Salt Lake when everyone else was bailing on Las Vegas. We stayed with her while we got it fixed. It took a couple days before we were back on the road. Dori had decided to stay with Bridey for a few days and then would fly out to meet us. The drive was just too much, she said. So Mikey and I took off, making it as far as Omaha where I called Bridey's house from a truck stop, only to be told that Dori was gone. Her story about flying out to meet us had been a ruse. She'd actually left for Texas, where her old boyfriend had ended up. I was crippled. There was no explanation. There was no forwarding number. Just the simple, gutting fact that she was gone. The rest of the drive was sheer torture. It was cold, gray, and drizzling the entire drive back and seemingly that way every day for weeks to come. I can't remember a darker, more depressing time in my life.

We landed in Worcester in Dad's basement. My brother was already there and the three of us crashed on folding cots in all the clutter. The cats scurried about and the fact that Dad was allergic didn't

matter because we didn't care. We had enough money now to find
our own place so Dad could relax, if while watery-eyed and sneezing.
We drove around Worcester trying to find a place. At some point
I nearly hit a homeless guy in the street. As a goof, I told Mikey
that the homeless situation was so bad in Worcester they'd made a
law that if you hit one, you didn't have to stop unless he was in a
crosswalk. Mikey was pretty bright but very gullible. Weeks later he
was behind the wheel with me in the car and asked, "Hey, if I hit a
homeless guy and he's not in a crosswalk, do I still have to report it
at some point?" I'd forgotten to tell him I was just fucking with him.
That could have been a goof gone horribly wrong.

We rented places in a three-decker building that had two apartments on each story. Our apartments were one on top of the other
on the first and second floor, one to live in and the other for an office. My brother was out—he'd had enough of this boiler-room shit
and went on to do his own thing. Jeff Brown would be coming back
to work with us but would get his own apartment with his coke-head
girlfriend. We had multiple phone lines installed and got a business
license—under Mikey's name—and a bank account. We'd be doing
business as New England Marketing.

We were all set up and everything was falling into place save for I
was still in a deep depression over Dori. It wasn't as though the relationship was even all that special. It was all just a control issue. I had
never been dumped, never in any serious relationship and never for
another guy. Nothing makes you love someone as hopelessly as when
finding out she's fucking somebody else. Having no way to contact
her, no way to beg and cry and tell her I was willing to change, made
it that much more desperate. All I knew was that she'd flown to Dallas. Her old boyfriend had been a phone room guy too, but nobody
uses their real name in a boiler room. Still, I called information
asking to see if his fake name was listed. "Nobody Home" from Pink
Floyd's *The Wall* played constantly in my head. I even went to the
embarrassing lengths of calling Dallas radio stations trying to request
"long-distance dedications" to her. I was that fucked up about it. As
a lifelong drinker, I can say unquestionably that I've done more em-

barrassing things because of love than I ever did shitfaced. Nobody else missed Dori. Mikey didn't trust her and Jeff thought she was a bitch. I never loved anyone more in my life, even if that only started when she left me.

The apartments were spartan. A couple of folding chairs and army cots from Dad's place. A spare table. The basics. We got a connection for merchandise. We'd be using the old "no-sale" pitch, but instead of advertising specialties—getting things printed would be too much of a pain in the ass—we'd be selling "executive pen and pencil sets," gift-boxed metal sets that we probably spent three bucks apiece on and sold for thirty-five. What you sold was never an issue—you could find the same scams selling vitamins, water-filtration systems, anything. We could be selling dog shit in a napsack. All that mattered was the allure of the "Big Award!"

We also decided to lowball the orders. Ninety-nine bucks plus shipping. We were working leads of people with track records of losing several hundred or even thousands of dollars a pop. When you're used to getting fuck all for thousands, trying to fuck you for only ninety-nine bucks didn't just stun you, it almost made the whole thing sound oddly legitimate. We didn't have credit card facilities so you closed the deal by sending FedEx to pick up a check at their business. Soon checks would be rolling in daily.

They'd buy the pen sets, and then down the road—only if or when they called to inquire about the big prize—they'd get sent a Pierre Cardin his and hers diamond watch set, the diamond being a chip of a diamond and our total cost being dick. Any complaints would be taken with the utmost care, sent to another number inside the apartment where a different-sounding voicemail would take a message and then forget to call back. The runaround lasted until they gave up, or if there were any real threat of it getting ugly, we would issue a refund. I don't know if that ever actually happened but that was company policy and we stood by it. "Satisfaction Guaranteed—Eventually."

The numbers weren't big but the pressure was little and the profits were all ours, so the money was as good as Las Vegas. The problem was that we were our own boss now, and our boss didn't call for much of a work ethic. There was no starting time and any work day could be called off entirely if Stan Cohen or my brother came over to drink beer and play cards. Those work-stoppages happened more frequently all the time. At one point someone had scored an entire sheet of acid which shut down production for days. I remember tripping heavily and walking into the kitchen for a beer. There was a rabbit sitting nonplussed in the middle of the floor. I stared for a while, and when it didn't leave or even flinch, I went back to my brother and Mikey and asked them to go in and tell me if there was a rabbit in there—in the city at night, in a second-floor locked apartment in the middle of our kitchen. Indeed, there was. Turned out later it was a neighbor's rabbit from the third floor which lived in a cage in the back stairwell. He'd gotten loose and come in through a broken screen we'd kicked out in our back door to use as a pet door. But that night we just accepted him as a magical rabbit and let him rule.

———

A FEW WEEKS IN, I AWOKE FROM A VERY VIVID DREAM THAT I STILL remember. I won't try to give details because that's annoying and you weren't in it. But the gist was that I'd sold my soul to the devil to get Dori back. I woke up in a fright—what I've since heard described as sleep paralysis—not knowing what was real for several minutes. A few hours later, Dori called from Dallas. She'd got my new number from Bridey (who I'd been harassing daily for more details, like a homicide detective bleeding a cold case file) and she wanted to come back. I had her on the next flight out. Nobody was happy about it but me, and I was all that mattered. I don't see the dream as anything but coincidence but it was a really fucking creepy one.

Dori came back and moved in with me while Mikey moved upstairs and lived in the office. Now that everything was perfect, I went right back to not paying much attention to Dori and spending all my days drinking and playing cards with my friends, fucking off and occasionally working when our bills became due and our backs were against the wall. Jeff Brown came back with his nuisance girlfriend and if nothing else, brought back that old ten-piece sectional that had ended up in their storage. Now we had furniture again! Jeff Brown was also a serious card player so the work hours were pulled back even more.

My time in the office leaving Dori alone, if only just a floor away, became more than a point of contention. She demanded that if I were going to be away from her that much, I had to get her a dog, which I did grudgingly. We went to the pound and got a shepherd/ husky mix that we named Otis, either after Otis Day and the Knights from *Animal House* or Otis Sistrunk from the 1970s Oakland Raiders, depending on when you asked me. He kept Dori content for a few months while I continued to be distant. Then she wanted a parakeet.

Mother came that Christmas and it was one of the better ones I could remember. We had plenty of money and could buy real gifts and decorate. Mother came with Deputy Mike who was now her third husband. Aside from me and Mike, almost everyone smoked pot heavily and we were all entertained by getting to hand a joint to a cop to pass along to the next guy in the circle, inside the offices of a fraud telemarketing outfit. He took it all pretty well. "Hey, I don't give a shit. I'm off the clock."

Mother would make Mike come into the office and watch me pitch people. They'd pull up chairs in front of my desk like Mother was seeing me in a school play. I tried to make it a show. I drew up a bullshit checklist—a legal pad with the word "bullshit" written on each line that I'd check off every time I lied.

"Hello, Ron, my name is Doug Reed."

Bullshit.

"You got a call recently from one of our representatives regarding a promotion."

Bullshit.

"I called to let you know you were selected for a major award."

Bullshit.

Bullshit on and on down the list. If that didn't make an impression on Mike, the FedEx truck delivering piles of checks every day must have. Mother beamed with pride at her son's ability to defraud people. She probably called it the "gift of gab" or something innocuous to make it more palatable.

Mother enjoyed having a daughter-in-law. My brother had married twice, the first to Jodi, who not only banged me when I was sixteen before his boot camp graduation, but then went on to fuck half the Marine Corps before they divorced. His second wife was just a marriage of convenience so he was allowed to live off-base. Dori was the first daughter-in-law that would have to pretend to like her. I don't know that she didn't but she'd still have to put the face on regardless. Mother's new racket was making handmade jewelry. This meant she'd learned how to solder wire around QVC gemstones. You know, the kind with healing powers. Each one had specific properties that would help all things body, mind, and soul, and she unloaded them on Dori who feigned all the interest humanly possible. But it still felt like an actual family Christmas. My brother was there. Mother was happy with her new man. I could visit Dad and Gail bearing gifts instead of having my hand out. For the first time back in Worcester, I was making my own way and had something to contribute.

SOMEHOW I NOW HAD CREDIT, AND THAT SUMMER I BOUGHT MY first brand new car, a charcoal-gray Plymouth Horizon. Dori and I, along with Jeff Brown and Tracy, broke it in by taking it to the greyhound track in Connecticut, and ended up winning a couple hundred bucks. We didn't want the party to end and had a bunch of acid. I realized that I'd never been outside the country so we dropped acid and drove to Canada, a four-hour drive that took us seven. The whole way they asked me if I was okay to drive. "Absolutely," I'd say while every moth flying into the headlights made it look like space travel at light speed. I have a warped recollection of the made-for-acidheads Chambers Brothers song "Time Has Come Today" coming on the radio. The part where it slows down like a record player running out of power made my skull melt. I wasn't driving. I was sailing.

We crossed the border at dawn and wouldn't have even stopped at the crossing if it weren't for needing to piss. There was nobody to check in with at the booth. Inside, I asked if I was supposed to check in with someone and they casually said, "Oh yeah," and we were officially logged in. No muss, no fuss. We found a breakfast place just over the border in Magog, Quebec that served alcohol, and a beer never tasted so good. After a deep breath and a plate of eggs, I said "There's no way on fucking Earth I should have been behind the wheel of that car!"

We asked around where we could find a lake or a pond or anything cool and nature-y. Nobody had an answer. I asked at a gas station and they just looked confused. I went behind the station to take a piss and after only a few feet of trees, I was staring at an enormous waterfall that went down at least six or seven tiers, with pools on each. Some people never look outside their own back door. We bought more beer and ate more acid and spent the hot summer day skinny-dipping in the most beautiful Eden-like playground on Earth.

The ease of the drive up, the lack of any border problems, and a day dancing around like naked wood nymphs only emboldened our false sense of security going back across the US border. We were so cavalier in crossing that Dori hadn't even bothered to wipe away the sediment from where she'd seeded out her pot on the passenger-side dashboard tray. They didn't hesitate to pull us aside for secondary inspection. We must have looked like reptiles, with our eyes so big and black. They searched our car, found weed as well as six hits of blotter acid in Jeff's pants-pocket. We were then taken in and strip-searched. Jeff was cited for the LSD. I can only guess he wasn't taken to jail directly due to the distance of the closest one to our remote location. What they really wanted was the car, and they got it. Under the Zero Tolerance laws they were using to seize yachts and planes for cocaine smuggling in Florida at the time, they could take any vehicle found to have drugs. We were released on foot, hundreds of miles from home. We made it to a motel at the next exit, got a room, and called Stan Cohen—collect—for a ride home. He'd just gotten off work, drove to pick us up, and got us back just in time to go to work again. That's a friend right there.

If I wanted to hire a lawyer, I could have fought them by saying that I had no idea there were drugs in the car, but it was easier just to sign a voluntary repossession, forgo the down payment, and buy another new car before the repo appeared on my credit report. Up until just a couple years ago, any time I played Canada I'd get stopped by US Customs when coming out.

"Looks like you've had some problems coming from Canada in the past."

"No. Twenty years ago you stole my car coming from Canada. You have a problem."

That "I'm just doing my job" hogwash went out with the Nazis. Take responsibility for your actions.

WE WERE SPENDING MONEY FASTER THAN IT WAS COMING IN. WE'D get a stockpile and then just stop working until it ran out. The rent was consistently late, and our landlord—Mr. Meenes—was harassing us daily. We made his life miserable. The thermostat for the entire building was in my first floor apartment and he was adamant that it was never to go above 68 degrees. We'd crank it up to 85 and open the windows during the day in the winter. He'd come up and knock on the office door. While I let him in, Mikey would run down the back steps, go through the back door to the first floor apartment, and turn it back down to 68. Meanwhile, I'd be assuring Mr. Meenes that it was set at 68 while fumbling to find my keys to prove it. By the time we got down there, sure enough, it was set at 68 degrees. I don't know how many times we had a worker come over to check the "broken" thermostat.

Mr. Meenes was the only impression I was ever able to do spot-on and I'd fuck with our pothead upstairs neighbor on the third floor relentlessly.

"Hello, Bruce? It's Mr. Meenes. I was just by the apahhtment and I smelled sumthin' funny comin' from undah ya doooo-ah."

"Um, ah what . . . I uh."

"Just fucking with you. It's Doug!"

When rent went unpaid, we always had some elaborate excuse for Mr. Meenes when a simple one would have worked just as easily. There was some Chinese trade embargo on our goods for our import/export business. The orders were lined up but we couldn't fulfill them until they released our product from customs at the shipping yard in San Ysidro, which could be any day now. Don't blame us, blame this Republican administration! So long as he believed we were on the precipice of a fat check, he warily let us slide.

Meanwhile, we were wondering why we lived in Massachusetts at all. Rent was really expensive, winter sucked ass, and the truth was that we could do this anywhere they had a phone line. Why were we doing this here? It only took so many afternoon cocktails to make this hypothetical into an absolute when we finally—literally— threw a dart at a map. It didn't hit Idaho exactly. It hit something in Wyoming that didn't have a town anywhere near it, maybe not even a phone. But Idaho was close enough and sounded funny. I called the Chamber of Commerce in Boise and drunkenly asked what rents were like. She started to refer me to real estate people, and I said, "No. Just tell me, what do you pay for rent?"

"Well, I pay four hundred a month, but that's for a four-bedroom house."

And with that, we were moving to Idaho. Like getting married, I committed to the joke. These were the drunk dials I delighted in calling Mother with out of nowhere.

"Hey, Ma! We're moving to Idaho!"

She was never surprised and always highly entertained. Her spontaneity had pretty much ended after her move to Florida and her third marriage but she could live through mine. And the fact that we'd recently watched Richard Pryor's movie *Moving* together—where he's transferred to "Boise fucking Idaho" made it funnier still.

Stan Cohen's marriage was on the rocks and he, also drunk with us that day, threw his hat in the ring. I told his wife that it would be okay, that he'd probably be back, that it was just a phase. The shit you're supposed to say. Jeff Brown was out. His wife didn't have a sense of humor and Idaho didn't sound like an easy place to score blow. So our plan was set that Stan and Dori would go out on point to Idaho as soon as possible to secure a place to live and an office to rent. Mikey and I would pack up the office, get movers, and tie up loose ends before driving out to meet them. Mr. Meenes could eat shit on the three months of back rent for each apartment.

The apartments now became an ongoing party for anyone who was left, which was everyone I went to school with who was still hanging around the corner years later drinking out of a brown paper bag. Of all these people, Rufus was a legend. That wasn't his real name. Nobody is really named Rufus, but we'd all called him that so long we couldn't even remember why. He'd always been a leech and a ne'er-do-well, always with a sad story and broke save for the pill organizer of his mother's medications he'd often steal. He didn't even know what they were most of the time. He'd just take 'em. But this night Rufus showed up with something to offer. It was the first time I did ecstasy. He had it in powder form and he'd twist it up in little hunks of toilet paper to make it into a sort of pill. In no time, I loved everything and everybody, I even loved Rufus! More importantly, I loved my friend Stan's jilted wife, hanging around so hurt and vulnerable. If there is such a thing as "making love"—and there isn't—that's what I did with Stan's wife that night, without any guilt or remorse. At least until I was no longer on ecstasy. We never spoke of it again.

10

Boise Fucking Idaho

WORD CAME FROM IDAHO THAT DORI AND STAN HAD SECURED A small office and a huge spread up in the hills of Boise, just underneath Idaho's billionaire potato magnate's mansion—JR Simplot, who had the contract to McDonald's french fries. It was the Idaho equivalent of living next to Spielberg in L.A. I said "Idaho equivalent." The movers had our shit on the way so Mikey and I loaded up my brand new Ford Escort wagon with Otis, the four cats, and the parakeet, and took turns driving nonstop from Worcester to Idaho in forty-eight hours.

The first thing that happened when we arrived was that the parakeet escaped. I should have taken it as a sign. Canary in a coal mine. The new digs were outrageous. Three bedrooms that it seemed like you'd need a shuttle bus to travel between. Keep in mind this is all in relation to what I'd experienced. If I were in that house today, maybe it would be just a really nice house, but back then it was the Playboy Mansion. Every bedroom had a jacuzzi bathtub. The ten-piece sectional looked small in the place. Stan looked shaken. He wasn't one to take chances like this and it showed in his face that he didn't want to be here. He just didn't want to be the one that chickened out.

Dori was still expecting me to pay attention to her when I had all this shit to do. She was fighting with me from the minute the parakeet disappeared. I tended not to fight back and ignore her but it was difficult. After one blowout argument that had everyone in the house on edge, I retreated to my big jacuzzi for a bubble bath and a beer. This was way fancier than our old arguments. Stan came into the bathroom in what appeared to be an attempt to smooth things over.

"It's funny. You get along so well with my wife and I get along so good with yours. Heh heh. We should just switch wives."

"Fuck that," I announced, still angry. "You can just have my fucking wife."

And with that, Dori was with Stan. I had no idea this had been already in the works, or that Stan had been semi-serious with his comments in the bathroom. He'd been fucking my wife not minutes after I fucked his wife! The nerve! Now he was in the bathroom talking about taking her away for good and I thought he was kidding around. He just walked out and told Dori that he'd talked to me and I was cool with it. I didn't even know what was going on. I woke up and my wife had left me, but only moved across the hallway. It would be a week until they could get their shit together and go back to Massachusetts. It could have been far more uncomfortable but I was fortunate that I'd learned from my dad how to ignore unpleasantness and smile when everything is falling down around you.

I took Dori an hour or so north to the mountains to some natural hot springs and tried to talk her back, but it was too late. It was over. Mikey couldn't handle the stress in the house and went back to Vegas at his first opportunity. Dori was in a bind now because neither her or Stan had any money and they knew better than to ask me for any. Just before she left, Dori called her mother for a loan. It was the first time in a year and a half I'd ever seen her call anybody from her past.

Within two weeks of showing up in Boise, I was now alone in this monstrous estate full of abandoned furniture and belongings without a friend in the world except Otis and the cats. I didn't work. I won tickets on the radio to see a cover band on my birthday, not knowing that it was something that anyone who called in won. I went and nobody talked to me. I joined a dating service, something only old people did back then. I called my first escort service. She wasn't a looker but she wasn't in a hurry. She told me that she'd been on the Boise vice squad until she found out how much money escorts made and switched teams. I was depressed as fuck. I even joined AA again for just a minute until I let some AA douche come to my house and he "helped" me by dumping out all my booze down the sink. I wasn't THAT into AA, sir. Relax.

I told the landlord the truth about the unexpected collapse around me. I told him I wouldn't be able to afford to stay there. He reminded me that there was a lease agreement. I reminded him about the Supreme Court ruling in the old case of *Blood vs. Stone*. I should have just given him the numbers to talk to my previous landlords. He should just be happy his dishes weren't at the bottom of a pool with cat shit in his closets.

I stumbled on some real estate magazine and saw a cabin up in Garden Valley, Idaho on the south fork of the Payette River, right up where Dori and I had gone to the hot springs. It said that owner financing was available. It was for sale for $45,000, with payments of around four hundred bucks a month. I jumped on it and signed yet another agreement. Before I left Boise, I got that first phone bill. On it I saw the phone call Dori had made to her mother. I had to know. I called her mother, who, after I explained whom I was, went straight into a tone of warning: "Did she tell you how old she is?" Turns out that had been the only thing Dori had told me that was true. Everything else was completely invented. The twelve siblings? Nope. She was an only child. Even the name she'd claimed was her maiden name turned out to be taken from a stepfather who'd disowned her.

I'd been P.O.W.'d. But unlike Wendell, she'd invented a relatively uneventful fantasy life, which is far stronger bullshit. Never give 'em a reason to fact-check. I called Stan and tried to warn him about it but she convinced him I was just making up bullshit to try to sabotage their relationship out of jealousy. He was in love and didn't want to believe it, and wouldn't until she left him two years later, taking his car and bouncing his checks all the way back to that same old boyfriend, now somewhere in Alabama.

I also did my first open-mic night at a comedy club before I left Boise. I always remember trying to be funny throughout my life. I was always a fan of stand-up comedians but I honestly don't remember any serious ambitions to be one before then, any more than a fan of rock 'n' roll daydreams about being Mick Jagger. I only did open mic in Boise as a cathartic opportunity to write and perform (stupid and universally unfunny) jokes about my now-ex-wife. I was now twenty-two and looked at least seventeen, and marriage material coming out of me came across as out of place as a veiny erection on an infant. My jokes sucked, nobody bought it, and I still don't count it as my first time doing comedy. Same as I don't count Maura as losing my virginity when we were nine. It didn't really count as doing comedy until I was old enough to come.

So I was off to the mountains. There were two names to my new town of four-hundred-odd full-time residents. Crouch, Idaho was where the bar was located, and Garden Valley was down the street where the post office sat. Evidently, they are technically different but considered to all be the same thing by the locals. It didn't matter, I was from Crouch. I was from the bar, and if moving to Idaho was funny, moving to Crouch, Idaho was funnier. It was soon apparent to both me and the pets that we were far outmatched for mountain life.

One of the first mornings in the cabin, I woke up to Otis going crazy, barking like he was in a fight. I jumped out of bed and realized that he was only at the top of the stairs of the loft, barking at the open front door of our cabin. He was seeing what I was seeing, the biggest dog ever—a deer hanging around just a couple feet outside the cabin door. We didn't know that was "normal." The next night I came home to the cats in the loft on either side of the box spring on the floor with something pinned behind it. I pulled out the bed and saw what I thought was a mouse until it started to fly. It was a goddamned bat. At this point of my life, all I knew about bats were rabies and vampires. There was no jack set up inside the cabin yet so the only way I could make phone calls was to plug my phone into the external jack outside the back door. I called Mother and Mike. Who the fuck else am I going to call? He's a cop for chrissakes and they are supposed to know what to do in any situation, and she is my goddamned mother! They laughed their balls off at me as I'd make different forays in to trap it, fail, and call back. I still had the bird cage from the parakeet and tried to use a spatula to fling it from the wall into the cage. I missed and it went launching around the room again. Eventually, it landed on a support beam way up in the ceiling and stayed there. I fell into bed, exhausted, and figured we'd call it even, you stay on your side, I'll stay on mine. And as soon as I lay down and put my hand under my pillow, something scurried through my already nerve-wracked hand and I leapt like I'd touched electricity. Turned out it was only a lizard but it was too much. I would have fled in the middle of the night like the Lutz family in *The Amityville Horror* if I had any place to go. The only other place to go was the bar.

———

THE BAR IN CROUCH WAS CALLED THE DIRTY SHAME, WHERE THEY let me know early on that they had a history of holding down hippies and cutting off their long hair. I knew this probably hadn't happened in decades if at all, but played along just for fun. The owners were a divorced couple—Ron and Jolene Yensen—who traded shifts. Jolene was a saint to me and took me under her wing, Ron not so much. Most of the regulars were grizzled and taciturn mountain men in Wrangler jeans and perma-frowns. I was the goofy long-haired kid that found the few rock 'n' roll songs on the jukebox and banged them out repeatedly. I was the weirdo who ate moths collected outside the neon beer sign for attention when I was drunk. I was the new guy who did that weird thing with his mouth . . . what's that called? Oh yeah. Smiling.

One of the regulars who was rightfully even more unfriendly than the rest was a burn victim that occupied the same seat most every day, drinking beer in a brooding silence, using his nubs like chop-sticks to get the beer to his head, which had no ears. Rumor was that the guy was having an affair with Jolene while she and Ron were married. According to lore, Ron had set his trailer on fire with him in it. Only, the guy didn't die. Instead, he just sat there silently drinking every day, making Ron stare at the gruesome spectacle he'd created. That's some serious fuck you. That's some Stephen King shit right there.

My father came for a visit with Gail. There had been a great scandal, especially in the humdrum context of their lives. Their church had a female minister and it had come to light that Gail had fallen in love with the minister's husband. They say don't shit where you eat, and Gail had taken a large, looping pile right in the heart of my dad's safe place. He wasn't religious particularly but had always immersed himself in the social functions at church, serv-ing senior lunch and teaching Sunday school. He'd been a deacon, whatever that means, but it meant something to him. Gail pulling some shit like this was a dagger and a humiliation. Still, dad had co-erced her into taking this vacation since they'd already planned and paid for it. He thought maybe he still had a chance to save it, like I had when I brought Dori up here to the hot springs. Gail was a bit younger than my dad, and while they both loved the outdoors, Gail actually did stuff outdoors other than just stroll around and whistle. She was an experienced white-water rafter and the Payette River was a pretty decent spot for that. My father, desperate to impress, booked us on an afternoon rafting. Dad had the agility of a giant drunk baby, and just watching him wobbling to get into the boat was cringe-inducing. The first and most important rule they told us was that when you hit the rapids, keep paddling! My dad was at the front left of the raft, and as soon as we hit white water, he did the opposite and recoiled back into the raft like we were about to hit an iceberg. It was sad to watch him trying so hard to prove himself, to be something he wasn't just to hold on to a woman who'd just publicly disgraced him.

Gail left my dad when they got home. He took it like a Buddhist. If she were happier somewhere else, why would he want to interfere? He'd make the best of it. It would all work out. I wished there were more of him in me. I was more like Mother. I wished he'd just burned her alive in a trailer.

I had the phone set up but didn't dial it very often. The Dirty Shame would open roughly around noon, very roughly, and most days I'd drive just drive back and forth waiting for Jolene to show up and unlock the place so I could start drinking. My bar tab was enormous and by now they were looking to repo my car for nonpayment. Good luck finding it up here. Mikey came back up to Idaho now that all the drama was done and got straight to work in not working at all with me. There was some fun to be had. That summer, the military were doing some kind of war game exercises in the mountains around Crouch. A few of them came into the bar one afternoon and Mikey and I ended up talking to them. After a few beers they had to head back to camp so we drove them as far as the roads could take them before they jumped out to hike the rest of the way. Later, we got drunk and thought it would be funny to try to infiltrate their camp. We drove to where we'd dropped them, and, armed with flashlights, beer, a paintball gun, and with our faces blackened with burnt cork (just for effect), we started hiking. After half an hour or so, we heard whispers and realized we were right smack dab in the middle of their camp. Not knowing what to do next, we just chimed up, told them we were local rebels, and asked 'em if they wanted a beer. One of the guys got in some shit for taking the ride earlier and giving away their position, but we were eventually designated "local friendlies" and had a few of the guys stationed at our cabin for a couple days as part of their war games. Here and there, we'd get to drive 'em to a bridge that they had to "blow up" with nonexistent explosives. Mostly we all hung around the cabin, them giving us souvenirs like freeze-dried food rations, and us giving them shitloads of beer. Later, their exercises got the blame—at least locally—for starting a forest fire that nearly forced the evacuation of the entire valley.

You didn't have to burn us out of Crouch. The complete dearth of single women did that naturally. We had a drinking buddy couple named Roy and Cathy Bunce. They were late-stage, death row alcoholics. Roy had 13 tons of steel dropped on him at a worksite years back, and now was toothless with a dented skull and the speech pattern of a deaf person. Cathy would get so intoxicated that she'd walk home just across the street from the bar with her pants down, pissing as she stumbled. Good-hearted, salt-of-the-earth folk. They had a thirteen-year-old daughter, Kolena—nicknamed Baby. One day we noticed Baby had tits, and when we started doing the math on how long before she turned eighteen, we decided we better just get the fuck out.

I'd heard that one of the Vegas phone rooms had opened a new room in Eugene, OR. I figured I would try that before caving in and heading back to Nevada. I lasted three days. There was no star treatment like I'd earned in Las Vegas and I couldn't even score an advance on commission. The only memory I have from that trip was sitting in a tittie bar called Jiggles, waiting for the World Series to start, when the San Francisco earthquake struck and canceled the game, one of the few exciting moments in baseball history. So around October 17, 1989, I went back to close up the cabin, give back the keys, and head for Vegas. Las Vegas had been the only place so far that had really paid off for me, so we headed back. I gave my washer and dryer as well as a lot of other small appliances to Jolene in trade for my tab. Not an unusual occurrence at the Dirty Shame. My furniture, including my good ole ten-piece sectional, went to the Bunce's. I packed what would fit in my car, along with Otis and now, three cats. Mother's cat had died in Idaho. I don't know how. She was just sluggish one day and dead the next. Like most parents of children, I was in no position to have pets anyway.

11

Vegas Redux

Fourteen hours later I was back in Vegas. I showed up at the door of a girl I'd known from AA named Rachel. I loaded the animals into her place and we got into her hot tub drinking beer. That AA baloney hadn't worked for her either. She asked me if I wanted a pill—I can't remember if it was a quaalude or a valium—but I'd never fucked with pills so I said yes. I had another beer and next thing I knew I woke up on her couch fourteen hours later. I'd slept as long as I'd driven. One of my cats had escaped and never came back. The remaining two went off somewhere not long after, and I'm ashamed to say I can't remember how or where. But pretty quickly, it was just me and my dog Otis.

Otis was a brilliant dog and it wouldn't be until I got stupid dogs years later that I realized it was his natural intelligence, not my dog-training abilities. In Idaho, I could tell him, "Otis, go get your ball out of the car!" and he'd jump off the couch, run outside and through the open car window, into the back seat, bringing back his tennis ball. He'd instinctively go for your balls when you were roughhousing with him, and eventually I trained him to do it on command. "Bite nads, Otis!" and he'd nip you in the nuts. It was a great party trick. People believed your German shepherd was trained to rip their balls off. They didn't know he was only trained to bite the person that said it.

I found a room to rent in a house that should have been condemned—or maybe was—from a hardcore heroin addict, spindly and emaciated, with shards of rotted black teeth. It was way out on the outskirts of the city limits in the desert on E. Charleston Blvd. The house was on what appeared to be a junkyard with the junkie living in a trailer in the back. It was straight out of *The Hills Have Eyes*. Very little of the plumbing worked. All of the common areas were covered in dust. If you've ever seen those remnants of houses they used in nuclear blast testing in Nevada, you get an idea. The other guy renting a room in the house was a guy working as a booking agent for a local rock 'n' roll club. The rare times he was there he carried a befuddled look on his face as if wondering what wrong turn in life wound him up here. He and the junkie had sat me down when I initially told them I wanted the room. They hemmed and hawed before explaining to me that the last tenant in that room had shot himself in the head in the bed. The bullet hole was still in the wall. The were relieved when I thought that was funny. It had good story value and the room was only sixty-five bucks a week, with Otis having full run of the junkyard. Dogs don't understand the word "squalor." It was perfect.

American Distributing had lost the grudge from my "customer abuse" departure of two years previous and welcomed me back like a hero, mostly because sales were sucking shit. Nevada had by now instituted more regulations and you had to get photographed and fingerprinted to be licensed as a salesman. Just taking out the people who had warrants would gut your sales force by half. The office was a ghost town. Thankfully, Tom Konopka was still there and we picked up where we'd left off as a telemarketing comedy team.

"Hey, Tom . . . get this. This morning at breakfast, my dog said, 'In the creation of comedy, it is paradoxical that tragedy stimulates the spirit of ridicule; because ridicule, I suppose, is an attitude of defiance: we must laugh in the face of our helplessness against the forces of nature—or go insane.'"

"That's a very astute dog."

"That's what I thought at first. Turns out he stole it from Charlie Chaplin. Fucking plagiarist dog," I said, having just read the quote out of the newspaper.

I made pretty good money still but now that I was legitimately over twenty-one, I was able to indulge in Mother-like gambling binges with no threat of being thrown out. I'd regularly leave work on Friday at noon, cash my check, and head directly across the street to the 7-card stud table at the Circus Circus. I'd play—poorly—for 13-14 hours sometimes until I was drunk and every penny was gone, knowing the junkie landlord was jumping from foot to foot waiting for my rent so he could shoot up. I'd have to pawn things to pay him. My paintball gun. My VCR. I even set up another yard sale that, like the last, became 24/7 when I was too lazy to clean it up.

I'd call Mother after marathon runs and sleepless nights on a roulette wheel to commiserate. I'd sometimes use suicide as a mental option for whether or not I should cash in the rest of my money for one more hand or another spin. If I lose it all, I can always kill myself. It was comforting to have that out. I saw how she'd gambled and wondered if she'd ever thought the same. Calling someone as fucked up as you always leads to diffusing laughter. You don't call your doctor when you have a hangover. You call your drunkard friends. The only reason that people on the TV show *Intervention* get intervened upon is that they don't stick with their own kind.

I lost all my money once playing bingo. Bingo was great when you were broke because you could play for an hour on $3 minimum cards—and you'd drink all you could drink for free. In between games I'd play nickel slots and drink for free for an hour until the next game. It takes a long time to blow a paycheck that way but somehow I managed. I'd go home and call Mother—an avid bingo player herself—and we'd complain about bingo. These were conversations you're supposed to have when you're both elderly. Mother would put Mike on the extension and we'd bullshit and ball-bust until the depression turned into gut laughs. The gambling losses. The suicide rental room on the junkyard. The junkie landlord doing the cool-jerk waiting for his sixty-five bucks. I was talking in comedy routines without realizing it. We were both really into watching stand-up and would always trade recommendations. It was rubbing off. She told me, "You should do stand-up comedy. You're funnier than any of these pricks on TV." I told her, "I'm only funny like this when I'm overtired. That'd never work. 'Hey Doug, you should get some sleep.' 'I can't. I have a gig on Wednesday.'"

I FELL IN MAD LOVE FOR A WEEK WITH ONE OF THE FEW WOMEN who ever worked the phones at American. Her name was Victoria and she was a scary, impetuous drunk and drug fiend. The kind that thought it was funny to steal someone's car at a company party and joyride it to go find coke. She'd come in hung over one morning, having got married in a blackout to one of the other salesman but unlike me, wasn't sticking with the joke. I got her back to my hovel that night and she stayed for a week, trying to ditch her new husband who'd taken it all too seriously. He was coming undone at the office since her disappearance. I swore to him I had no idea where she was. She loved the desperation of my rathole and couldn't get enough of the sketchy, junk-strung landlord. She gave me her wedding ring on a necklace. Before she left my place to move back to Phoenix she left me a note saying, "When I am on the cover of *Rolling Stone* and being interviewed, I will ask you, Doug Stanhope, to present yourself in my life again and then I want my wedding ring back." I didn't bother getting a subscription but I kept the note.

One day I came back to the Spahn Ranch and found a three-day eviction notice. Seems the junkie hadn't been giving whoever owned the place any of that rent money after all. I confronted him and he just shrugged it off with, "What did you expect, man? I'm a junkie." It was the parable of the Scorpion and the Frog. He was a junkie and therefore it was his nature. Or, as Mikey would have said, "Just cuz."

Meanwhile, I'd been dating/banging a girl named Pandora Tranowski, a seamstress who also worked part-time as a hostess at an S&M dungeon. I'd been set up on a blind date with her and it was very casual, but now that I was out on my ass, I conveniently wanted to take it to the next level. Otis and I moved in with her and, while the sex was kinky, once I am finished, you're no longer a dominatrix. Now you're just a bitch. It's fine shoving something up my ass while we're fucking but as soon as I'm done, I have my own shit to do and bleaching the toilet isn't it.

There was a 24-hour bar/grill right by her apartment that I'd eat breakfast at every day. It was summer so I'd let Otis hang in the shade outside the front door. He was a smart dog. He wouldn't run off. One morning some guy leaving the bar spotted him out front and came back in asking everyone at the bar if anyone owned him. I was on the restaurant side and hadn't heard him. The guy took off with Otis before I ever knew he'd asked. I was frantic. I left my number with the bartender. I put an ad in the classifieds. It was June 24, 1989. I still remember distinctly. Or maybe it was the 28th.

I checked in with the bar several times a day to no avail. And then, a few days later, my phone rang and it was the guy who had my dog. I couldn't believe it. I'd given up. I told him what a great dog he was, how smart and kind he was, all the different tricks he could do. We made arrangements to meet at another bar that night to pick him up. In my excitement, I forgot to ask for his number. I must have oversold what a great dog he was because the guy never showed up and I never saw Otis again.

Bite nads, Otis. Bite nads.

12

Stand-up Comedy

I DON'T REMEMBER WHY BUT AROUND THEN I LEFT AMERICAN Distributing for another job at a place called the Tower Group. The scam was credit card protection and the big prize was a worthless vacation. I was disinterested and working on autopilot. Andrew Dice Clay had just broken big and I knew his album by heart. I'd parrot Dice incessantly around the office any time I wasn't on the phone. The owner of the company was a stout, mustachioed rugby player named Buzz who also had a cover band as a side gig. Seeing me getting laughs with all this Dice material, he offered me a spot opening for the band at a local bar. I explained to him that it wasn't my material and he said he didn't give a fuck. He ran a scam boiler room, you think he has artistic integrity? At least I knew it was wrong and turned him down, but just knowing that if I did have my own material, I could get a gig that easily started me writing.

I found an open mic at a bar called the Escape Lounge II on Maryland Parkway. I'd go every week and watch the comedians, always asking if I could go up the next week. I'd go home after and spend all week writing down jokes, premises, or even just funny words. "Sea monkeys" was funny so I wrote a (horrible) bit around it just to be able to say it. I'd get on the phone and try it all out on Mother. Every week I'd go back and Ron Putnam, the enormously fat and tender guy who ran the show would ask if I was ready to go up. I never was and it became a running joke every time he'd see me. I'd watch the show, go home, and write some more. Pandora started to hate me. I wasn't getting shit done around the house. I wasn't making much money with all my time and headspace going into writing.

Finally, on August 28, 1990, I put my name on the list. Pandora and her mother, who was visiting from California, were in tow. I finished most of a pitcher of beer before I went up. That doesn't work for everybody but it did for me and I killed. This isn't to say I was any good but it's common in stand-up for comics to do well their first time and then eat shit for months or years afterwards. Your first time you have the comics to play to, and comics are a good portion of an open mic audience. Comics are generally supportive of each other and usually root hard for first-timers. Once they've already heard it, though, you're dead. So as much as I hate the cliché, comedy is like a drug in that you are always chasing that initial high, which is never as good. Also like a drug, it will eventually wear you down and ruin you. It will destroy relationships and make you drift away from old friends in favor of new friends who do your comedy drug, still chasing the dragon. After a time, you don't even enjoy the drug anymore but keep doing it out of habit. It's all you know. It's also a gateway drug that, if you stick with long enough, might lead you to harder drugs like television. You can see how deep you've fallen into the abyss. You want to go back to who you were but it's too late. The withdrawal back into a 40-hour work week would be too much to bear. Then you get shunned from circles when you get too sloppy at your drug and they have no more use for you. Open mic Tuesday. Go ahead, sign yourself up.

1990 was still at the tail end of the '80s comedy boom, and there were plenty of bars to do open mic. After my first night success, local open micers put me up everywhere. I did six shows at different bars in my second week of comedy. I had no idea that I sucked. Like growing up, you don't realize how stupid you were until years later. Besides, everyone else sucked as much or worse than I did so it was all relative. I'm sure a lot of the problem was that I'd work out all my material with Mother and she'd laugh at everything. Even on her deathbed, she'd bring up old bits from my open mic days like naked baby pictures. Most were truly embarrassing but she'd repeat them as though they were comedy classics. Remember the bit about the used car salesman working the drive-through? Do you want fries with that? What's holding you back from the fries? What's it gonna take to put you into these fries today? Please, Ma. Let it go.

I hit comedy with the same timing I'd hit the phone rooms, at the end of the boom. I wasn't concerned, I never had eyes on making a living doing comedy. It was something to do just to see if I could pull it off, and in a pretty short time I was a big log in the small toilet of Las Vegas open mic comedy. Drinks were always free and that was usually all you got. My first paying gig in town landed me a whopping ten dollars. But that was a landmark night because getting paid any amount made me—technically—a professional. I could now in good conscience say I was a traveling, formerly homeless, experienced male prostitute, con artist turned drug-smuggling mountain man, and a formerly recovered then active alcoholic prone to inter-racial transgender sexual interludes. I was keen on not being full of shit, if only technically. And I was quick to denounce myself on the technicalities once the joke was told, unlike serious bullshit comedians I know today. But that night I became a professional comedian. That fact I didn't consider a mere formality. It was real to me. I called my brother to tell him I'd officially turned pro in comedy. He asked if that meant I no longer have to wear the oversized gloves and the protective headgear anymore. He's a funny cunt, too. I called Mother to tell her about my new status. I couldn't have done it without her.

Comedy was also getting me the eye from the ladies here and again, the same kinda gals you can score doing really good karaoke. Things with Pandora were already strained and the new female attention I was getting didn't help. It came to a head the night of the Tower Group company Christmas party. Somewhere in the night I'd lost the keys to Pandora's car and we had to get a ride home from another employee. Back at the apartment, she went into a full-blown rage. We ended up nose-to-nose, screaming, when she cocked back and punched me straight in the mouth. Never tell a woman that you'd never hit a woman. They'll store that knowledge. I dared her to do it again under threat of retaliation and she didn't hesitate. She kept punching me in the head—really not my weak point, especially when I'm full of alcohol—until I could restrain her, push her out the door, and lock it.

I waited a couple minutes for her to calm down. It was December and it was cold out. Once she assured me she was done, I opened the door just far enough for her to barrel through the rest of the way and resume punching me in the head. Then she went after my stuff, throwing things out into the street one at a time. A toaster, a notebook, a pile of clothes. I called the police. When the cop showed up, he walked in to assess the situation and Pandora yelled, "He tried to kill me!" Yet another reason my go-to charity is The Innocence Project, pro bono lawyers and students fighting for the wrongly accused.

I'd told the 911 operator that I just wanted to get my belongings out without violence and I told the cop the same thing. He stood there trying to calm her down while I humped armloads of shit into my car. I'm still wearing a tuxedo from the party, with blood dripping from my split lips.

"Other than that, officer, it was a pretty good party."

This got a laugh and it sent Pandora over the top, whipping an unopened beer can at me right in front of the cop. Her "he tried to kill me" rouse was sunk. I got my shit and got the fuck out forever. I found Ron Putnam and some of the local comics at a bar while the blood was still fresh. Most people will never know the beauty of the ball-busting and laughs you can get out of being the victim of domestic violence. Most people will never be comedians.

(Before starting this book, I did an Internet search for Pandora. The first link I found sent me to a series of mugshots out of Texas for drugs and prostitution arrests, each more disheveled than the next—like the Faces of Meth photos. The second link was to her obituary. You should feel kinda bad in these situations but sometimes you simply don't. You can't force yourself.)

I found refuge on the couch at Mikey's place. The next few months were a montage of comedy, weird strippers, poor decisions, and leaving bars at seven o'clock in the morning. I won a couple of competitions at local bars and eventually got my first official road gig at Sandy Hackett's Route 66 Comedy Club in Flagstaff, AZ, co-headlining with a ventriloquist act. The club was in the bottom of the Monte Vista Hotel, an old, historic hotel where your bed would rattle every time the train went by across the street, which seemed like every few minutes. I only had to do 30-35 minutes, but everything I'd ever written—including the epic "Do you want fries with that?" diatribe Mother loved so much—totaled 25 at best and I was scared. The puppet act was even more afraid. He'd never worked comedy clubs before, mostly just state fairs. He was neurotic as fuck and wouldn't even stay in the hotel. He was afraid that due to the age of the place, it may burn down and take his dummy with it. He told me that one time on a cruise ship, some drunk threw his dummy overboard and that he'd rather pay for his own hotel than to go through that again. Welcome to the road, Stanhope.

As if I weren't nervous enough, Victoria had gotten in touch with me. She was living in Phoenix and was going to come up to the show. That psycho fuck-up from American Distributing who had stolen my heart was gonna be at my first road gig. I called Mother in Florida—again collect—and worked out as much ad-lib stuff about the hotel, the room, the train, anything to pad my time. All those lines killed—at least on the phone with Mother. On stage, they did better than my prepared novice act but there was no epic victory by any stretch. I don't think I ever did more than twenty-eight minutes. Nobody was clamoring for more.

Victoria showed up—sober now—and I was in love again. She told me I should move to Phoenix with her. I didn't ask a lot of questions. I'd been driving Mikey out of his mind living on his couch and it would probably be good for me to live in a state that

Me and my brother Jeff with Mother, about to learn to swim by getting chucked in a pool. Later we'd learn not to fuck with giant ant hills the hard way as well. Florida vacation, 1972

Mother with our pig-fucker step-father John Kirk. Paxton, MA 1978

Can't tell by the cute class photo that I was plotting people's deaths. Paxton, MA 1979

Graveyard shift at the all-night gay diner on Halloween. Worcester, MA 1984

Bare, stained mattress in my basement studio with MaryAnne Hanley and Dragon. Hollywood, CA 1985

Eating Pussy! Mom's bed in Crystal River, FL 1986

Mother in the Oscar Madison role in *The Odd Couple*. I still have VHS copies if you want to sit and watch it. Crystal River, FL

Mother lets my brother and I take a squeeze of her new tit job. Las Vegas, NV 1987

Rick Bell, me, Jeff Brown, and Mikey outside Midwest Enterprises wearing garb from Mother's thrift store CARE packages. Standing at the Yugo I was supposed to win. Las Vegas, NV 1987

Working the phones, rocking the mullet. Worcester, MA 1988

Otis at the cabin. Crouch, ID 1989

Mother at the Vail Comedy Festival. Vail, CO 1995

Keeping light on Death Row with Victor. Raiford, FL
1997

Goofing off with Mother on the road. Somewhere in the 1990s

Jeff visiting Mother and me. Los Angeles, CA 1997

Leann the Neighbor Chick from a stalker's perspective. Los Angeles, CA 1999

Me and Mother. This is a love story. Los Angeles, CA 2000

Mother poses with a white chocolate cock popsicle. Los Angeles, CA 2000

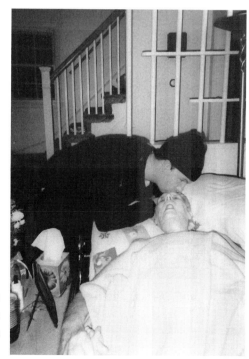

Dad, minutes after he died. Show me a baby picture, I'll show you this picture—so you know how the movie ends. Providence, RI 2001

Mother in all her splendor on set of *Memphis Bound and Gagged*. Los Angeles, CA 2001

Drunk in Love with Renee. Aspen Comedy Festival, 2002

Mother and Tanya Lee Davis playing cream-of-the-crop strippers dancing for P. Diddy on an MTV roast of Carson Daly. Los Angeles, CA 2003

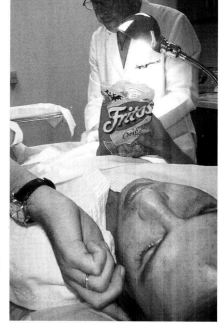

Chatting on the phone, eating chips while the doctor cuts open my ball-bag. Don't look down. Vasectomy, 2002

Mother's boy is on a billboard! Los Angeles, CA 2003

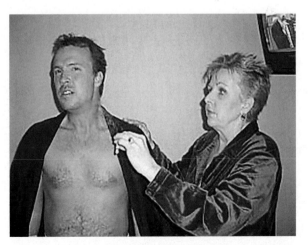

Mother as my corner person, boxing Tonya Harding. Can't drink and smoke yourself with the gloves on. Los Angeles, CA 2004

Promo shot of Mother from an independent flick. Los Angeles, CA 2005

Crazy love notes from Bingo's troubled head. Bisbee, AZ 2005

One way to meet your new neighbors. Yes, she really thought she was talking on a phone. Bisbee, AZ 2005

Photo shoot at Safeway. No, we won't be needing wallet size but thanks. Bisbee, AZ 2006

Last Call for Mother and her grandkids. Palominos, AZ 2008

On Thursday, Mother came over to kill herself. Bisbee, AZ 2008

had a last call on alcohol. But mostly I wanted to be in love over and over again.

Of course, I called Mother after every show. She wanted to know how each bit I'd riffed to her had gone over, like she was coaching me from prison. After the last show I called again.

"How'd the show go?"

"Great! I'm moving to Phoenix!"

13

Going Pro in Phoenix

WHEN I SHOWED UP IN PHOENIX, VICTORIA WAS HOUSE-SITTING for some rich dude in Scottsdale. I fell into a plush bed in a huge house, woke up to float in the swimming pool while she brought me breakfast, sharing the disgusting, dreamy-eyed bliss of being in love. Those were amazing days. About three of them. Then the dude came back and we moved in with her parents. In hindsight, I think her parents were more than tolerant of me being there mostly because they were just happy she was staying sober and not around the drug addicts and enablers that she usually ran with. I was an up-and-coming goddamned stand-up comedian. That explained why my days of chain smoking, drinking coffee, and reading newspapers at the dining room table could be written off as "work." And that actually was the work. Pretty soon I got a job as the house emcee at a local failing comedy club called the Comedy Cove inside the Days Inn lounge in Phoenix. My pay was a free room, all the free food I could scam from the kitchen, and more stage time than you could ask for in those early years, doing a full 10–15 minutes on stage seven shows a week every week in a regular comedy club as opposed to open mic nights.

The comedy clubs in Vegas never touched local acts. They got all their people from Los Angeles so the open mic pool there was a stagnant pond of incest. You never met anyone who actually did this for a living. At one point Ron Putnam hired a headliner from the Riviera to come down between shows and close the open mic at The Escape Lounge, trying to raise the image of the show. He got comedian Geechy Guy, who had just won *Star Search*, the *America's Got Talent* of the day. Geech got heckled and came back with the softest version of the most hackneyed comic comeback of all time: "Hey, I don't come down to where you work and unplug the Slurpee machine." The *back* of the room fell apart! The comics were dying laughing at the most overdone response in heckler history! We were so sequestered from actual working road comics that it was brand new to us . . . even comics who'd been doing Vegas amatuer comedy for years.

In Phoenix, I now would be working with actual road comics every week as opposed to just the locals. I finally made contacts. I saw that I could actually do this for a living and I worked my ass off, even if I didn't have any kind of voice. I don't even think I had opinions yet. But I wrote endlessly and I was immersed. And as I got more swallowed up in comedy, Victoria got back into coke and methamphetamine and some lighting guy for Cheap Trick. You follow your heart.

———

I MET MAT BECKER IN THE LOCAL PHOENIX COMEDY CIRCUIT. He was an odd duck. His jokes were out of the league of the boilerplate that everyone else was doing to amuse the dregs that Free Comedy attracted. But his confidence was shit and he tended to give everyone the creeps, both in the audience and in the back of the room. He was the comedian's comedian's comedian. We fell in love straight away. By now I'd been introduced to what they called "Tribble Gigs" that were infamous at the time and still are legend. David Tribble was and is a booker out of Washington state who ran a circuit of one-nighters throughout the Northwest, known for shit money and incomprehensible drives between shows. One night in Pocatello,

Idaho, the next day seven hours to Billings, Montana only to double back the next night to Missoula. You'd make 125 bucks plus hotel per night as an opening act, not including off nights. Having to drive from Arizona even to start the runs, you'd be lucky to break even. Who gives a fuck! I'm working on the road as a traveling stand-up comedian. I'm fucking girls with similar mullets. I'm driving through Yellowstone National Park between gigs like it's city traffic, yelling at tourists for lolly-gagging and making me late for work. I've never to this day had more fun in this business.

Becker would come out on Tribble gigs with me. I was only the opening act but I'd put him on upfront to get stage time, and all the money was communal. Becker's scamming abilities were worth as much as the cash. He'd buy a video camera so we could film our sets. He'd get one with a "30-Day No-Questions-Asked" return policy, and then return it 29 days later.

"Was there a problem with the camera?"

"Well, now, that's a question. Your sign says "No Questions Asked" and here you are asking me questions. LISTEN UP, PEOPLE! DON'T BUY ANYTHING FROM THIS STORE! SIR! DON'T EVEN THINK OF BUYING THAT TV! SEE THAT SIGN? IT'S ALL BULLSHIT! THIS GUY WON'T HONOR MY RETURN! ITS A BAIT-AND-SWITCH! BAIT-AND-SWITCH, I SAY!"

Becker would get his refund, go back the next day to a new place to buy another. Sometimes even the same place. Fearless. I still envy his balls. We got a single-room apartment in a shitty part of Mesa, AZ, mostly as a place to leave our shit when we were on the road. It was in a huge complex that looked like the projects. I'd find that a lot in the Southwest, that the buildings all look so similar—all cookie-cutter beige, brown, or salmon stucco, be it a gated community or public housing—that you don't know a bad neighborhood until it's too late. We knew that this complex was the ghetto immediately but the price was right. The building manager walked us to the second-story unit that we'd be renting alongside the courtyard, complete with a greenish, algae-riddled pool.

"Oh look, we're right over the pool!" says Becker. "I guess that means we'll be testifying in court a lot!"

Then she showed us the place. Searching for any selling point at all, she mentioned that the cabinets had just been painted. A closer look showed a cockroach on the edge of a cabinet door that had been left and painted over, possibly alive. We signed the lease on the spot. We knew comedy. Everything horrible in life was money in the bank on stage.

—————

EVENTUALLY, I HAD ENOUGH WORK TO WHERE I DIDN'T NEED TO keep coming back to Arizona. In December of 1991, I packed my shit into my car and headed out on the road. Like I had in L.A., I got a voicemail service and a mailing service so I had a permanent number and address. I'd call in for messages using prepaid phone cards and have my mail forwarded any time it stacked up and I was somewhere on the road long enough to collect it. If I had days or weeks that I couldn't fill with a gig, there was always a comedian, a waitress, or a fan from the audience willing to put you up. That's the great thing about being young and following your dreams—people are excited for you. They want to encourage you, help you out, and send you off with a sack lunch. If I were forty-seven and living out of my car, people couldn't sprint away from me fast enough.

I lived out of my car for three years almost to the day. Or I should say six or seven different cars. They'd break down and if it were serious, it was usually cheaper to dump it and buy a new piece of shit than to fix it. I couldn't call Mother for money anymore. She'd pissed all of hers away and was living paycheck to paycheck the same as me. I had Dad's credit card number written on the back of a business card for emergencies. That saved my ass on many occasions. One Christmas he came out on the road with me for a week. We were driving on barren two-lane stretches between Rock Springs, Wyoming and Montana. I don't think there is a more desolate stretch of road in the country. We were dead in the middle when snow started coming down in a wall. I could tell my dad was scared shitless.

"Jeez, guy. What would you do if you ever broke down out here?"

"I don't know, Dad. That's usually when I call *you!*"

For the most part, those years of gigs were at the lowest level of stand-up comedy that still paid money. If you've seen Jeff Bridges at the beginning of *Crazy Heart*—staying in a ramshackle motel, drinking alone, and playing to hayseeds at the roadhouse across the street, that's a pretty good representation. I loved every minute of it. I never worried about my status in the industry, never even considered it. I was making a living onstage. I was getting girls, some of them not even that ugly. I never had to pay for a drink unless I sucked. That was the only incentive I had to maintain any professionalism. I was better than most of the other guys working shit gigs in hotel lounges. That was my only barometer of quality. There was no thought of a bigger picture. This was more than I could have ever hoped for.

14

Movin' On Up

BY 1995, I WAS WORKING PRETTY STEADY, MOSTLY BECAUSE I WASN'T
picky and generally, I was rarely an asshole. People forget that it's
important to be a decent guy. A lot of the gigs were terrible but
those made for the best stories. I'd moved up to headlining most
one-nighters and as a middle act in comedy clubs, but still took any
shit gig I could get to fill in the holes. At one point Becker and I
booked a gig on a tour bus taking the blue-haired elderly from Minneapolis to the Indian casino forty-five minutes away. I was booked
first, and Becker, who was booked for the next weekend, came along
for the ride. I got on board and sank into immediate terror. Save for
the driver and the tour director, there couldn't have been anyone
younger than seventy on that bus. To make things worse, the seats
were facing each other, with tables in between so half the people
had their backs to you. The microphone played over the bus's loud-
speaker. I turned to Becker and begged him under my breath to take
my place. Even my cleaner material had no relevance to these an-
cient relics. At least Becker had jokes. He flat out refused, knowing
that watching me eat shit was worth way more than they were paying. As the bus started up, the tour guide piped up like Julie from *The
Love Boat* and announced that everyone was in for a treat! I leaned
into Becker and told him to keep count, that I'd give him five bucks
for every one of his jokes I did. I proceeded to do Becker's entire act.
So it's hard to say exactly who died on their ass.

At some point early that year I was working a shithole dance club in Pueblo, Colorado as an opening act. A hundred twenty-five bucks and a room. You weren't gonna get rich and you weren't gonna get famous, so all you could hope for was to get laid. Problem here was that people didn't give a fuck about comedy. They'd slowly filter in as the show went on, patiently waiting for you to shut the fuck up and finish so they could line-dance. Being the opener, you're also waiting for the headliner to shut the fuck up so you can work the few chicks that actually saw you on stage. I'd lost a contact lens at some point weeks earlier and, rather than dip into beer money, I had been surviving with only the one. Even poor vision couldn't make the ladies look good in Pueblo.

That night, the headliners' manager, Judi Brown, who was from Colorado, was in the audience. After the show she asked me if I wanted to participate in the fledgling Vail Invitational Comedy Competition she was running. They were having regional competitions around the country, with the top comics advancing to the semifinals in Colorado. There were promises of big-time agents and network execs, exposure and the like. I was skeptical but I had nothing to lose. I was on my way to Minneapolis anyway where a regional was set at an Indian casino. I signed up, hoping it wouldn't be for the audience from the bus.

That next morning in Pueblo, I was woken up by the programming director from the local radio station that had sponsored the show. She'd come to take me to breakfast before I left town. I was hungover like a pirate. I opened the door and flopped back face down onto the bed, groaning at the light. She went to the sink, emptying a glass to rinse out and bring me a fresh glass of water. It was a minute before I realized that glass had my sole contact lens soaking in saline solution. She'd dumped my only contact lens down the drain. I had to drive a thousand miles to Minnesota squinting like Mr. Magoo, blind as a shrimp.

I won the regional competition. I won something like five hundred bucks and a pager and went on to the semifinals in Boulder, Denver, Canon City, Colorado Springs, and back to Pueblo. I got to work with some of the funniest comics I'd ever met. Jim Norton, Derek Edwards. Infamous road lunatics like James Inman and J. Scott Homan. I presumptively flew Mother out to see me take the crown. Neither of us really cared when I didn't even make it to the finals. The comics like me that didn't advance still got to do sets in Vail. As promised, there was indeed industry present and I got noticed, but I had little or no idea what to say to the suits. I was a dude who lived out of his car and spewed filth at saloon audiences. I wasn't Hollywood-industry savvy. I didn't have a sitcom idea or a screenplay I'd been working on. They'd ask me what I wanted to do with my career and I thought I was already doing it. I didn't know that all they wanted to hear was, "I'm moving to Los Angeles." They'd tell me what I wanted to do with my career once I got there.

Mother had seen me perform once or twice before but nothing on a scale like this. The stink of chasing the big break was all over the place. Most of the comedians were frantic to get noticed. I was stupefied just being in the scene. Mother shined. She was a cocky, arrogant ball-buster. I remember her sitting around a lounge table of suits and comics when a plate of oysters came out. "Look," she said, picking one up with her fork, "Pussy Del Mar! That means 'Of the sea!'" She claimed her status of "Comedy Mom" to all the comedians and nobody balked. She wasn't wowed by the industry. They'd say, "You know you have a very funny son." She'd say, "No shit, Sherlock."

A management couple, Mark Lonow and Joanne Astro, blew the largest plumes of smoke up my ass. I liked them because they didn't seem desperate. As much as every comic wanted to stand out, I could see the same thing in how the industry big-timers needed to look important. I remember one suit who was either the manager of, or agent to, comedian Tim Allen, who was huge on TV at the time. I remember him sitting outside the hotel one afternoon where all the comics were hanging out, having a very loud phone conversation with Tim Allen. We knew this because he kept using Tim Allen's full name to Tim Allen while he talked to Tim Allen about Tim Allen and Tim Allen's career.

Mark and Joanne had none of these bullshit airs about them. They seemed just as happy to be there as I was, and if something were to be gained, so be it. They were a couple who managed a few comedians. Mark Lonow was partners with Budd Friedman in The Improv comedy club chain. They raved about me—to me—which is always awkward but better than the opposite. To listen to them, you'd think I'd be flying out of there in a Learjet. I didn't care if they were lying. I had nothing for them to take. They wanted to manage me and I had no idea what that entailed, but I couldn't see how it was bad. They took me out to some gothic, upscale wild game restaurant and we ate buffalo, boar, and quail. I hadn't ever been in a restaurant that actually had someone at the table taste the wine. That shit only happened in movies. The bill had to be in the hundreds of dollars. I couldn't imagine paying that much for a meal. That's what I'd pay for a car. There was no way I'd be signing with anyone else at this point. The meal had already paid for itself before I even had dessert.

I could forgive my mother for missing my one amazing catch playing football. Because she was there in Vail when all the hype actually materialized in slow motion. And all while she was paying attention and cheering for me, not looking away because she was afraid I'd get hurt.

Joanne flew out to meet me on the road a few weeks later at a club in Wichita to sign the contract. She seemed amused at the abject destitution of the road. She'd done stand-up comedy for a minute but I don't think she'd ever seen the road like this. It was like Hollywood sent in a Navy SEAL team to save me.

Just a few months later, in the summer, the same people held the Vail Comedy Festival. Same shit without the competition. Just shows in front of industry, only now I had management to field the questions I didn't know the answers to. Agents and networks were waiting to meet me. Mother was waiting by the phone to hear what they said. I signed with APA as my agent and they told me that HBO wanted to sign a development deal with me. At the same time, the San Francisco Comedy Competition had just accepted my entry for the fall. Unlike Vail, San Francisco was a pedigreed comedy competition of legend. Even if its most iconic years were behind it, it was still the biggest competition in the country.

There was no doubt now I'd be moving to L.A. I made a few forays in over the summer. I was still living out of my car, but in L.A. there was always a place to crash. Comedy clubs were like AA meetings in that you always had some kind of disjointed family you could find in any city. And everyone eventually winds up in L.A. I'd have pointless meetings with networks and lunches with agents. Agents love to get lunch. Nothing was ever accomplished but they always picked up the tab. I'd grown my mullet out to full rock 'n' roll hair . . . sitting on Sunset Blvd., with my sunglasses on, listening to agents and managers tell me how big I was going to be, waiting to cash the check.

———

I WAS STANDING AT THE BAR OF THE IMPROV COMEDY CLUB ON Melrose in West Hollywood. It was August of 1995. Barry Katz was and is a legendary comedy manager. I'd met him at the Vail festival. He was tall and gangly, with long hair and a hook nose, like a blond Howard Stern. He'd told me I was going to be a big star. He said he could always tell. I passed him at the bar at The Improv and he stopped me. He said he'd heard I was gonna be doing the San Francisco competition. I said that I was.

"One of my guys is doing it too. You wanna bet prize money against him?"

His "guy" was Dane Cook, a comedian client of his who I'd never heard of. Nobody had heard of either of us at that point. I declined the bet, which was silly anyway. The competition was a month long, with forty comedians. The chances of either of us even being in the top five to get prize money was a long shot.

I'd been staying with Mitch Hedberg and his girlfriend Jana Johnson since I'd moved there. Mitch and I had originally bonded over an insane acid trip in Minneapolis when we first worked together at Knuckleheads Comedy Club at the Mall of America a few years before, and had worked together a bunch more over the years. He'd moved to L.A. shortly before me and was starting to get noticed. He was doing the San Francisco competition, too.

The competition was split into two groups of twenty. The top five from each of the first two weeks would go on to the semifinals, the top five from that week on to the finals. Mitch and I were in the first week, along with Dane Cook. The first night of the first week of shows took place at the Punch Line Comedy Club in San Francisco. Mitch and I both had decent sets but didn't make the top five. Dane Cook placed second for the night. First place was taken by a girl who pretended to be deaf. It was a character she did regularly but in a short set she never broke character. If the comics weren't crying foul, they were murmuring it. Mitch and I were drunk and dejected. We talked about quitting right there and not even finishing the week. I passed Barry Katz at the bar. I was pie-eyed and irritable.

"Aren't you glad you didn't bet me priiiize money now?" he said with his easily-imitable drawn-out sneer.

"You know what? Fuck you. I'll bet you a hundred bucks I win this whole fucking thing regardless of your guy." I was enveloped in false bravado.

"You don't wanna make that bet."

I kept my hand out until he shook on it. I had the rest of the week to make it up and I did. Mitch didn't make it out of the first round but it didn't matter. There wasn't a comedian there who didn't see that Mitch was miles beyond us, including Mitch. When he learned that he was mathematically eliminated before the last show of the week, he just went on stage and did his act until the light went on that told you your time was up. The second the light went on, he'd just stop talking in mid-sentence and leave the stage. Brilliant.

The San Francisco Comedy Competition was legendary for the people who had done it in the past. Dana Carvey, Ellen DeGeneres, and Kevin Pollack had all been previous winners or finalists. Robin Williams came in second place in its inaugural year in 1975. But those days were gone and the luster of the competition had worn off. This was their twentieth anniversary. The winner still got $10,000, but nobody in the business really gave much of a fuck anymore. But I gave a fuck now. I bet a hundred bucks talking out of my ass, and I wanted that hundred more than the ten grand or the benign accolades.

The rest of the competition went like a script. Dane Cook and me neck and neck throughout, all the way to the finals. One of the nights was at Harrah's Casino in Reno. After the show, a few of us were gonna go to a tittie bar. I asked Dane if he wanted to come along. He declined, saying he was going to his room to work on his set. What is wrong with this guy? Going to the tittie bar *is* working on your set! And for me, it pretty much was. Honestly, my material was shit at that point but I allowed myself to riff a lot and that made all the difference. Anything you could come up with about the town, the venue, the other comics, or the night before that made it seem real and loose made all the difference. It gave the illusion that it was not packaged, not an act. The competition was grueling, and not just on stage. You weren't getting paid, and, aside from that night in Reno, you didn't get a hotel. There was plenty to riff on with just sleeping in your car and taking sink showers. Having nineteen other comics in the back of the room was like having a whole second audience to add laughs to your show if you could play to both.

During an off night the first week, Mitch and I went to a comedy club in the East Bay where his friend Arj Barker was scheduled to MC. The show was about to start and Arj still wasn't there. He'd been caught in traffic. They asked Mitch and me if one of us would cover for him, saying it would pay fifty bucks. We both knew we needed the money so rather than draw straws, we went up together as the comedy team of "Arj" and "Barker." Fuck it, his name was already on the marquee. We knew each others' acts well enough that we could just set each other up in silly vaudeville style.

"Hello! I'm Arj!"

"And I'm Barker!"

"And together, we're the comedy duo of ARJ & BARKER!"

"So, Arj . . . I hear that you don't like it when people hand you flyers?

"Yes, Barker . . . it's like they're saying, 'Here, YOU throw this away!'"

Twenty-five bucks each, free drinks, and I went home with the single-mom bartender. One more night without having to sleep in my car.

If Dane Cook and I had anything in common, it was that we were both mama's boys. Every night after a show we'd invariably wind up at the same bank of pay phones, calling our mothers to tell them how we did. It was always awkward for one of us. Whoever had placed higher that night had to muffle his conversation so as to not be bragging in the other guy's face. We were civilized in that manner. But it was clear that we were rivals, and by the finals it was clear that Dane Cook wasn't going away easily.

The last night of the finals week was held at the Herbst Theater in San Francisco. I'd bought a suit, tie, and shoes at a thrift store for a total of $16. I got there early and did what every comic had been doing before and after shows for the last month—annoying the scorekeeper. Scoring the competition was a series of convoluted arithmetic, dropping highest and lowest scores from each night and averaging the rest. The scorekeeper had left his book open in the green room and I started crunching the numbers. I went over them repeatedly, and even with my cruddy math skills, it kept coming up the same result. Mathematically, I was a lock. I couldn't be beaten. My pulse went batshit.

I pointed this out to Jon Fox who ran the competition.

He looked at the numbers. He balked and evaded giving me a straight answer. He said it looked good for me but that anything still could happen. I went through the numbers again like a defense attorney, demanding he admit that I had already won. He wouldn't say. I thought of the Yugo I was supposed to win at Midwest Enterprises. I knew that some fix was in and I was about to get robbed again.

I crushed onstage from what I remember. Or maybe I didn't. My nerves were so haywire and I was so worn down that it was as blurry as a fistfight. Backstage was the gallows waiting for the scores to be tallied. Each comic telling the other how good they did, hoping the judges didn't agree.

They announced the finalists in order. It got down to me and Dane Cook, waiting in the wings for first and second. I looked at my feet pacing in small circles.

"And in second place . . . Dane Cook!"

I fucking won! I fucking won and these cocksuckers knew I'd won the whole night and wouldn't tell me. I'd spent the last three hours with acid burning through my guts thinking I was about to get railroaded. I wished I'd never looked at the numbers. Instead of a victory, it felt like I'd been exonerated of a crime I didn't commit. Sure, I was happy to have a ruling in my favor but I didn't feel like I'd hit the lottery. It felt like I'd broken even. In hindsight, they did the right thing in not telling me. I could have easily walked out on-stage and taken a shit in a wine glass as my act, knowing I couldn't lose. And there'd be no thrill in announcing the final five in order if it was already known backstage. But even realizing that, the truth was that there was an emptiness in winning that final night.

They had champagne in the green room and four other spent comics offering me sad congratulations. There was nobody to cele-brate with. I hated that night. I'd known going in that all competi-tions were bullshit, that it was just a lottery based on the opinions of random judges, most of whom had nothing to do with the busi-ness. Radio DJs and newspaper entertainment column hacks. But it really sunk in afterwards in that green room. I've always felt a special kinship with comedians. A cliché, yes, but they really are family. Those years on the road where it's just you and one or two other comics against one hostile audience after another. You made friends and bonded very quickly. Even if you didn't like each other or laugh at their material, you had each others' backs. Pitted against one another in a competition made for a really shitty climax. You wanted to beat the audience, not each other. I wanted to apologize to the other comics, not high-five an empty victory. I drank my champagne, got my check, and got the fuck out. The party didn't start until I called Mother. I probably cried on the phone to her, but then again, eat a pail of shit.

I left my car at the Herbst and went to the Punch Line where I could gloat outside earshot of my competitors. Beers poured and shots flew. I woke up in bed with a waitress I didn't know. I'd left my car on the street at the theater, which was a tow zone after 7 a.m. Seeing it was well past 7 a.m., I ran out without waking her up and flagged down a cab. The relief of seeing that my car was still at the theater was quickly erased when I saw that it had been broken into. Someone smashed out the back window and stole everything I owned. I stood there, reeking of booze and strange pussy, still wearing my $16 suit, with a check for $10,000 in my coat pocket, wishing there was someone with me to share the surreal moment.

I called Mother again with my new development. She would listen to my stories so enraptured that it made me want to fuck up even more just to entertain her. She couldn't believe my luck, the seeming insanity of it all, and that I just seemed to skate through adversity time after time. I think I needed to see it through her eyes to make it all real, or unreal maybe. If it was all an incredible movie to her, it could be to me as well. She was my rock and my muse and my only fan that mattered.

Of course, I called my dad but he didn't quite get it. He'd come to my shows both in Worcester and out on the road a few times. He didn't get the jokes but he liked seeing other people laugh at them.

"They really seemed to enjoy the heck out of you!" he'd say.

I called to tell him I'd won in San Francisco. He thought that was just great. I tried to explain to him the lore of the competition. He didn't know stand-up comedy from marching bands or extracurricular pussy. I knew he'd at least be aware of the extremely famous Robin Williams. To try to give him some scope of what I'd just won, I explained that Robin Williams had done the first-ever SFCC and only come in second place. He thought that was just great. It wouldn't be until years later that I found out he'd been telling everyone in the family I'd just beaten Robin Williams in a comedy contest.

The most important call I made that morning was to the office of Barry Katz. Congratulations were the first thing out of his mouth. I want my hundred dollars was the first thing out of mine. I think he thought I was kidding. I wasn't. It took me a year and three different payments to collect it from him but eventually I got it in full. I'd have framed it if it hadn't come in so many small bills.

Dane Cook became my official comedy adversary in those weeks of the competition. I didn't like his comedy much but it was never personal. Everyone laughs at different shit. He became my go-to reference for hokey stand-up long before anyone really knew who he was. In fact, what bothered me most about his rise to fame and subsequent backlash was that I felt robbed by people jumping on my bandwagon. I hated Dane Cook back when he was just a garage comic.

Dane was also now Mother's arch-rival but she took it seriously and never let it go. For years after you'd hear her say, "I saw that fucking Dane Cook on TV. He's fucking awful! I can't believe these fucking people think he's funny," to the point that I'd end up having to defend him. The Yankees don't hate the Red Sox as people, Ma. I like to hate Dane Cook. But it isn't personal. It was just fun to have a nemesis. Mother acted like he'd molested me as a child.

Ten thousand dollars in one lump sum was staggering. I had the money to move to L.A. now. I had two more months of road dates to finish first. On December 13, 1995 I officially moved to L.A., almost three years to the day that I began living out of my car.

15

The Big Time

I STAYED WITH MITCH AND JANA IN WEST HOLLYWOOD FOR A short time while I looked for a place of my own. Jana said she had a friend who had a place opening up in her building just a few blocks away—and it was rent-controlled. To this day I still don't have any idea what rent-controlled means legally but I know it equals cheap as fuck. I looked at the place, a one-bedroom in West Hollywood, walking distance to all the comedy clubs. It was perfect. It was also only $410 a month. I gave them six months up front just to secure it. Between thrift stores and the Dollar Store, I was set up in days. I had a TV, a VCR, a bed, a chair, and a desk. I had my own food in my own refrigerator. I had $14,000 in the bank. There was nothing else I needed. Nothing else I wanted. So there was nothing to spend it on, which made it seem momentarily worthless. It was a disquieting moment of clarity. How can you go from splitting a $50 gig with Hedberg out of sheer necessity to having fourteen grand in the bank that quickly and be depressed about it? The reason cigarettes are so fulfilling is that you're going to want another one very soon, and immediately you are able to satisfy that need. I'd drink coffee in the morning not to wake up but because it made me want a cigarette. What good is a cigarette if you don't feel like you need it? Having everything I needed in L.A. made me feel complacent and dull in that moment. I was scared and I was out of my element but I'd adapt. L.A. has a way of making you feel like you need shit.

———————

MOTHER HAD BEEN IN FLORIDA NOW FOR OVER TEN YEARS AND that is going to take a toll on a person. Florida is good for no more than four days. I have put in the time now to know. I saw her a few times early in 1996 while doing college gigs that I was completely ill-suited for. Colleges prefer clean, goofy acts for those young students who still had hopes and dreams. Mother drove out when I played with Mitch on my birthday in 1996 at the University of South Florida, and later alone at Embry-Riddle Aeronautical University in Daytona. The Embry-Riddle gig was in a cafeteria during dinner where nobody even seemed to know they were having a comedy show. Students just loaded their trays full of gruel, which they devoured, and occasionally they might look up. Mother was the only laugh to be heard, exaggerated and screeching through the silence, always followed by her hacking smoker's cough. I loved that cough. She'd had it since we were kids. We could find her in the grocery store by just listening for it like a rescue beacon. Now I could find the only person enjoying the show by hearing that cough. One person laughing is way worse than nobody laughing. Your mother being the only person laughing is humiliating. But the check was good and we ran like thieves back to Crystal River. Mother never saw a Doug Stanhope show she didn't love.

She had gone back to nursing school and blown off my brother's wedding for the graduation. She couldn't miss any kind of spotlight. For the graduation, she dressed up as an old woman with a fake colostomy bag, spilling it all over herself and other students. Way funnier if she'd done it at the wedding, but funny still. Now she was actually working as a nurse and hating every minute of it. All the same shit from her bartending days, always someone was a cunt, always somebody else she couldn't work with. She was making Michael's life miserable too, constantly trashing him for simply being himself. He couldn't do anything right. If you didn't do exactly what Mother would do, you were an asshole. Unless you were me.

Mother was also becoming racist, or at least speaking their lan-guage. We'd watch the news and she'd mutter "fucking niggers" under her breath. This was the polar opposite of the mother that raised us. I didn't know if being married to a cop was what started this, but Michael never showed any sign of being anything but a sweet, fat, lazy dude, incapable or too lazy to hate anyone. Mother defended herself with rhetoric that belied her intelligence, basically the Chris Rock bit that there are black people and there are niggers, only without the rational, funny parts. I knew the difference be-tween black people and niggers. One of those words Mother would have slapped me for saying when I was kid. Unless I made it funny.

In short, Mother seemed to hate every single thing except me. She loved me to the point that it was uncomfortable sometimes, like I was the only thing in her life that was good. She made no secret that she was living her life vicariously through me. Even though there was a certain sadness to that, it still stroked my newly-emboldened ego that I was something to be admired.

She visited L.A. just after that trip for the first time. I brought her to The Improv, my new home, and they treated her like royalty. She fell right back into the life of the party like she had in Vail. Agents and managers took us to lunches and dinners, and I wasn't embar-rassed when she stole Sweet-N-Low packages off the table. You pic-ture your grandmother doing that. Mother was only fifty. Younger than even my managers. Fuck it. Steal away, lady. These other people picking up the tab are all interchangable out here anyway.

I had a gig booked in Santa Ana and talked her into opening for me as herself, my mother. She did plays so she was game so long as I wrote her what to say. She went up with this, very bashful and demure.

"Hello boys and girls. I'm Bonnie, and I am Doug Stanhope's mother. Are you looking forward to the show?

"Well, I just wanted you to know that if you're not familiar with my son's show, that he does have a bit of a potty mouth.

And he does have a tendency to go into the gutter. So I just want you to know that he was raised in a good, wholesome middle-class environment with my good values and morals.

So if at any point you're offended during his act, it should not be a reflection on me."

At this point, Mother dropped the sweet act and started cranking up the vitriol into a lather . . .

"If you want someone to blame, try that dip-fuck father of his! That stupid asshole's idea of discipline was, 'Here's a Tootsie-Pop, don't do it again!' What the fuck is that? I'm trying to bring up wholesome, upstanding children and this pansy-ass cocksucker just let them do any goddamned thing they wanted to! **HE** wanted to be 'Pals' with his children! Well, get this, 'Pally-Boy,' check out the foul goddamned mouth on this son-of-a-bitch, you bastard! Are you happy now, you rotten prick?"

And now in full spitting hatred . . .

"So if any of you sniveling douchebags came here looking for a family show, don't get pissed off at me! I'll give you his father's number and you can call that motherfucker collect!"

Then back to catching herself for a beat, and then going back to adorable . . .

"But it's all in good fun . . . So are you ready for a show? Let's hear it for Little Dougie Stanhope!"

She destroyed. She couldn't ask enough times how well she did. Every compliment was like a drop of water in drought-stricken soil.

———

BACK AT THE IMPROV, A FEW NIGHTS LATER, I SAW BARRY KATZ AT the bar. He still owed me money for the Dane Cook bet. I'd caught him once there and asked for my hundred dollars. He said he only had forty. I said I'd take it but that he still owed. This night I had Mother work collections.

"I'm Doug Stanhope's mother and he says you owe him sixty dollars."

"Uuuuh, heh heh. Well . . . I only have twenty."

She took it. I laughed from across the room as he fumbled through his wallet. I got the last forty the next time I saw him there. I'm surprised he hadn't just stopped going to The Improv altogether to get out of paying.

Mother had a blast in L.A., save for the traffic which horrified her into clutching the dashboard and constantly pumping her imaginary passenger-side brakes. She loved being recognized and congratulated if just for being my mom. Like everyone else in L.A., she again took all the credit she could. But she deserved it.

She went back to Florida. Michael got fired from the Sheriff's Department for "some trumped up bullshit" that I never got the full story on. They divorced shortly afterwards. I still really don't know why but nobody was surprised. I think he'd had an affair. God knows he deserved one after all the shit he took. Mother had a way for running people out of her life.

Meanwhile, between gigs on the road, I floated around L.A., waiting for this famous shit to happen. I did a million showcases for the suits. Showcases are live stand-up comedy shows where the audience is monopolized by industry people looking at new talent. I did showcases for networks, for festivals, for late night shows. I remember doing a showcase for the Letterman people. Afterwards, the Letterman booker told my manager, "Yes, he's really funny. But the 'Doug Flutie's flipper baby' bit isn't going to be on Letterman any time soon." There was a lot of places my jokes weren't going to be appropriate. Still, I did get a small development deal with HBO's production arm, which had just put out *Everybody Loves Raymond*. Development deals work in that they give you a chunk of money to develop a sitcom for network television. Hedberg had just got one for $500,000. Mine was only for $15,000, with another $30,000 for a half-hour HBO special to be taped the next year. I wasn't complaining. The worst that could happen is it all went in the sewer and I went back to being happy living out of my car. If I didn't have confidence, I had low standards and apathy down pat. Hollywood moves slow as milk-spit and I wasn't in a hurry. You get a deal and then you wait forever while agents and lawyers and managers finger-fuck the details. Everyone has always got a call in to so-and-so, and waiting to hear back on such-and-such, and then you'll be famous. Take your time. I'll grab a drink.

L.A. wasn't home until Mitch and I found our own bar, the Coach and Horses, on Sunset, only a couple blocks from where we lived. We'd walk past it all the time but it seemed sleazy and possibly dangerous, even by our low standards. It was open but you almost never saw people coming in or out of it, and when you did, they looked like hoboes or old war veterans. One day, bored, we ventured in.

Ginger the bartender was a bedraggled woman between sixty and seventy-five who looked homeless and talked like Momma from *Throw Momma From the Train*. She was mean like a wounded animal and the bar was empty because of it. She'd evidently worked there for seventeen years and the owner was too much of a drunk to bother with the trouble of replacing her. We'd hear legendary stories, like about her throwing a blind man out for having a dog. When one of the few regulars tried to explain the situation, that he was blind, that this was a seeing-eye dog, she screamed, "I DON'T CARE! THE SIGN SAYS NO DOGS!" I don't doubt the story. I was in there one day when the guy next to me at the bar was talking to his friend. Ginger picked up his empty beer bottle and mumbled a hate-filled "You want another?" When he politely said that he was fine for right now, she shrieked, "THIS ISN'T A BUS STOP!" I still use that today when people aren't keeping up with me. Ginger became our unrequited soulmate simply because she was insane and we made the Coach our regular bar. Anyone who dared to come in we were friendly with, since it was always ugly and mostly empty. That made it an easy target for people who didn't want to be seen. Michael Keaton came in a few times. Kiefer Sutherland on other occasions. Mitch and I bought shots for Quentin Tarantino one desolate afternoon. We didn't know what "being that guy" was. We just recognized him and that was a good enough reason to drink Jagermeister at 4 p.m. Not everybody has a life that allows them to drink Jagermeister with Tarantino in the middle of the day. We owed it to those people.

RON ZIMMERMAN WAS A WRITER AND A DRINKER I KNEW AS A regular at The Improv bar. He was also a poon-hound. One night at the bar he asked me if I wanted to be set up on a blind date. In return, he wanted me to set him up with one of my lady comedian friends. Any one of them. He was friends with a girl who had been a child star on a show called *Head of the Class*. He said she was a tall redhead who'd been one of *People* magazine's "50 Most Beautiful People." He told me she drove an $80,000 Corvette. He thought we'd hit it off. I couldn't understand why he'd think someone like that would have anything to do with someone like me. I didn't consider he just wanted me to set him up on an equal level. Maybe he'd been shopping this blind date to anyone he thought had hot friends. Didn't cross my mind. Didn't matter. I said, "Absolutely."

Becker had come through town and was staying with me for a while. Everyone stays with you for a while if you live in L.A. and have a couch. Some will stay forever if you let them. That's why I tell comics in L.A. never to own a couch. Get a love seat. They will develop scoliosis before you ever have to tell them to leave.

I told Becker about my blind date. I had no idea where to take a girl like this. I had no idea what to even say to a girl like this. Becker and I plotted out a plan of action. My car was a 1984 Olds Cutlass I referred to as The Pig that always seemed to be on its last legs. It was the same car that had been broken into in San Francisco, now with ratty duct tape where the window had been. It just wouldn't die. On one of my rare gigs in the Southeast a couple years previous I'd visited Mother. The Pig was going through a quart of oil every couple of fill-ups. I mentioned it to Mother and Mike and they sent me to their mechanic. He took a look at it and told me that it was leaking oil from every possible place a car could leak oil. The mechanic advised that I should just drive it into the ground and be done with it. I left town and it never leaked oil again.

For the date I decided that, if nothing else, I should put new duct tape over the smashed-out window on the off-chance I had to drive. That's how you spruce up for a date with a hot celebrity. New duct tape on your car window. Coming up with no ideas on where to take her, I finally told her just to meet me at the Coach and Horses and we'd take it from there. I got there plenty early to drink up my swagger.

I took two seats at the door-end of the bar. Evan was a regular at the bar and was sitting on the corner across from me. She was the kind of dive-bar regular that only exists in movies. She was tall, Nordic-blonde, and gorgeous if somewhat weather-worn. She was only twenty-nine but carried herself like she'd been drinking alone at the same barstool for just as many years. Sometimes I'd come in during the day and she'd be sitting in her usual spot at the far end of the bar, chain-smoking Carlton 100s and drinking Miller Lite. I'd come back after shows late that night and she was still in the same spot, still drinking, no worse for the wear. There was always something about her that was unapproachable. The fact that nobody else at the bar ever seemed to hit on her—an otherwise sitting duck in a bar full of predators—confirmed this. This night was the first time she wasn't down in her regular seat and the first time I talked to her.

I told her about this famous girl I was supposed to meet, that I was nervous and out of my league. She gave me shit and goofed on me for even caring. She was childlike in her cruelty. I needed the abuse. I needed the beer even more, panic-drinking. Khrystyne walked into this landfill bar like it was a red carpet. I didn't need any social skills, she had them all. I asked her what she wanted to drink and my soul sunk when she said she didn't really drink. Evan rolled her eyes behind Khrystyne's back and tried not to laugh at me audibly. We never left the place. We sat and talked while I got progressively more intoxicated and somehow everything seemed to go fantastically. She was verbose and fun and she didn't seem to care that I was piling down beers and shots like it was the eve of Prohibition. She didn't want dinner or a movie. She was just fun and interesting and even seemed interested in me. Every time I gained a bit of confidence, I'd see Evan behind her shaking her head like I was a stooge.

Finally, Khrystyne said it was time to go. I walked her to her Corvette, swapped numbers, and we agreed to go out again. Then I came back to drink some more. Evan dressed me down. She'd essentially spent the entire date with us without Khrystyne's knowledge. She made me feel like an idiot but conceded that she thought it was a huge success. I eventually stumbled home but not before stopping to feed the kittens. Across the street just past the 7-11 we'd found a litter of kittens that were living behind the trees in front of an empty house. Now it became tradition to buy a bag of cat food on the shuffle back to the apartment and hang out for a minute petting the kittens. I still think animal shelters should be open an hour before last call and right next to a bar. Or even in the bar. Adoptions would quadruple.

That night I was love-struck, drunk, and giddy. I lay down with the kittens, shitfaced and beaming. I thought I might even sleep there in the small cluster of trees. A car full of Mexicans pulled out of the 7-11 and up to the curb. One guy got out and walked into the trees where I was laying down. He started to take a piss and, unknowingly in the dark, was pissing directly on me. When I made my presence known by vaguely rustling, he just said, "Don't move." He probably thought I was a homeless guy and pissed all over me. I was in no condition to do anything about it. In fact, had I been sober and alert I'd still be in no condition to do anything about it. When he got back in the car, I got up to leave. He drove off, shrieking with laughter—"I fucking pissed all over you, dude!" That is why I think all Mexicans are bad people and two out of three black women are men. That is also why I think all homeless people aren't homeless at all. They just fell in love with a wealthy starlet and decided to sleep in the bushes with stray animals to celebrate. I am a product of my environment.

Becker was waiting up when I came home. Everything went perfectly. She was beautiful. She was rich and famous. She didn't seem to care that I was a drunk. She hung out at my bar for hours and wanted to see me again. And I was covered in piss from a Mexican gangbanger. The night was a complete success.

———

AROUND THIS TIME I'D STARTED UP A CORRESPONDENCE WITH A Florida death row inmate. He had placed an ad in the LA Times classifieds in the pen pal section. I loved and still love reading the newspaper in the morning with a cigarette. It makes you feel like you're doing something. And unlike the Internet, the newspaper eventually ends, so you know to get on with your day. Even if you have to get down to reading classified ads out of boredom. His ad read:

"Death Row Inmate, 35 w/m, 6'3" 185, answer all correspondence" with the name Victor Farr and an address in Raiford, FL.

I sent a letter that said:

"Dear Victor, I saw your ad in the LA Times and was intrigued, more so with the fact that you included your height and weight. You're on death row, for God's sake. Did you think someone wouldn't write to you because you're a bit too chunky? If you're going to include your height, why not just say you're a 3'9" midget looking for a fat girl to smuggle you out of prison in her ass? At least that way your mail would be more entertaining." I included my name and address but didn't expect a response.

A week later I got a reply, thanking me for the letter. He said that I had no idea how important and rare it was to be able to laugh in a place like death row. That's all I needed to hear. The biggest payoff you get from doing comedy isn't on stage, it's from making people laugh unexpectedly and when they really need a laugh that's the most rewarding. A frustrated waitress or store clerk laughing is way more gratifying than a paying audience. It's the difference between a girl blowing you because she likes you versus blowing you for money. You don't critique a free blow job. You're just grateful for the courtesy.

I wrote to Victor for several years. At some point early on I asked him to keep my letters and send them back to me when they built up. This way I could keep them as a de facto diary that I'd otherwise be too lazy to write. Those letters are a large portion of the reason I was able to piece together some of these years.

He sent me his picture. I'd bring it with me later whenever Khrystyne would bring me to functions where there were famous people. I'd ask them very politely if they'd mind taking a picture with my retarded brother's photograph. He's a big fan and couldn't be here, well, because he's retarded. Stars can't say no to retards. It's part of an oath, I believe. Khrystyne could get us in anywhere, invitation not necessary. She made a sport of it. From Oscar parties to the American Comedy Awards, I got pictures of Victor with everyone from Weird Al and Dennis Rodman all the way up to Nicole Kidman and Winona Ryder. I don't know how popular you can be on death row but I'm sure it couldn't help but boost Victor's reputation.

THE THRILL OF DATING A FAMOUS CHICK—AND A BEAUTIFUL ONE at that—wore thin quick. My jealousy was palpable. We'd walk down the red carpet at a premiere and photographers would yell out to her for a pose.

"Thanks . . . yeah, uh, but could we get a 'single'?" would invariably follow, a polite way of saying, "Hey, Mr. Nobody, get the fuck out of the shot."

It all shit on my newfound ego. I was supposed to be the up-and-coming talent here. Her show ended six years before. Since then she'd done straight-to-video classics like *Scanner Cop II* and *Cyborg 3: The Recycler!* I was the one now getting all the meetings and auditions. I was getting spots on TV, goddamn you! But any time I was out with her, I felt invisible. She'd guest-starred on a short-lived sitcom with veteran comedian Richard Jeni called *Platypus Man*. When he'd come into The Improv, he'd hit on her like a viper. She'd always introduce me to him as her boyfriend and as a fellow comedian. He'd nod and go straight back to hitting on her. Later, at the Montreal comedy festival, he was hosting a late-night show and introduced me, saying, "I haven't met this next guy but I've heard a lot of good things . . . "

I opened with "You haven't met me? You've met me a dozen times when you were hitting on my chick right in front of me at The Improv in L.A., and then continued hitting on her after you knew it was my girlfriend!" Now that I've been doing comedy as long as he had been then, I not only understand hitting on other people's girlfriends, I am certainly aware of not remembering shit. I love it now when I'm out with people on the road and someone starts a story about crazy shit we did in days gone by. Even though I'm a part of it, I'm as interested as anyone else at the table in finding out how the story ends. But at the time I guess I thought I was a lot more remarkable than I was.

———

MOTHER WASN'T DOING WELL IN FLORIDA. I REALIZED THAT THIS was really the first time she'd truly been financially on her own in her life. Even during the brief periods between husbands she'd had alimony or Grandma's "Dead Money" to support her as well as friends and family around her. That was all gone now. She couldn't seem to hold down a job at all. For the same reasons as her bartending days. There was always someone she couldn't tolerate, some cunt employee or boss that was an asshole or a moron. Always someone else's fault. I could tell she was scared and sometimes I thought she was losing her bean altogether. She was working graveyard shift in a nursing home and would snivel about all these horrible patients she had to deal with. To make her point, she brought a mini-cassette recorder along on one of her shifts to tape these awful patients she told me about. She mailed me the tape and I listened to it for about fifteen minutes with my jaw on the floor. It was Mother crudely and menacingly trying to get some terrified old woman into a bathroom.

"Please be gentle. You're hurting me."

"Oh, shut up. I'm not hurting you. Just sit down. Jesus Christ."

"Pleeeease!"

"Just Shut Up!"

It was straight-up elder abuse and Mother honestly thought she was the victim, having to man-handle elderly dementia patients. Like Ginger throwing a blind guy out of the bar. I tried gently to tell Mother that she was in the wrong but she wouldn't hear it. I understand losing your cool in a frustrated moment, but to calculate tape-recording it and then—with the benefit of hindsight—still justify it? I'd seen her afraid, courageous, meek, helpful, polite, and even rude. But being mean to the weakest of the weak, and arguing—complaining even—that it's her job? That's what bad cops do. It's hard to look at your mother in that light.

She was still doing local theater and occasionally I'd float the idea that maybe she should move to L.A. and try her hand at acting out here. I was still developing a show and had gone so far as to write in characters based on Mother, Mitch, and Khrystyne. They'd partnered me with a writer named Stan Daniels who'd gotten his start writing for *The Dean Martin Show,* and had gone on to win Emmys for *The Mary Tyler Moore Show* and then *Cheers.* You think my references are dated? This was 1996. I was twenty-nine. Stan Daniels was sixty-two but he might as well have been 106. We'd write at his house in the Valley, underneath his shelf of Emmys. In the script, he'd have me quoting Immanuel Kant. I had to ask who that was. I had to know the references before I could understand that the jokes weren't funny. At one point in the script, he has Khrystyne's character going to the bathroom to get me "mecurochrome," an antiseptic popular when my elderly father was a child, for a cut on my hand. Even my spell-check puts a red squiggly line under it now when I type it, that's how dated a reference it is. I wanted to tell Stan, "Why don't you just have her say she's going to apply the leeches?" but instead I just shut up and looked at the Emmys. What did I know? Every sitcom on television sucked as far as I was concerned. *Mad About You? Suddenly Susan? Third* fucking *Rock From The Sun?* How could I tell what they thought was good? Maybe our shitty sitcom was exactly the kind of suck Hollywood was craving.

I did the Florida Comedy Festival in 1997 in Jacksonville. Mother came out but made me come pick her up. She wouldn't make the two and a half hour drive by herself, preferring me to drive five hours round-trip to come get her and bring her there. She was suddenly too scared to drive, too scared of getting lost. It didn't matter that I was coming from across the country with a head full of material to put together. That chapped my onion for a minute but once we were there, she went straight into vulgar and hilarious not-your-typical-mother mode. She opened one of my shows with the same schtick from Santa Ana, and killed. The festival included a competition night as the finale. The contestants had been preselected and I wasn't one of them, but there was a wild card spot up for grabs for the Best of the Fest from the week ramping up to it. I thought I had it nailed but was informed that I wouldn't be eligible because you had to be TV-clean to do the competition. When I assured them I could work clean, they caved in and gave me the spot. As the wild card entry, I had to open the show. The shit spot. Taking the bullet. I was still riding a TWA Flight 800 bit from the previous summer, the flight that blew up or was shot down over Long Island. It was a particularly cruel piece berating the families of the victims for putting undo pressure on an overworked medical examiner to identify bodies, him trying his best to piece together body parts like Mr. Potato Heads. The story was just old enough that an audience could overlook the initial savagery and see the righteousness inherent at the core. I had to change one necessary "motherfucker" to "mothertrucker," but otherwise, as bombastic as the subject matter was, it remained TV-clean. Like the Doug Flutie flipper baby, it was never going to be on Letterman, but it crushed and I won the competition as a huge underdog with Mother there to see it. Unlike in San

Francisco, I had my biggest fan to celebrate with. We tore that night down like we were king and queen of the prom.

————

BEFORE THE END OF THE FESTIVAL, I TOOK A DAY TO GO UP TO Florida State Prison in Raiford, Florida, less than an hour away, to drop in on Victor on death row. After being thoroughly searched and then undertaking the menacing walk through a chain-link cage passageway across the yard, death row turned out to be pretty relaxed, at least in the visiting area. It wasn't sitting on a phone looking through a safety window like you'd imagine. I didn't have to press my tits up against the glass while Victor masturbated like Brad Davis's character in *Midnight Express*, though I would have just for the story.

Death row visiting was a large room with about fifteen stainless steel tables with four seats each, all affixed to the floor. Inmates were dressed in orange jumpsuits but otherwise un-cuffed and free to walk about. Most of the tables were full and everyone was laid-back if not almost festive. These guys don't get out very often and visits are rare, so everyone was on their best behavior and jovial. You could tell immediately that Victor was a known goof and a charmer. He shot jokes back and forth to other inmates and guards who'd always smile. There were vending machines and we loaded up on junk food. He introduced me around. He'd lean in and point out different prisoners and whisper to me who and how they murdered, who he did and didn't like, who was going to die next, etc. Death row gossip. We were like silly women.

As for Victor's case, he'd been outside a bar in Lake City, Florida and asked two women sitting inside a car for a ride. They refused—rudely, according to Victor. Being new to town, he did what most people would do. He shot them both. They both lived and probably still don't pick up hitchhikers. He then carjacked another car with a couple inside. The guy fled and Victor took off with the girl still in the car. A police chase ensued and he wrapped the car around a tree at 70 miles per hour, killing the girl. Felony murder. Any felony resulting in the death of another person was a capital crime. He'd been on death row for seven years. Now we're eating vending machine Pop-Tarts while I snuck into the bathroom for an occasional smoke. Life goes on. For a limited time only.

I hung out for longer than I could come up with conversation. I knew he'd rather sit around with nothing to say than go back to his cell. They offered Polaroid pictures for five bucks a shot just like they used to do with featured tittie dancers at strip clubs. We got a couple shots before I left, one with him pretending to choke me. He'd later tell me he'd almost got written up for playing along. On death row, I can't imagine what the punishment would be.

After the festival, Mother and I went back to Crystal River for a few days. I went to visit her at work overnight at the nursing home. That was the real death row. Victor's death row in prison was a bachelor party compared to the elderly and infirmed at night in the nursing facility. Moans echoed down otherwise silent corridors along with the rhythmic beeping of machines. People who'd been there for years with strokes, dementia, lost, and in pain. Bedpans and catheters. Fed through tubes. Just like on death row, they were incubated in small rooms with a small television and probably just as few visitors. If family did visit, they probably went unrecognized. No need for bars or fences when you can't even walk. So and so just broke a hip and that guy keeps pulling his tube out. Occasional shrieks from pains or night terrors. And that's your reward for ninety-seven years of good, clean living. It was gruesome. It didn't excuse Mother's treatment of the patients, but like the prison guards on death row and living in that shitty town just outside the razor wire, you could see where it would drive you into depression, sadism, or insanity.

Anyone who says that suicide is never the answer hasn't heard all of the questions.

16

Breakdown
Dead Ahead

WHEN I GOT BACK TO L.A., KHRYSTYNE WAS GETTING READY TO leave on a last-minute trip to London, Paris, and then on to the Cannes Film Festival. She did a lot of gallivanting like this but never with me. She was being invited to dinner with Rod Stewart or a weekend with one of the Kennedys. O.J. Simpson was an old friend who'd flown her to a Super Bowl when she was a young actress. Just after he was acquitted, he called her to go out on a date. As possessive as I may have been, I could only laugh at the absurdity of that showdown. "Hey, stay away from her, dude! She's with me now! Hey, has anyone seen my sunglasses?" She didn't return his call.

Khrystyne would show up occasionally at my gigs on the road and in L.A., but when she took off on some global excursion, I was never invited. Now she was going to Cannes where some big-shot ex-fling of hers was going to be. I was leaving to drive across country on a seven-week tour. I was resentful and being petty. She said that she wasn't sure where our relationship was headed. Something to that effect. Pre-dump chatter. I smelled it. The writing was on the wall and on the windshield for the 2,400-mile drive across the country. Like when my wife Dori had left without warning and disappeared on the drive from Las Vegas.

From a letter to Victor:

"Poolside in Charlotte, NC. Drove here. Left Friday, stayed Saturday and Sunday in Tulsa, got here Tuesday a.m. Thought about the girl the whole way. Torture. In France, out and about with the rich and famous. Right where she belongs, right where I want to be. But not as someone's guest. I need to be the celebrity. Otherwise, it's all tinged with jealousy.

"Twenty-four hundred miles with nothing but painted white lines and the fear. I've brought the fear on myself, I presume, but there is no backtracking. Just miles more to go, weeks more to wait. I left L.A. with only the knowledge that she was somewhere unreachable in the south of France, in the same place as her famous longtime lover and that I wasn't invited. Just enough knowledge that it was easily transformed by the road into a cancer that spread with each mile. Was she now being helicoptered to his palace, so enamored by his status and his title that no mention of me ever crossed her lips? No thought of me, not a glimpse in her mind? Another border, another rest stop. Was she wondering how to break it to me, that she'd decided to snub me for her old flame? Another mile. Should I leave her now as a preemptive strike? Could I bear to feel this way again? Not only jealous and untrusting but also ashamed to feel this way to boot? Do I feel this way because I have no faith in my own constitution if the roles were reversed? My hypocrisy is thick enough. A hundred miles under my belt and still no messages. My imagination run wild, exhausted. I picture finding her and her ex on the cover of the National Enquirer, his 14 inches of cock laying across both of her outstretched palms. An insert photo of me, little-dicked and potbellied, with a tear in my eye.

"Sunday afternoon she calls, no idea why I've left so many panicked messages. There is no way to explain what the hours can do in your mind, how thoughts can manifest into realities, how the imagination can run free and turn ugly on you. Especially with a guilty mind.

"He hadn't stolen her away. In fact, he'd snubbed her on the phone. No danger, no imminent collapse. Not even an understanding of why this fear had come about. It's not hers to comprehend."

I could have just written, "Wow, I blew that shit outta proportion like a fucking moron." But that wouldn't have sounded so despondently tragic. I had been completely out of my mind on that trip. I'd left dozens of needy, helpless messages on her voicemail, begging her to call. I even actually looked at tabloids in truck stops. All just to finally get a "What the fuck is your problem?" call from France.

The next week I was back in Florida and visited Victor again. That night, I stayed with one of his legal aides and called Khrystyne who was back in L.A. She said she doesn't know what she's doing with her life and she doesn't feel like she's my girlfriend anymore. She doesn't think she's in love with me anymore but she loves me and doesn't want to lose me, and I'm her best friend but it's not going to be like it was and she just doesn't know it. I was getting dumped! I fucking knew it! How can you do that to a guy, alone out on the road banging his death row buddy's legal staffer? Have you no soul? I drove twelve hours through the night from Florida to Texas, where I had three nights off before my next gig. I spent six hundred bucks on a last-minute flight to L.A.—about what I was making for the Texas gigs—to see her face to face.

When I got back to L.A., she came to the apartment. I asked her if she'd seen her ex. She said that she had. I asked her point-blank, "Did you fuck him?"

She said, "No." But then she said that other things had happened.

Why couldn't you just stop at "no"? Technically that wouldn't be lying.

We were done. It didn't matter that I'd cheated on her every possible chance I got on the road. She wasn't the type to ask a lot of questions. But those were just road girls. My sewer-grade infidelities couldn't compete with global A-listers. This is where I was going to be cute and say that I won't tell you his name but I'll tell what he does for a living—which would tell you exactly who it is. The lawyers have shat upon that. Lawyers don't like cute and are afraid of getting sued by bigger lawyers. I'll save it for the stage.

Now I had to fly back out for five more weeks of horrible roadwork in redneck hell with all that shit in my head. There's things you don't do. You don't be cruel to animals, you don't hit a woman, and you don't dump a guy when he's on the road. I guess with my torturing caterpillars and punching my stepsister, I had it coming.

I've had plenty of nosedive, wayward, tanked sets in my career but I can't imagine anyone deserving a refund more than any poor chump who had to witness my sullen and morose act on the rest of that trip.

———

By the time I got back to L.A., I'd slightly recovered and if only out of spite, I went in search of anything and everything I could drop my cock into. I went on a tsunami of poon and not all of it horrible. One, in fact, was quite fantastic. I was standing in front of a nightclub called Union, waiting for it to open for a show I was doing that night. They were late in opening and a few people were gathered out front, including one girl who had to have been the most beautiful girl I'd ever seen. She was alone and asked me for a cigarette. The attraction tripled. I started drumming up some small talk. Just bullshit, asking who she was here to see, hoping it wasn't a comic that sucked. Nothing worse than shitty comics getting beautiful girls. Her name was Renee. We carried our conversation to the bar and I was emboldened when she kept up or ahead of my drinking. She didn't fuck around. She was twenty-two and had just moved down from Oregon to get into acting. That's usually a horrible sign but she seemed as apathetic about the business as I did. L.A. was just a place you had to show up and tolerate. The show started and we watched together from the bar. She laughed—or more importantly, didn't laugh—at all the right times. I never told her that I was a comedian, much less that I was going on. I just waited until they announced me from the stage and excused myself.

"Hang on, I'll be back in ten minutes."

Smooth.

I killed. I came off stage, sat back down, and ordered us another round as though nothing had happened in my absence. If I couldn't close this lead, I didn't deserve the paper. I took her to the Coach and Horses. Everybody hit on her. I was afraid to leave to take a leak. We were drunk quick and she came back to my place. I woke up to a note and a phone number. I was afraid to call. I knew from the road that sometimes you weren't always the only one waking up and making fun of your poor drunken choices from the night before.

Renee was the rebound girl and sometimes you cling to the rebound with ten times the zeal as the relationship you are recovering from. I guarded myself from going overboard but I would have moved her into my apartment that day if I had the option. She was living with three girlfriends just on the other side of the Coach and quickly became a regular there. And while I'd see her often, I couldn't ever quite nail her down. I tried to be cool about it. She was eerily taciturn and secretive about her life, like she may be part of some covert organization or touched inappropriately as a child. I often wondered if she was some high-class call girl on the side. Either way, it gave her an air of mystery that piqued my curiosity to levels that could easily be confused with love. She would command the attention of any room she was in without saying a word. She also had a habit of having to be carried out of the bar. I didn't have the upper-body strength.

The Coach was changing. Ginger had been fired after seventeen years. All the regulars knew she was unemployable otherwise and worried what would become of her. There were a few Bigfoot sightings of her sitting at bus benches but not waiting for a bus. She called me once to hint at her staying in my apartment. I remember that day because that was the day I bought Caller ID.

April was the new bartender. She was young and cute, very cheerleader sweet and peppy. That was great but it also turned a genuine dive bar into dive-trendy seemingly overnight. Young, hip, and cool people now started filling up the seats without our caustic Ginger to scare them off. "This isn't a bus stop!" was sorely lacking. It was becoming wall-to-wall without her, the small handful of regulars crushed into the back corner and none too pleased about it. Some nights it would get so overfull that I'd barback for free just to get out of the crowd. I'm very claustrophobic. One night Janeane Garofalo was sitting at a booth with some other people including SNL's Chris Kattan. She came to the bar while I was back washing glasses and asked me if I could stop one of the drunk patrons (a regular) from bothering Kattan. I told her very calmly and honestly, "I don't work here," as I continued washing dishes behind the bar. She rolled her eyes at me like I was the biggest shitbag in the world.

Working for a living is admirable in most parts of the country, but in L.A.—in show business—it's looked at as a disease. There's a reason they say "Don't quit your day job." A day job means things aren't working out. It was funny when comedians who knew me peripherally would come into the Coach and see me loading beer into the coolers. I was supposed to be this new hot property in L.A. What happened? They'd look at me sadly like they'd walked in on me masturbating with crippled hands. I never explained.

I was still getting nowhere with Renee and it made me crazy that she was now part of my bar but still a free agent. She flirted in a "one-of-the-guys" kinda way that made her all the more appealing to everybody. There was one guy named Lorca who was a semi-regular. There were three kinds of regulars at the Coach. The ones you hugged when you walked in, the ones you high-fived, and the ones you nodded at. Lorca was a nodder. He was also a leering, dour drunk, probably in his mid-twenties, who always seemed to be on the edge of a fistfight. He also seemed to be sitting with Renee quite a bit. One night I'd been playing cat-and-mouse with him and Renee. They'd be sitting together and when he'd wander off, I'd jump in and steer her my way. Becker and Ralphie May showed up at some point. They knew my infatuation with this girl. Renee and Lorca were both as shitfaced as I was. In my mind, it was a Mexican standoff for who was going to leave with her. A few times I caught him glaring at me. I couldn't discern if he was trying to stare me down or if he was just wasted. I'm against violence as are most people who aren't good at it, and the mere hint of it in his eyes had me on edge. Ralphie and Becker, also both big paranoids, convinced me that, yes, he was overtly being a dick. Still, he hadn't done anything outright to warrant me saying something to him. I'd be hard-pressed to take him aside and say, "Quit being creepy," so I just allowed it to silently ruin my night. I hated being a coward, and I also hated being so deluded by a girl that I couldn't tell if I needed to be brave in the first place.

Finally, April called last call, and shortly after we were all invited to get the fuck out. The bar cleared out onto the street. Ralphie, Becker, and I walked out the door and turned left up the sidewalk. Lorca, a few steps behind, ran right out into Sunset Boulevard and was killed by a speeding car. It knocked him literally out of his shoes.

I didn't expect the night to end like that either.

RENEE AND I LOST TOUCH AND SOMEHOW I WAS BACK TOGETHER with Khrystyne. I don't know how it happened. You've had those relationships. You don't know how they happened. They just seem to go away and then recur like herpes. I was never much for being single. Or faithful for that matter. I've always been with a girl except for the three years I lived on the road, and those girls went by like mile markers. And I fell in love with a lot of those girls, too.

My TV pilot had died but that just meant another pilot was going to happen. You switch writers, pitch a different network, find a new production company. Even with a brand new concept, every pilot still included characters for Khrystyne, Mitch, and Mother. When HBO's pilot for NBC shit the bed, they also dumped my half-hour special. I still got paid but I would have much rather have had the show than the money. My stand-up was really doing well but the rest of the LA nonsense just seemed to drag. I sucked at acting and it didn't help that I'd get sent to auditions for parts I had no business playing. I hated auditions. Actors are generally horrible, empty, vapid people and writers install temporary personalities into their voids. You go to an audition and it's a room full of desperation, as though three lines for an insurance commercial is the sole donated kidney and everyone in the lobby needs the transplant to live.

It got to a point where I knew I was going to suck and just had to get through it. A lot of times I'd read for the same casting agents for different things, and even they knew I was going to suck. I could always get a laugh in the room but never with the lines I had to read. Outside the room was a different story. Try cracking a joke to break the tension of actors preparing. May as well fling shit in their hair.

I'd been cracking wise outside of some audition and getting glared at by the half-dozen other guys in the room. I'd stopped giving a fuck. The audition was for a single sentence, something generic like, "Looks like you're gonna need a new transmission." Everyone is gonna read the same stupid sentence and somehow I'm fucking up your mojo by adding a little levity to the waiting room. I got called in to read. The casting lady knew me from stand-up showcases and really liked me, but she'd also auditioned me for several things before and I was always fell flat.

In an audition, you are in a small room with the casting person and usually one or two other humps with clipboards and one guy filming you. I said the line. They stared at me like I'm out of focus. They asked me to read it again. How many fucking ways can you read that? It's a simple sentence. There's no context. I read it again exactly the same. Then I get the ubiquitous "Thanks, we'll let you know." Knowing the woman and being fairly friendly, I said, "I know I'm not getting the part but will you do me one favor? All those assholes out there act like they're about to play the new Batman. So, the second I open the door to leave, will you give me a huge, screaming round of applause like I just blew the roof off the place?"

They looked at each other and started to smile. I'm sure they were tired of the monotony of a thousand douchebags saying the same benign sentence. They agreed. I opened the door back into that funeral parlor in the lobby and an extended bellowing, foot-stomping roar followed me out. I turned around and took a couple of half-bows and a wave as I backed out of the room. The actors sat slackjawed and incredulous. One of them asked, "What did you do???" I just offered a cunty shrug and a "Good luck" and walked out of the place.

The final straw came when I was given a script for a lead role in a feature film. If it wasn't *Dude, Where's My Car?* which I'm pretty sure it was, it was something equally inane. My agent handed it to me like it was *The Godfather.* I sat with Mitch that night in the Coach and tried to read my lines to him. I wasn't trying to act them out, mind you. I was just reading them to show how utterly embarrassing they were even to say out loud. I was horrified that I'd actually have to deliver this mucus in front of strangers like it was funny. I drank heavily. We kept going through the script, finding more lines even worse than the ones before. At some point Mitch casually said, "Yeah, just don't do it." I'd honestly never considered this! I always just did what I was told to do. It never dawned on me I could simply say, "No thank you." What a beautiful drunken epiphany! In the morning, I called my agent and said that I wasn't going to the audition, that it just wasn't me. The phone fell silent like I'd just thrown a stack of cash into a campfire.

I didn't want to act. I wanted to be doing stand-up. All these auditions were doing nothing but making me depressed. I remember telling Mitch in an embarrassing voice of drunken pomposity that night at the Coach, "I don't even want to act. I want to be so real that someday people want to play *me!*" Oh, the arrogance of fear mixed with alcohol. Regardless, the sentiment was true. I hated acting. Acting was Mother's thing. She loved this shit. She should be out here doing this.

17

Mother's Big Move

I DID A ROUTINE ON ONE OF MY RECORDINGS ABOUT MOVING MY mother to L.A. If you heard the bit, I chalked it all up to one drunken phone call. Stand-up comedy doesn't allow time for detail. The reality is that it was probably several drunken phone calls over a period of time. But I did achieve my goal.

I flew out to pick up Mother on May 4, 1998. We rented a U-Haul truck that we would tow her car behind. Mother was an agitated wreck. She had piles of shit in and out of boxes and she was frantic. She wasn't even close to ready, and me being in a hurry made her even more sniping and abrasive. Where we were going to put all this rummage when we got to L.A. was another problem but we'd deal with that when we got there. Most of the shit she was bringing was completely unnecessary but there was no telling her that. The cats were cordoned off into one bedroom so they wouldn't run off while we loaded the truck. They were used to being free-range cats and weren't happy about being locked in a room. They didn't realize it was only going to get worse. All the way to L.A. in cat-carriers. Solitary confinement.

I was terrified at the idea of just having to drive the U-Haul, much less towing the car on the back. Fortunately, what I lack in driving skills, I more than compensate for in stamina. My record nonstop drive at that point was twenty-seven hours. I figured we could make this in forty-eight hours in a straight shot with Mother only having to take the wheel when I needed to grab a couple hours to recharge. Boy, was I fucking wrong. Mother didn't take the wheel once, although she might as well have been driving with all her unusual invisible brake-stomping and other gesticulations and critiques. I was a lot more patient then than I would be now, but even then, I was getting pretty fucking irritated very quickly. The cats were stacked in carriers behind us and were constantly yowling. Mother kept hinting that we should get a motel at some point later for the night, and as I ignored her, the hints turned into demands. We'd barely made it eight or nine hours before we were checking into some off-ramp trucker motel. This didn't mean simply stopping to sleep. It entailed finding a motel, unloading our own shit—me, a toothbrush—her, a suitcase, a pocketbook the size of a suitcase, a cooler, her bags of snacks, etc., etc. Then we'd have to sneak seven cat-carriers up to the room as well as cat food and a litter box. Motels may be pet-friendly but this was starting your own no-kill shelter, and you could hear the cacophony from the parking lot. In the morning, I realized that I'd fucked up and parked in a way that would force me to back out in a very complicated fashion. It's one thing to tow a car but I have no idea how to angle it in reverse. After the same clusterfuck of getting the cats and all our shit reloaded back into the truck, I gave several frustrated attempts at getting out of the parking lot, each more fucked up than the next. Then it dawned on me—Mother can do it! She was a truck driver! She's trained to do this! But Mother didn't. Or just wouldn't. She wouldn't even make an attempt. I can only assume now that Mother's trucking days were mostly spent when her partner let her drive on long straightaways, like letting your kid steer the car in an empty parking lot from your lap. Eventually, I flagged down a trucker leaving the motel to get it turned around for me.

We'd end up getting a motel every night. Along with having to stop to pee every two hours, my forty-eight-hour trip lasted five days and I knew I'd probably just bitten off a huge chunk of mistake.

THE APARTMENT WAS FILLED UP WITH MOTHER'S DEBRIS TO THE point of breaking before we'd unloaded even close to half of the U-Haul. The rest would have to go into storage until she got her own place, something she wasn't eager to discuss. Any time the talk turned to setting her up on her own in either a job or an apartment, she went into her own five stages of manipulation—ignore, dodge, barter, panic, and finally, cry. But never acceptance.

"But I like it *here*."

So Mother started building her nest. She preferred to stay in the living room on the bunk bed because she wanted to be in front of the TV. Then she had her table with her ashtray and her 32-oz travel mug of diet soda. Mainstays. Then her tissue box where used tissues overflowed and spread like dust bunnies. Then assorted snacks, M&Ms, as well as pens, Post-It notes, TV guides, alarm clock, lighters, and cat toys until she was completely enveloped in her own semi-circle of comfort-refuse. The nest then spread to my desk, which was just a folding banquet table. Here she set up her make-up table that could have painted a circus. Plastic drawers, hand mirrors, double-sided table mirrors, hair brushes, eyelash curlers, all that shit. I didn't have a lot of stuff to begin with, which is good because I'd have been overrun.

The good news for my relationship—whatever state that was in by now—was that Khyrstyne was deathly allergic to cats and couldn't come inside anymore. She didn't hang around much at the apartment beforehand anyway but usually spent the night. Now she could only talk through the screen door. That was fine by all parties involved. I wasn't dying for Khrystyne to spend a lot of time with Mother. Even when I did find Mother's eccentricities amusing—and I didn't right around now—it wasn't Khrystyne's sense of humor. Khrystyne was all-Hollywood and could plaster on a fake smile in order to game show host her way through any type of social situation. I'd even brought her up to Crouch, Idaho once to a BBQ with some of the old mountain-man Dirty Shame Saloon folk and she had them eating out of her hand. But she wasn't going to be doubled over laughing at Mother jacking off cats and cranking out farts. Mother hated Khrystyne right away. She said she was a "phony," and she might have been correct, especially if you think being polite and smiling when you really want to say, "You repulse me on every level of humanity" is being fake. It was the only girlfriend I remember Mother disliking and the timing made that stand out. I don't know if it was territorial or if she didn't like that Khrystyne didn't put enough effort into listening to her run-on stories and playing the daughter-in-law part. But their paths didn't cross often enough for it ever to become an issue.

The funny twist was that, in all this time, I had never once been in Khrystyne's house. Khrystyne also lived with her mother and her mother wouldn't allow strangers in. The only time I'd met her mother is once when Khrystyne brought her to my place for dinner. I remember spending a long afternoon trying to de-porn the place. All the accoutrements and decorations in my apartment were obscene to the point it was hard for me to recognize all the things that could be upsetting. My refrigerator alone was covered in smut. There was a centerfold of a naked 400-pound lady from some obese-porn magazine that Mother had sent. A cut-out picture of a woman with her knees at her ears and a large yellow onion stuffed halfway up her asshole. A snapshot of Joey CoCo Diaz slinging his Cuban uncut egg roll off the bunk bed. Every time I thought I was done cleaning up, I'd spot something else. The inflatable sex sheep on the top bunk. The penis pump over the wine bottle in the front window. It was all just normal bric-a-brac to me, and hiding it all was my only focus. Funny that I was never troubled about the fact that I couldn't cook.

Now, because of our mothers, neither Khrystyne or I could go to the other's place.

An excerpt from a letter to Victor:

"Mom is settling in like an old dog taken from the pound. Scared, unsure, needy for attention yet still stuck in her old ways. The TV is on round the clock. She panics every time she has to leave the house alone. Gives me puppy dog eyes when I leave for the bar, asking me if I'm coming home. Takes it as though she's a burden when I don't. But she'll grow out of it.

Hopefully sooner rather than later. Otherwise I'll have to have you give her a car ride.

"The cats are going to be a problem. At least until they die, and considering the way she pampers them, that may never happen. Those cats may well live to be a hundred. Walking around with artificial legs, IVs on rollers, plastic heart valves. Others lying in oxygen tents of life support systems with nurses round the clock. I'm only afraid one day it will be discovered that I have the same blood type as one of these little house rodents and I'll have to spare a kidney or a lung. Most of that herd of vermin should have been dead years ago. One looks like a burn victim, one is blind in one eye, some are missing fur. Looks like they just did a tour of duty in 'Nam. And Mom will sit around all day talking to them. And when she's not talking to them, she's talking about them. She will sit with a stack of photos of her cats laying around in different places and make you look at them, all the while the actual cats are laying around in different places right there in the room.

"'Ma! If I wanted to see Charlie sleeping on a box, I can just look over there! I don't need a fucking picture!'

"Don't misunderstand me, she's got good qualities but there aren't jokes in the good ones. In fact, there aren't any jokes in me at all anymore. The woman has sucked all the funny right out of me. She talks so fucking much that half my friends are afraid to call. I should give her your address. She'd bore you to death quicker than you could say 'OLD SPARKY!' She can do nothing for six hours and then spend six more hours telling you about it."

A lot of this would wind up in my act. I'm still not sure if I was trying out material on Victor or getting the material from writing the letters I'd write. Probably some of both. He was like my personal private open mic.

It was time to lay out "ground rules" for Mother just like I got when I moved in with her in Florida at eighteen. I understand you're chasing your dream but you still have to look for a job. I can't be paying for everything. Get rid of all this unnecessary shit. And, for fuck's sake, find a place to live. I was more than willing to help her look. In fact, I looked for her when I saw she wasn't looking at all. Finding a place in L.A. that would take seven cats would be difficult. Finding one I could afford would be nearly impossible and Mother wasn't scrambling to find work.

I was fully aware of Mother's manipulations and she was very aware that I'll generally cave in. But not on living with me in a one-bedroom apartment. She had visions that we'd sit around together on the bunk bed, watch TV, and read *National Enquirers* together like when I was eighteen and lived with her in Crystal River. Now I had a whole world of comics and comedy clubs, bars and parties, girls and a girlfriend on the side. I had meetings and lunches for fuck's sake! Can't be hanging around the homestead farming cats! I got shit going on!

I stayed away as much as possible. I had a good amount of road work that summer, giving her time to settle in on her own and figure out the neighborhood.

In July, I got a hand job from God. The apartment two doors down was opening up and it was also rent-controlled. I jumped on it. Not only was it vagrant-cheap, but I was still within shouting distance from Mother. And still she couldn't understand why I'd want to move out when I'd still be literally 25 feet away. I think she liked cock-blocking me from Khrystyne. The sad fact was that I had to ask Khrystyne for the money to move in. It killed me but she knew it was a miracle find and we probably hadn't had a place to fuck since Mother got there. I eventually paid her back, it just took me fifteen years.

My manager Mark Lonow taught both acting and comedy classes and took Mother into both. Shortly afterwards, they signed her as a client. I hadn't figured out the whole L.A. scene quite yet but there was no mistaking that this was a polite gesture on my behalf and I appreciated it. It gave Mother something to do. She was pretty good at getting on the ball acting-wise, getting head-shots and resumes made up right away. But anything that involved her leaving the house by herself was fraught with terror. I understood on some level. L.A. could be overwhelming to anyone, and after a dozen years in a place like Crystal River, it had to have seemed like utter bedlam.

She started submitting herself for parts in the local acting rags—mostly student films and the like. Her first audition was in September and she got the part in a short film as the mother of a breast cancer survivor. It didn't pay anything but I was not that much of a prick that we didn't celebrate. I'd never got an acting role and I'd been to shitloads of auditions. Money was tight but maybe she could actually do this.

What she couldn't do was stand-up comedy and unfortunately, through Mark's class, she was trying. Her class did their final set live at The Improv in front of a real crowd. I wished I'd faked cancer to get out of seeing it. She stumbled and stammered her way through jokes that would have still died even if she nailed them. The premises were predictable. PMS vs menopause. Growing up in the fifties and sixties. Bad TV commercials. A lot of it was personal, and she even made reference to her first suicide attempt at fourteen. It just wasn't funny. I couldn't even offer the fake chuckles of her classmates, the ones she gave me when I was bombing. It takes a lot of courage just to walk on the stage and I wished my mother didn't have that courage. She could be very funny. Offstage, people would always tell her, "Now I know where Doug gets it from." Not tonight. This was like the bloody miscarriage of the audition I did for Mother's play in Florida. Not that she would ever make that analogy out loud. Not even if I was dead and she were writing a book.

This probably makes me sound like an unsupportive dick. But I was supportive. I just knew that no matter your pedigree, you can't make someone stage-funny in a class. Mark Lonow didn't even have pedigree. He owned a comedy club, he didn't perform in it. While I loved him for pretending to give a fuck about Mother, I knew she couldn't write a joke to save her life. I tried to help her but save for just writing her an act, there was nothing I could do. I couldn't write from the perspective of a fifty-three-year-old woman, and if you can't write on your own, there's no point in doing this. Even if

I could write it, stand-up is different than acting on stage. I always found it curious that Mother could act in a play but fell apart doing her own material. I could do stand-up but I couldn't act. It feels too phony. Maybe that's where actors find some kind of shield. Maybe for Mother, stand-up felt too real.

She took another stab at comedy. This time it was at the Union on Sunset where I'd met Renee, where I was a regular. I just hoped that it wouldn't be *as* horrible. I gave her some tags to shore up her jokes and massaged some verbiage in her bits. Before the show, someone came up to me and said that comedian Joe Rogan from the show "News Radio" was coming down to see me. He heard that I was funny and of a like mind and wanted to see my show. I'd met famous folk over Khrystyne's shoulder but never because they sought me out.

Mother went on stage and was dead in her first sentence. She forgot where she was immediately and never recovered. A minute into her collapse I saw Joe Rogan's head—a smaller version back then—poke through the door. I ran over to run interference. I didn't want him seeing this. I introduced myself.

"Did someone say that's your mother?" he said, transfixed by the spectacle on stage.

"Uh . . . yeah. Hey, let's go outside and talk!"

It probably wasn't as bad as I remember. Or, it was as bad as I remember, but I'm probably the only one that thought it was that bad. Seeing your mother suck at what you're known for right in front of you and your peers is fucking excruciating.

Mother stopped doing stand-up to focus on acting. I applauded her decision.

I had to talk to her about getting a job several times, sometimes calmly but mostly irate. My free network money was gone and even though our rents were cheap, it was still double the rent. Every classified section and actor's rag had ads for people to do medical testing so I talked her into being a lab rat. If she wouldn't work, then she could be a guinea pig. She did a few of those trials. I have no idea what for but she never grew an extra limb or got gigantism like I'd secretly hoped. Eventually, she got a job at our favorite thrift store,

Out of the Closet, on Fairfax. What better place for a hoarder to not just get a job but an employee discount! Shit, she could have been setting the prices for all I knew.

Every dead cat was replaced by a thousand pieces of junk or clothing she didn't need. But she got it for $1.50, and do you know what these things cost new? Even though I now had my own apartment, Mother stayed on in that bargain-basement bunk bed I'd left behind, which only exasperated her chronic back pain. Her bedroom was now being filled with her thrift shop treasure. You never know when you might get an audition and need a security guard outfit for wardrobe. And it was only three bucks. The worst was when you actually did need something randomly and she had it. One D-cell battery would justify all of her clutter and she'd rub it in. Fuck it, it wasn't my problem anymore.

Once I no longer had to live with her and she was working, we got along pretty well. She was there to handle paying the bills when I was on the road and I could wait until I had enough beer when I got home to go listen to her bitch ad nauseum about her facile world. As I started selling CDs and later DVDs and t-shirts on my Web site, she'd take care of shipping merchandise. Fans knew the merch was authentic, as the t-shirts would be covered in cat hair and reek of cigarettes. This also gave her the opportunity to force my product on any living human being she came into contact with. Mailman, cable guy, her co-workers, anybody at all would be forced to take a recording of my act. If she came into contact with them again she'd haunt them for reviews. I'd love to get that email from a fan who only knew of me because he was fixing Mother's plumbing and she jammed my CD in his toolbox.

Our apartments were on the second floor of a two-story building facing the street motel-style, with one apartment in between hers and mine. It was loud, no question, and Mother never did adjust. The traffic made her crazy, anyone playing music in the building was contemptible. The dog across the street would bark constantly, its owner would fruitlessly yell at the dog, and Mother would scream back at the owner.

Street parking was rough but to Mother it was a prison fight. You had to move your car every week on street-sweeping days. Monday one side and Tuesday the next. Some old prick that lived around the corner owned a gargantuan, early sixties tub-of-shit jalopy the size of a parade float that he never actually drove save for re-parking it in choice spots before street sweeping. It made Mother livid and I was with her on this one. One day I noticed he'd parked barely an inch behind a car across the street with an open space behind it. I ran out and pulled my car not an inch behind his, knowing he'd be coming soon to move it across the street before morning to avoid the ticket. We watched through the window when he showed up and assessed the situation with all the slapstick of a silent movie. Check the front car, walk back, and check the room to the back car. Scratch his head angrily. Get behind the wheel. Get back out and do the whole thing over again, looking around for someone to blame. Finally, he started the beast and we laughed like fools watching him make a 75-point turn over a good fifteen minutes to free himself. He never parked where he could get blocked in again but still continued to clog up coveted spaces. Now Mother and I just went old school and would sit up on the outside rail in front of our apartments raining eggs down on his car. A lot of people say that their parent is like their best friend, but when you're thirty-two and you're egging cars with your mother with tears of laughter rolling down your faces, it really feels that way. Because that's the kinda shit best friends do.

The neighborhood was a mixture of gay and Russian, and they kept a civil peace. Russians never acted gay, gays never acted Russian. Probably because of those atrocious hats. One of the fun things we learned was that if you didn't want something anymore, you could just leave it on the sidewalk and the Russians would scavenge it before you got back upstairs. Dump it and run. An old couch, a broken TV, a table missing a leg. Just leave it out for the Russians. Once as a gag Mother filled my apartment with at least sixty or seventy inflatable bunnies that were being jettisoned after Easter at the

Dollar Store. I came home from the road and was too tired and irritable to find it funny. It was late at night and I just wanted to crash. So I just started throwing them over the railing to the sidewalk. Within twenty minutes, every single one of them had been adopted by the Russians. So afterwards, Mother and I started occasionally leaving shit out for the Russians just to see what they would and wouldn't take, to find their limits. The inflatable sex sheep went fast. A five-dollar bill smeared thick with vaseline also went with a little more trepidation. But the Russians took everything eventually. I can't imagine what their hoards looked like compared to Mother's.

———

MOTHER GOT A COMMERCIAL AGENT AND SOON BOOKED A SUBARU commercial. Not only was that cool as fuck and a legitimate gig, it also could have meant money for her. I still don't exactly know how commercials work but I knew back then that if it ran a lot it could be serious bank. This commercial didn't, and wasn't, but by the time we knew that, we'd already celebrated and didn't care. It was a legitimate credit.

I got an audition for a hidden camera show for the Fox Network. I'd cut my hair, which I am sure helped stop me from getting pegged for the stoner/surfer roles I used to be inundated with. I fucking love hidden camera when it's done well. We grew up on *Candid Camera* and couldn't get enough. Later, shit like Ashton Kutcher's *Punk'd* sickened me with its lack of creativity and smarmy tone, but I'd still watch even if only to make me angry.

That audition was the first one that didn't make me squirm in the guts. Instead of reading tripe in front of bored phonies, I would have to come up with some gags to film on Hollywood Blvd. using just a hidden eyeglass cam. We went to a mailing service and tried to have a package shaped like a cat wrapped in tin foil shipped. "My ex-girlfriend has been bitching at me that she wants her cat back. Oh, you're gonna get your cat back, alright."

I stood in front of McDonald's and offered people a free Big Mac as part of a promotion. All they had to do was sign a contract I had printed up—in thick legalese—selling their soul to the devil. We were shooed out pretty quickly by the McDonald's people but not before we had enough footage to get me the job. I'd have my own segment on every show called "Beware of Doug" that my friend, comedian Henry Phillips, wrote my theme song for. It was my first real TV show that wasn't just stand-up spots. I had a big head but only needed small hooks on which to hang my hat.

Meanwhile, Mother landed a role in an independent full length film called *Memphis Bound and Gagged*, co-starring with Betsy Brandt, now known as Walter White's shoplifting sister-in-law from *Breaking Bad*. It didn't pay but it was a lead role in a serious production. Tamar Halpern, who was there the day Mother died, was the director. She wrote me a long email while I was writing this book, chronicling the times she spent over years with Mother, a lot of things I didn't know at the time or until I read it. I've broken it up throughout the book. It began with this movie.

From Tamar:

Bonnie J. Kirk (aka Gladys)

In analog times, actors submitted head-shots through the US post. A landslide arrived daily at my doorstep during casting of Memphis Bound and Gagged. Bonnie stood out immediately because she was old enough to play the part of Gladys, the Elvis-fanatic aunt of The Director, played by Betsy Brandt. That got her in the door along with a bunch of other old coots. Turned out she was the only one who could act.

Under special skills on her acting resume, she listed "Sober for 17 years and that ain't no . . . "; I can't remember the last word. I've tried to remember for years, given the haunting shit that happened later.

That ain't no joke!

Or

That ain't no small thing!

Or something witty, but I remember thinking, "Inappropri-ate." I brought her in anyway because there aren't that many old people willing to act for free. Turns out she stole the show. And she got all her outfits—spangly get-ups befitting an Elvis freak—even got her hair did as high as it would go did so she could really be the part. She was method.

She would do her scenes as Gladys, a slightly tremulous and feeble-minded woman who was camera shy and accidentally charming. When I'd call cut, she'd come over and tell me why one of the other actresses was a cunt.

Her character was a gentle, addled woman who claimed her son was the result of a night with Elvis, but who was wholly afraid to say it on camera. Between takes, Bonnie told us bawdy stories from the pages of her own checkered past as a nurse and a truck driver, an alcoholic mother, an ex-wife. She was a reve-lation. She nailed the role. She made us nervous. The switch be-tween her character and her real self was such a gaping stretch, we didn't know how to respond.

That first week, while twenty of my cast and crew traveled through Paso Robles, Bakersfield, and other glorious locations, she pressed Doug's first comedy CD into each of our palms, begging—nay—insisting—DEMANDING with those blue eyes that were not afraid to laser point, that we listen. Now.

"I will, Bonnie. Soon. Let me get through making my first film," I'd say as nicely as I could.

"He fuckin' brilliant. Swear to God." Her truck driver swag-ger and refusal to accept that anyone on the film was too busy to listen finally drove us, on the fourth night of filming, to say fuck it, we gotta get her to shut up about her stupid son. So we throw Doug's CD in the van stereo. With Bonnie safely in the other van, we could listen without her eagle eye. We assumed it would be mediocre at best. We didn't want to fake laugh through it in front of her. For all her toughness, it was clear her baby was her everything. And she was obviously delusional because every mother thinks her son shits diamonds. I think mine does, so I get it.

The first bit on the CD was about . . . Bonnie! We gasped, because it wasn't very flattering. It was hilarious. We laugh-cried together hysterically—me, the AD, the DP, a couple of the actors—and shrieked, "That's Bonnie's VAGINA he's talking about!!" We couldn't fucking believe it. Bonnie was right. Her son WAS fuckin' brilliant. At her expense. And she was proud! Shout it from the mountain proud!

We could barely look her in the eye when the two vans pulled up and we tumbled out, telling her we heard the first twenty minutes and we were Huge Instant Fans.

"Yeah," she said, beaming. "Isn't he fuckin' brilliant?"

"And he was talking about you! Your cats! Your Polaroids of your cats! Your insistence that people look at your Polaroids of your cats! YOU WATCHED HIS PORN."

"Yeah."

She didn't care what Doug was talking about. Her being in his routine was just a by-product. She just wanted people to hear what he had to say. She was the best publicist a son could ever ask for. It was weird. And refreshing. I felt like I finally understood her. She wasn't an act. She was real and fuck anyone who didn't appreciate it, especially that one cunt actress.

Week two, Bonnie saw I was starting to fall apart. Stupid boyfriend stuff. She caught me lying on a bench outside the restaurant where we were having dinner after a long day on the road. In two seconds, she had me sitting between her legs while she massaged my shoulders and neck expertly. It was exactly what I needed and I told her so. "Oh no," she said, waving me off. "You don't know. I've had this exact fantasy that someday I'd be on set, acting in a movie, and the director would need a massage." I think she almost teared up. It made me nervous. And made me love her.

I knew none of these details at the time. Most of the conversations with her about her movie revolved around all the negative aspects, the driving and the traffic and the people who were hard to work with. She loved to complain. Her complaining sounded like my act without the jokes. But I could still tell she was thrilled to be doing it. I was just happy that we both had projects and that the whole idea of her moving to L.A. might be paying off.

———————

MY FIRST EXPERIENCE WITH REAL TELEVISION PRODUCTION WAS like my first dog Otis. Bright, fun, and uncomplicated. Subsequent ones were stupid, blundering, and didn't like me all that much. The show, originally called "When Hidden Cameras Attack," featured large-scale gags on sets mostly but my segment was strictly guerilla shit like my audition had been. I had my own producer, Gerry McKean, a Brit who was also a drinker like me. The head of Rocket Science Labs, the production company, was Chris Cowen, and Chris was a dude, not a suit. Baseball hat, Cleveland Browns fan, lived for taking chances, even if he knew it would probably never make the air. We'd pitch ideas just like comics at a bar. When we had enough pranks green-lit, Gerry and I would fly out on the road with a cameraman and a pocketful of rough ideas and just start shooting shit. It was primarily an eyeglass camera that the camera guy would rig me up with, and if necessary, he could back it up with a briefcase camera for secondary shots. If the ideas weren't working, we'd hit the bar at the end of the day and come up with new ones. Completely rogue. No crew, no oversight. Just three fuck-ups with toys.

A lot of shit would never see the light of day. In Austin, we did a petition drive on the UT campus to change the name of the tower to the Charles Whitman Memorial Tower. Whitman was famous for killing sixteen people with a sniper's rifle from the observation deck of the clock tower in 1966. I said we were with the NRA and wanted to commemorate Whitman's incredible aim. Of course, that never aired, but Chris Cowen still found the footage of people going batshit hilarious. Doing it primarily with the eyeglass cam, it was important to make that single shot as engaging and active as possible. We'd go to thrift stores in the morning and look for props I could hold up in the shot, and then reverse engineer it from there. We even borrowed a baby and brought it into tattoo shops, trying to get its lip, nose or nipple pierced, the baby being lifted in and out of the shot around the horrified face of the mark.

Cops would be called frequently when we'd done nothing illegal, just for being creepy. In Minneapolis, I went into dive bars in a hospital gown dragging in an IV on a roller. I'd tell the bartender I'd just left the hospital from a liver transplant and really needed a drink. I'd try to get them to pour it straight into the bag.

One week we'd wrapped filming in Houston and were driving back to Austin to spend the night and fly out. Shortly into the two-and-a-half-hour drive, Gerry got a call on his cell phone. You could tell right away it was bad. I assumed the show was cancelled. It was far worse. His younger sister had been killed in a car accident. It was the most silent, interminable car ride back to the hotel. We hit the bar like a corporate takeover the minute we pulled in. Within two drinks we started putting our toes in the cold water of gallows humor. Several more drinks and we were deep into the ugliest black humor that could be thrown out at the table, all of us laughing like kids at night in summer camp. Some people use the word 'cathartic.' But it was comedy where comedy was its most important. Not just to make you forget about your shitty, quotidian life. Not just when laughter was the best medicine but the only medicine. Like my dog Otis once said, "We must laugh in the face of our helplessness against the forces of nature—or go insane."

Then it was back to L.A to regroup, write more gags, and head back to the road. We probably filmed far more that would never air than the approved bits, but we had to maintain a balance between keeping ourselves entertained and pushing the limits.

My favorite one was a little too much for the equipment we had but we tried it nonetheless. Gerry and I got a mannequin in a body bag on a gurney and would roll it up to someone's door and ring the bell.

"Do you know Derrick Barger?"

"Uh . . . no?"

Then we'd explain that we were from the morgue and the new policy is that a corpse not claimed after two weeks had to be delivered back to the person's last known address. Mr. Barger must have lived here at some point before you. Then we'd start unloading the body onto the person's porch.

"WAIT! You can't just leave that here?!? What am I supposed to do with it?"

"Oh, you just call the Department of Public Works. They'll come out and pick it up. In 10-14 business days."

It was a funny gag but too big and clumsy—wheeling a corpse in a body bag and all—to capture well on just an eyeglass cam, but funny enough that when we got back to L.A., they told me to re-write it and other ideas, and they'd use it—and me—in some of the regular full-scale gags. I fucking loved that my work was being recognized. They knew I was a chump when it came to business, and they weren't paying me much but recognized my ability and effort and gave me more money without even an agent having to get involved. I didn't know how rare that was in L.A.

The next day, I came in with pages of written outlines for the big gags, where you take over a location and the mark comes to you. Chris Cowen shuffled through them aghast like they were written in sanskrit. I was terrified that he thought they sucked. He slowly turned through pages and started to smile in a way that I knew was at my expense.

Shaking his head and laughing, he said, "Did you write these on a *typewriter?*" I had. I guess I was the only person in L.A. without a cell phone or a computer and was blissfully unaware that I needed them. I think this endeared me to them even more, like the homeless guy with the golden voice. I was writing and doing big gags as well as my Beware of Doug segment. I was being treated like I was an important voice on the show. I was getting enough money and having a blast. It was the most hopeful that I'd been in L.A., and that freedom would spoil me for every other TV show I'd ever get.

Mother was wrapping up shooting her own film.

Continued from Tamar:

The last week of the shoot, Bonnie MADE Doug be in the film. He didn't want to. He was in the middle of shooting a hidden camera show and had spent the day in a hazmat suit. She forced him. She told me all about it. 'Doug's tired. The hazmat suit was a fuckin' inferno. But I told him this is Really Important.' That was that. I got to have Doug Stanhope improvising about small dick porn on camera. That woman could move mountains and just shrug it off like it was no biggie. I remember thinking, I hope when my kid's older, I can still boss him around like that. (Newsflash. Nope.)

The love we all had for her was because she was such a spark of adventure, who gives a fuck, and why the hell not—we couldn't help but be fiercely charmed and slightly repulsed by her. It's a powerful combo and she made a huge impression.

I remember watching dailies with my DP who said, "You know what, Tamar? Your gift as a director is casting. And you know who the breakout actor in this film is?"

"Betsy!" I blurted out.

"Bonnie," he answered. "Look at how the camera just loves her. She was made for this."

After the film, I would receive all sorts of gifts from Bonnie, the best being what's known as The Honker—a huge, fake diamond ring she bought off QVC when that blonde chick from Three's Company was hawking her wares. It even came with a certificate of authentication and Bonnie presented it to me at the Kodak Theater when we had a press screening. I shook hands with people and impaled them with the thing.

She'd have me over for complimentary massages. There were a lot of cats, and true to Doug's stand-up, I was introduced to the tower stack of Polaroids. I told her, I can see the cats right here in the apartment, so she just showed me the photos where the cats sit awkwardly with their little paws dangling by their hinterlands. She thought it was hilarious. She had like fifty of these kitty porn shots.

The place was a junk hole. Two bunk beds in the living room covered with books and bills and coffee cups and coupons. She explained this had been Doug's apartment but he got another one down the hall. I imagined them sleeping in the bunk beds, with Bonnie snoring contentedly while Doug lay awake, freaking out about the next time she'd lean down in her baby doll nightie and he'd accidentally see her 'crushed spider.' The massages were great by the way and, because I was a smoker myself, I didn't mind the haze.

The statement that Mother "made" me be in the film was presumptuous. I certainly was exhausted from a day filming in a hazmat suit but the opportunity to actually be in a movie with Mother, I wouldn't have missed for anything. That was the whole reason for her to be here. It didn't matter if it was a blockbuster or even if the movie didn't paid anything. We were in a fucking movie together! This was the shit we'd dreamed of doing. I was only worried about sucking and embarrassing her like I did in that audition for her play in Florida.

ON THE LAST DAY OF FILMING GUERILLA GIGS FOR THE HIDDEN camera show in Salt Lake City—including taking over a pawnshop, and, after rejecting whatever valuables people were trying to pawn, tried to talk them into selling body parts for black market transplants—we broke and had our own three-man wrap party. It was late afternoon and we were drinking and cavorting to the hilt. I got up to take a piss and checked my voicemail on the pay phone. Khrystyne was on the set of some awful movie and left a message saying she was thinking about me, that she loved me and couldn't wait to see me. And then she thought she hung up.

After some garbled static and phone rustling, she started talking to someone on the set.

"No, that was my ex-boyfriend. I have a new boyfriend now and I don't think that's probably going to work out either but . . . " and then back to being unintelligible. I sank. I went back to the table dead-eyed. Gerry asked me what was wrong and I told them. A stink wafted over the party. I was stunned. I was pissed. I was heartbroken. And after I let that sink in for a minute, I realized that I was at the wrap party for my first TV show with my band of guerillas. If Gerry wasn't going to let his sister's death bring the group down, I certainly wasn't going to let this spoil the fun. If there's anything a drunk secretly loves, it's those moments of ruin where society would not only dictate that it's OK to drink but that you *must* drink! To excess! Death of a loved one and being dumped are like a true alcoholic's St. Patty's Day and New Year's. And we relished it.

When I got back to L.A., I used that voice message like a shrewd prosecutor who would lead a cross-examination knowing he was going to close on the damning piece of hidden evidence. Your sworn testimony was that you called and said you miss me? You said that you were thinking about me and loved me? Your Honor, if it pleases the court, may I play the rest of that voicemail?

She told me that, in reality, our relationship had been over for a long time. Really? Maybe you should have told me that a really long time ago. I was pissed off and hurt but there was something evil in me that relished having her over a barrel with indisputable evidence that painted me clearly as the fucked party. I'd spent most of the relationship absent or in the company of others. She had every reason to run off. But now I felt like I was out-dumping her inadvertent dump of me.

Our on-again-off-again three-year relationship was solidly over. There'd be no going back this time. Nobody was happier than Mother.

_____

MOTHER AND I GOT A NEW NEIGHBOR IN THE APARTMENT IN between us. She was as painfully beautiful as she was very intimidating, or intimidating because of it. Spiky blonde hair, athletic and raspy-voiced, but all business. Her name was Leann and she managed a trendy bar called North right behind the Laugh Factory. It happened to be the same place I'd tried to fake-pimp myself out with Jules back when it was a gay bar almost fifteen years before. I'd try to create casual run-ins with her when I heard her coming up the stairs. She'd politely say hello with a service-industry smile but nothing more.

At some point we crossed paths in the laundry room and she asked if I'd kindly put her shit in the dryer when it was done. I was just happy she talked to me. Rather than fumble for sentences, I wrote the first of the "Leann Letters" and posted it to her door. It read:

My Dearest Leann,

I just wanted to convey what an enjoyable time I had putting your things in the dryer, in what I consider to be our 'first date.' I've been reeling in severe depression ever since you stood me up for our last 'first date,' when you suggested we might spend a lovely afternoon carrying heavy boxes from the back of your truck, an event I prepared for with a regimen of rigorous exercise with a personal trainer who had me lifting his own heavy boxes for weeks until it was obvious you no longer needed me. Now with this whole 'dryer' thing, I will once again sleep comfortably knowing our relationship is on solid ground. Though, as you know, I'm not the type to shower the ladies with romantic gifts (hell, I rarely shower at all), it so happens that today I received the master for my CD 'Sicko,' a copy of which I have enclosed. Enjoy it free for thirty (30) days. If not completely delighted, simply return the CD to the laundry room. Or keep it and every month receive new and exciting promotional items such as The Doug Stanhope Action Figure or The Doug Stanhope Lunch Box. Never any obligation to buy. Cancel at any time. One other thing, I've noticed that occasionally it sounds as though you are being brutally murdered in your bedroom, a sound I can hear quite clearly even though your Hole CD is playing at top volume, and that worries me. Therefore I've asked David the manager to install a doggie-door between your hall closet and mine so that I can check on you in these rare instances.

God Bless,

It was the classic comic fake-hit-on-you move, where at best it works, and at worst I could say I was just kidding. It got nothing but a passing "I got your letter, very funny" on one of the calculated times I pretended to be just going out when she was coming in. But just her even casually or politely saying it was funny kept me going. Now I'd write far fewer letters to Death Row Victor and a lot more to Leann.

THE HIDDEN CAMERA SHOW WAS WRAPPED AND SO WERE THE paychecks. Now it was a matter of just waiting for an air date. I wondered if I'd go on talk shows to promote it when it came out. I don't know how all this shit works. It's network television. Prime time. I was the only regular cast member each week. Am I a buffoon for daydreaming about being next to Jennifer Aniston on Letterman chatting about these gags we pulled? All I knew is I wasn't rich or famous and was about to be broke.

A letter arrived from the IRS. It wasn't a long one. It said that I owed them to the tune of some $35,000. Seemed I failed to file my taxes. Ever. It was just one of those things in life I didn't really understand. You know, math and keeping records. What sucked the most is it was for a lot of the years I'm sure I lost money and was well below the poverty line. Living out of a car piled with filth and all my belongings, eating drive-thru value menu or free happy-hour spreads. Driving endless hours to make 125 bucks, and then driving some more. If I made fifteen grand, it probably cost eighteen grand to make it. Was I supposed to keep a filing system for receipts somewhere under that wasteland of McDonald's bags and dirty laundry? Evidently so. Remember that, young comics. File your taxes. It's worth it.

I got an accountant who eventually got it knocked down to about $24,000 on payments, but that was still a kick in the banana. I scrounged for any road work I could get.

———

HOUSTON HAD BEEN A BIG COMEDY SCENE THAT I FREQUENTED IN those heydays. I'd tape 3 CDs there in total and had made a bunch of good friends. And like any city that nurtures a strong comedy scene, as soon as it piques, all the best comics (as well as a lot of the shitty ones) flee to L.A., and every one of them looks for a couch to crash on until they get situated.

A friend of mine, Selene, who was not a comedian, was part of that Houston circle joining the exodus. Being newly single with my own apartment, I gladly offered up staying at my place until she found her own. Not only was she funny and a fellow booze-bag, she cooked and cleaned and we'd occasionally bang with no strings attached. But mostly she wasn't Ralphie May. He was moving out from Houston too, and if I already had Selene staying with me I wouldn't need to explain why my cheap fold-down futon couch was not structurally sound for a 500-pound comedian.

Selene stayed for a while and even had other girlfriends and comedians come and go. I wasn't complaining. I was stocked up on road work most of the time, and coming home to half-dressed drunk girls with hot meals was wonderful. All it might have been missing was pillow fights with feathers blowing and titties bouncing. But that's still how I remember it. It was the beginning of a short golden era. Plus, Mother now had new play-friends who thought she was a riot.

The next couple years seemed like one constant party at the apartment whenever I was home. I was gone most of the time on the road but when I got back it seemed even more of a green room. The faces evolved but there were always people there and Mother never complained about the noise so long as she was invited. Sometimes they'd talk her into smoking pot and delight in her going into campy sixties hippie antics. "Wow, duuuuude. Check out all the colors, maaaan!" like an over-the-top Carol Burnett character. I had a wheelchair in my apartment that they would bring down to her place, just for show to wake her up, roll her back, and get her high. Sometimes people at the party didn't know her and thought she was really some old woman neighbor in a wheelchair that we hijacked to smoke out like a puppy in a fraternity. She was still sober but had fucked off AA for a long time now and didn't care that smoking weed might have counted against her credits. I don't even think she really wanted to smoke it but there was no way she was going to miss out on the attention and the laughs she would get. Mother was a pain in my ass quite a bit but I never got tired of other people liking her. It was easier for them than for me.

The problem with Mother mingling this much with my friends is that she'd pry them for information. Of course, she'd always be trying to pry information out of me and most of it was none of her or anyone's business. I knew if I told her things, she'd tell everyone else. Gossip is currency to Mother. There are some things you don't say to Mother and not just about skanks you banged behind your girlfriend's back. You learn quickly in L.A. to shut your fucking mouth about possible projects. Everyone is being pitched on some big project, and 99 percent of the time they go nowhere. I still had people asking me when my HBO special was coming out because I'd been shooting off my mouth about it when I got the contract. I'd been paid 30K but that money was long gone even if I cared to answer by waving it in the air. Some things—women and business—you didn't talk about, especially in front of Mother.

———————

I FELL IN LOVE AGAIN ON THE ROAD. THIS TIME WITH A COMEDIAN named Betsy Wise from Miami. She was a Jewish lawyer who quit law to do stand-up. She'd been my opening act. Now I was a phase she was about to go through and I was pretty aware of that from the beginning. It lasted a lot longer than it would have if we weren't both constantly in different places on the road but we got together often enough to have a lot of fun. It didn't last long after she decided to move to L.A. Getting fucked up after shows on the road seemed like the norm, part of the business, but when she realized that's how I lived all the time at home as well, that my apartment was also carrying on like an overcrowded green room, maybe it was best if we just smiled and said goodbye.

––––––––

AROUND THEN, IN 2001, I GOT MY OWN COMEDY CENTRAL HALF-Hour Special. I'd have to submit my material for approval. A woman from Comedy Central called shortly after I'd sent in my bits, very upbeat. She asked what I wanted for a backdrop on the stage. A lot of comics would have very elaborate sets and they usually looked silly and distracting. I couldn't think of anything so I told her just a regular curtain would be fine. She said everything looked great with my material and she just had "a couple of things" to go over. Over the next twenty minutes she'd go on to tell me that pretty much everything in my set couldn't be used or had to be altered. A bit about suicide was nixed because it could open them up to lawsuits. Drug material could only be used if it were negative about drug use. No names of brands could be used so no possible sponsors would get chapped.

"So what you're saying is that everything in my act is fine except for my act?"

"Well, don't look at it like *that*. It just needs to be *tweaked* a bit."

I hung up, thought for a few minutes, called back, and said, "You know what, this is what I want for a backdrop. Just a cartoon of my head with the cheeks blown out and duct tape crossed over my mouth."

I thought that was very clever, although since then I've seen it done by other comics over the years and have to assume probably more comics did it before me. It wasn't meant to convey that I'm so dangerous, only that I wasn't allowed to say a fucking thing.

My father had been diagnosed with colon cancer at seventy-three, and after a couple of surgeries, was declining quickly. As my tape date approached, my brother called to say that I'd better get back pretty soon, dad was going quickly. My dad was at Jeff's house in Rhode Island. I was taping on March 16th in New York and would get on the first bus to Providence after the taping.

The taping didn't go well. I'd like to blame it on being too wrapped up in my father's impending death but that would be a convenient excuse. When you are in that kind of spotlight for the first time, your entire family could be being murdered in front of you and you'd only be scrambling to ask if that one segue worked. Comics that night taped in pairs. Each audience of 1,200 would be switched out for the next pair, keeping you from having to play to a burned-out crowd. I was going to go up first on the first taping. The warmup guy—as I now know is common for live audiences in taped television performances—kept fluffing the crowd like they were preschoolers.

"Now what are you going to do when we introduce the first comedian?"

Wild cheers.

"C'mon, that's not good enough! Let's try it again! What are you going to do???"

Bigger screams and they were never good enough. Comedy Central can't look like they were filming some nobody! You can always do better than that! By the time the announcer called my name, the crowd screamed like they were waiting to see gladiators being eaten by pigs. It felt entirely duplicitous.

I got to the mic and said, "Wow . . . it sounds like all my fans are here!" and a bigger wave of applause. As it slowed, I said, "Okay . . . what's my name again?" pointing the mic towards the front row.

The silence bled into uncomfortable titters. They'd been trained like monkeys to roar like I was their favorite Elvis and now I slapped 'em for jumping through the hoop. I never won them back. All of my bits were clumsy, saccharine versions of themselves and all my timing was blown. Instead of saying the transvestite was "sucking my dick," I had to settle for a hand-bobbing-over-groin gesture. It was horrible. When my material was done, I said goodnight, but before I could leave the stage I was told from the wings I'd only done twenty-seven minutes of the thirty-five I was supposed to do. I stood there onstage in silence asking them what the fuck they wanted me to do. I closed on an awkward argument with producers onstage in front of 1200 silent people. They only needed twenty-two minutes for the special and they'd have to get what they needed out of what I gave them. To their credit, they sweetened it up a lot before it aired and made it look like I was far more well-received than I'd been. But they did cut out the "What's my name?" part, making a hideous, obvious cut from a wall of applause to a quiet opening joke. When I see it now I'm like an old woman looking at a porn film she did in her younger years. You don't care about the bad dialogue. You're just enraptured by how much better looking you were back then.

Later that night I watched Louis CK film his half hour. He went up and said whatever the fuck he wanted, including "fuck" and everything else I was told I couldn't say. I was rocked. I asked him afterwards why he was allowed to get away with that. He told me that they tell everybody what they can and can't say and that he just ignores them, knowing that they've spent all this money to film so they'll just bleep stuff out rather than not air it. And never do the amount of time they ask for. The less time you give them, they less they have to make you unfunny in the edit. I wish he'd told me that before I went up talking about the mouth-fucking transvestite using children's language. Lesson learned.

Funny. My spell-check has no problem with "mouth-fucking" but is confused by "mecurichrome." I should have written this on a typewriter.

I SHOWED UP TO MY BROTHER'S HOUSE A CRUMPLED WRECK BUT just in time. My dad was in a hospital bed in the living room. I'd seen him six months before, and he looked sick, but now it looked like he'd already died weeks before and it took all the air out of me. I took his hand and he looked up at me as if I were from a dream. He smiled wide. My voice broke apart when I talked to him.

"You look great, Dad."

He groaned out a "Yeah?"

"Not really. You look like shit." I tried to make light but the reality of the joke put me in tears as I said it and I had to turn away.

He never showed any other signs of being alert or aware. We spent the day waiting. The humor was hard to come by. Jeff's wife and her brother were there along with Jeff's two small children. Even my leech stepsister showed up but this was no time to hold grudges. That could wait for tomorrow. There were a few times that we couldn't tell if he was dead. Jeff remembered the old trick from the movies of putting a mirror under his nose. We both leaned in very close, me from the side and Jeff from over the top of the back, waiting with an eerie tension to see if it fogged up. We waited, and at some point when we made eye contact, wide-eyed like we'd been waiting for a bomb to go off, we burst into ridiculous laughter. The family was horrified when, after he finally died that night, we started taking a lot of pictures with the body. I kept a picture of me kissing my dad's corpse on the forehead in my wallet for years. I'd break it out any time someone showed me a baby picture, just so they would know how it ends. Jeff has always shared my sense of humor and I love him for being there to laugh when times are the darkest.

For all I know, Carla was and is a decent person. I was a pile of shit as a kid and quite a bit of my adult life, so maybe I never saw her inner beauty. Perhaps one day she'll read this and we'll have a good laugh. I did not, however, feel that way at the time.

Dad had once asked us very earnestly to be kind to Carla after he was gone, and we promised him we would. We broke that promise as soon as possible. I never understood his soft spot for her when I saw nothing but a parasite. But now that he was gone, I didn't give a shit. When we cleaned out his house, we threw all of her belongings out the same window Mother had thrown out our toys when we were kids. We left it all in a pile in the side yard. That was our room anyway and she didn't even live here anymore. She just used the place as storage. We then filled underneath the back seats of her car she had stored there with raw chicken and rolled it to the bottom of the hill where it would get towed. Fuck her. We've never heard from her again.

———

IF I COULD NEVER PINPOINT A TIME WHERE MOTHER WENT FULLY bonkers, I know that my father's death was my first taste of true hostility towards life. He was a wonderful man with never a bad word to say, didn't drink or smoke, and although he'd eat Welsh rarebit—canned cheese sauce poured over toast—and he'd nibble butter right off the stick, I always looked at him as healthy because he'd go outside and take a stroll sometimes. I was angry that he had to die so cruelly. If my mother was my best friend, my dad was my rock. He was always there at 20 Rich St. for anything I needed. If I didn't have room, I could store things at his house. If I didn't have an address, I could have it mailed there and it would be taken care of. If I needed money, he'd bail me out. It didn't matter that I never thought I'd need it; I knew that no matter what could ever go drastically wrong in this surreal life I was leading, I could always come home again. Now all that was gone. For the first time in my life, I had the full realization and weight that I was now officially an adult.

———

THIS COMPREHENSION THAT I WAS NOW TRULY ON MY OWN MADE me start to look at Mother in a harsher light. Now that I was fully aware that I was genuinely on my own, I realized that I also had a dependent. Don't think of it as losing a father; think of it as gaining an adult baby. I was never cut out to be in any position of responsibility. My entire life I'd lived as a goof. Now I felt conscripted into a position of seniority. My having to pay Mother's way for so long, her unwillingness to find adequate work while she constantly complained, wasn't going to cut the same slack. It was an immediate about-face. Mother was now an unwanted child so far as all things child-like. No more playing it up like you're some feeble invalid. Our roles of parent and child had slowly been reversing. If there were a moment of an exact flip, it was now. I was throwing her chest of toys out the window for being insubordinate. I didn't know what she was secretly going through on her own.

At this time after she'd finished *Memphis Bound and Gagged* with Tamar, Mother began an exercise from the book *The Artist's Way* that suggests writing three pages a day in a notebook called "Morning Notes." As soon as you wake up, write three pages about anything at all that comes to mind. I found the notebook while writing the book. It was immediately too painful to read. She kept the writing up for barely two weeks, but those pages paint a very clear image of a woman lost in her own terror of rejection, inadequacy, her loneliness, or abject emptiness. Her words detailed every paralyzing fear, every perceived failure and her endless, clawing need for acceptance and meaning. And invariably, her deliberation with suicide. I had no idea the extent of the anguish she was keeping from me.

Although the full context of her forty-two pages truly drives home the depths of her depression, I've whittled it down to a "Best Of" out of fear the reader would want to kill themselves after reading the full version. Besides, Mother's cursive handwriting is like trying to decipher cave wall etchings.

2/16/01
    Ok, ok I'm up. Shit, I hate having to get out of a nice warm bed. My neck hurts, my mouth is yucky. The cat is bothering me—go away Margaret! I feel so guilty that I can't pay for more medical care for her. Have to find AMTA [massage] papers.

Should have organized paperwork long ago. If all else fails I can call or try computer. Have to change credit cards on HSN and QVC. Why didn't I do that 6 months ago? Got to get out for a couple of puffs—bad bad girl. Can't do anything right—have to fuck it up somehow. So sick of this alone emptiness. I like alone time to do what I want but not this empty feeling of loneliness. Disconnected—that's how it feels. No real intimate closeness with anyone. Had two puffs. Love the rush/hit and hate the constricted feeling and guilt.

So afraid of losing my mind. Went and ordered red earrings from HSN. I have to wash the floor soon, too. Cats keep sniffing around like there's something strange on it. And they have to walk on it and clean their paws of whatever I track in here. No wonder they're sick. Haven't seen sunshine in three years!

Keep thinking of all the medical/dental work I need and how much it will cost. Back hurts. Overwhelmed I can't do it all.

2/17/01

It feels like I'm going to lose it major. Anger, frustration, guilt, fear. If all else fails, I can lock myself into making money and forget about acting. Ho ho ho. I'll kill myself first. I keep forgetting that I am smart and creative and fractionalized and demonized and I am fighting so many things to emerge to what I set out to be. Want to strike out and scream at everyone and everything to Shut the hell up!

2/18/01

Back is tight and right hip hurts. I want to smoke so much—not the side effects just that hit of smoke to wake up with. Cough is getting almost as bad as it was. Got to change the bed and start a list for Monday. Can't think of any one thought except when I can sneak a cigarette. Jimmie's [her cat] cough sounds worse than I do. Eyes are still puffy and still feel guilty and overwhelmed with things to do. Want to spend more time with Doug but he's always too busy—just like that song We'll get together soon, son.

2/19/01

The noise in this fucking neighborhood! Shut the fuck up! Jesus Christ on a rubber crutch! Folks behind have the TV up so loud! And fuckwad in #1 with his noisy fucking yippy dog and 16 relatives with noisy cars, and #6 with his noisy car, friends and penetrating voice and the screaming fag yuppie who yells at his dog across the street—what a fucking place to live!

2/21/01

Here we go again. Overwhelmed by the day ahead. Here we go here we go. What holds me back? What am I afraid of? Why am I afraid to check out the city? Why am I afraid to try new things, to meet new people and find my way around town? What is the big bad thing about having fun? Like it's some kind of waste? Good and hard talk with Doug last night. Still can't figure out if he loves me or hates me. Sometimes it seems as if everything I say, don't say, do or don't do is wrong. Seems like I can't win with him. Maybe I can get more answers tonight on the way to the airport. Got to check Fantasy Five numbers. Sure wish I could win and make up some of this debt with Doug. Why can't I get out and do things?

2/22/01

Back is stiff. Car is up around corner, need to clean up and do so much more before I can get out and get it. The day is half shot and I've accomplished nothing. What the hell did I do last night? Maybe I should just kill us all—cats and me and try again in the next life. Everything seems so overwhelming and seems to need attention all at once. Got to take my vitamins today and try to eat right. Too dizzy. Felt so good and confident last night and had to go and blow it. Why do I sabotage myself?

2/24/01

I got myself together enough to go try for a job at Massage Therapy Company. Just in time for orientation on March 7th. Felt really good going in and at least trying. And while I was there, I got paged by a producer and I got a part! And Tiffany who is the receptionist is an actor too so we yakked about that and I left feeling really great! Have to get my date book organized today! Then I got 2 extra clients at work and when I checked my messages found I have an audition Monday for the Man Show—cool! I watch it and I know Doug likes it. And he's doing a show for Comedy Central & it would be really neat for me to be on a Comedy Central show too! I'm so thrilled to get the part. It has done wonders for my self-esteem, and hope for my acting career. I think back 2 days to when I was so down and ready to commit suicide and see how many times I've had that rollercoaster up and down mentally, and right after I hit bottom something happens to make me think: I'm so happy I didn't kill myself or I'd have missed this!

Need to find a jewelry outlet. Maybe I can make some money that way. Doug will get to me and make me feel like an idiot. Guess I did that to them. Oh, the seeds we sow. Little sprouts.

I don't remember my mother ever making me feel stupid although surely it had happened. Even when I did stupid things, I only remember her making me feel like I was funny in doing them. I can't say the same for myself. If I made her feel stupid—be it regarding her faith in psychics, self-help gurus, alternative healing, or magic beans—it was out of a need to protect her from charlatans and false hope. I could never stand the idea of my mother being made a fool. But within the month after she was writing these daily thoughts, I came home from the death of my father as a newborn adult. And she bore the brunt of it. There was no way I could have known at the time the daily phalanx of terror that she already woke up to every day. Every minor task left her incapacitated. To me, she was just bitchy and manipulative, putting more responsibility on me than I could handle. I know I could be short with her around then, pointing out the problems without knowing the reasons for them. It seemed justified. I didn't know she felt far worse about herself than I did.

While she was writing "Cat's in the Cradle" references about spending time with me and contemplating suicide, I came home like a drill sergeant. If I have to be responsible, so do you! I don't know that you're currently fucked out of your skull! Straighten up and fly right! You've had enough time to get your shit together. I can't do it for you anymore. Go get your massage license and get a real job! You have to take care of yourself!

And, for fuck's sake, stop bitching at our hot neighbor chick!

Leann,

Today I overheard Mother chastising you for the volume of your music. You were very kind to turn it down but there are a few other things that have been upsetting to her peace of mind. For instance, she's noticed that when you move around your apartment you have a tendency to use your feet. This can create a 'walking' sound that tends to interrupt her long conversations with the cats, forcing her to start over and further annoying the cats. Rather than all the boisterous 'walking,' maybe you could try slithering belly-down like an earthworm. Another thing that sticks in her craw is your extremely impolite habit of getting phone calls. You don't hear anyone calling Mother, now do you? No, you don't. Also, and I hate to sound nitpicky but your chewing is getting a bit on her nerves. The constant smashing of your teeth against one another is disturbing her Home Shopping Network. Maybe you could buy baby food or foods that were pre-chewed by caring others. Thanks. Mother understands that you're young and will occasionally do things like bathe. Perhaps a membership at the YWCA would benefit all parties. The sound of running water can make Mother incontinent. And any more of this breathing while you sleep will force Mother to bring in the police. It's unnecessary and mean-spirited. Please try to keep these things in check so we can all live together peacefully.

Doug, the guy two down from Mother

P.S. When you throw this letter out, try not to crumple it. Mother hates crumpling sounds.

Priorities! There was no winning Leann's heart but Mother was finally getting her massage license and I had maneuvered my way through Betsy leaving and my father dying. No reason not to crank up the party a bit more. The apartment was still rocking any time I was home. Comics and ladies and lady comics came and went. While there was never a sober phase of my comedy career, there were times that were more drunk and free than others. This was one of those eras. And who shows up out of the blue right after Betsy dumps me? That old love-of-my-life, drunken heartthrob Renee from the Coach & Horses. Renee had gone off with some boyfriend on a traveling adventure and showed back up single and as impenetrable as always. But she came back flashing just enough glimmer of "maybe" that I was more infatuated than I ever had been. No matter the debauchery at the apartment, Renee never left my subconscious. She now lived above a bar in Santa Monica and worked at a flower shop down the street. She'd come by or call just often enough to keep me perpetually wanting. Mother loved her because she remembered Mother's favorite flower and would bring her those flowers on the off-chance of a random visit. What kinda flower? Beats the fuck out of me. And I'm not calling Renee at this hour to find out. It was a nice flower. I think it was white. Is that good enough?

Let me explain how intimidating Renee was to me. A couple of years ago, my manager was contacted by some big Hollywood agency saying one of their clients was looking to talk to me. They said it was Johnny Depp. Turns out Johnny Depp was a huge fan. Maybe you think that I am way cooler than I am and that this would be no big deal to me. You are hugely fucking wrong. He wanted to meet me. He flew Bingo and me to London for a first-class all-expense-paid vacation to hang out with him in London. To say that it was surreal would be like saying a thing that is far less surreal was surreal. I've hung out with him a few times since and we stayed at his house for a few days. Since then he's all but offered the keys to his house any time I want to come. I don't take him up on these offers because I'm afraid to call. I'm afraid he'll have changed his mind and no longer think I'm funny. I am afraid in the same way to call the Howard

Stern Show to ask to come back as a guest, even more scared of Stern than Johnny Depp. I've been on the Stern Show at least ten times since my dad died and I am still so skittish of being turned down that I drink heavily before I dare even ask. Easier not to call at all than to call and get rejected.

I was that afraid or more of calling Renee. She was honestly that beautiful and extraordinary that the fear of being dismissed made it petrifying to risk a phone call. Unless I had a really good excuse, and I was always searching for one. This was evident in that the first thing that went through my mind when 9/11 was going down—before the Towers even fell—was that I had a great reason to call Renee without it seeming like a cheap ploy to ask her out. I was coming back from an all-night drive from a Montana run with Becker. I was on the far outskirts of L.A. when the shitty cassette player in my car ate my book on tape and it went straight to radio. The news was frantic and I listened in stopped L.A. traffic to the chaos reigning down, the Pentagon, more flights unaccounted for, the threats to every city, the impending doom. And my first thought was, "Hey, here's my 'in' with Renee!" It was a cheap ploy to ask her out.

She didn't answer so I just left a message: "Wake up! The World is Ending!" Then I called Becker, whom I'd dropped at the Salt Lake airport earlier on the drive back to fly home to Alaska. We've always had a running thing where we try to be the first one to break tragic news to the other. I knew he'd be asleep in Anchorage when the Towers fell, and I won. Every generation has its own Pearl Harbor, and unless we live through another generation, Becker will never be able to beat my 9/11 "Hey turn on the news!" moment.

Renee called back later and we got together a few times over the next couple months. Although I could never land her as my own, she always gave me just enough light to keep chasing it. She came to a show one night in West Los Angeles, some regular weekly gig at a brewery with a long lineup of comics. I got a rare standing ovation. Afterward, we went to where her friend was staying nearby, house-sitting for Rodney Dangerfield, to spend the night. Renee passed out drunk in the tub. I had to pull her out for fear of her drowning. In the morning, we walked to breakfast and spotted Jillian Barberie at a nearby table. I'd done the Stern Show with Jillian previously. Before I could say anything, she noticed me and screamed "DOUG!!!" and came running over to the table. I couldn't imagine her ever remembering me. After talking for a minute, I realized she'd thought I was a regular member on Stern when she said, "I'd *really* love to be on the show again!" Still, Renee was unaffected. I'd just gotten a standing-o the night before and now here I am at breakfast getting recognized by a real celebrity and somehow getting nowhere with Renee! Even my Comedy Central special and the old hidden camera show that had been shelved for years had finally been airing! These were all supposed to be the elements that land you the impossible girl! What do I have to do to impress you, for fuck's sake?

I did what one is supposed to do in this situation, given the opportunity.

Other women.

A lot of guys write books that are nothing but a compendium of women they've had sex with. Those guys are vapid assholes. Yet there are times when getting laid can pull your ego and confidence up from the ashes, especially when you are young and honestly feel out of your league. It's meaningless in the long run but at the time it works. I know women whose only misguided sense of self-worth is through the men trying to fuck them. And they're usually the craziest fucks on the planet and the roots of the funniest stories. Truth and decency are not always on the same plane. Unlike farts, fucking gets old. But for a lot of my younger days, it was everything.

———

SELENE HAD MOVED ON TO HER OWN APARTMENT BUT MY FRIEND Patty was staying with me now with two of her other girlfriends from Chicago, every one of us a drunkard. I'd met Patty a few years before at the Chicago Comedy Festival where she was a waitress at Zanies. I'd done a show there on the Saturday night and afterwards drifted to the table in the back where the comics and waitstaff would congregate to inevitably bitch about the audience. Remember that. We judge you, too. Maybe even harder. The night wore on and soon it was just me and Patty at the table while she counted her checks, ignoring me. You could count on me being there circling the last waitress like carrion. I finally asked her if she was coming to the bar around the corner to meet up with the other staff and comics. She stopped, looked at me with disdain and said:

"I saw your set tonight and I just want you to know that I find you *completely disgusting.*" She walked off without another word or glance back. I was almost relieved. I thought she was about to call me out for so obviously hanging around to try to fuck her. She should have found out first if I was going to be on the final show there the next night. I was and she wouldn't know it until I started laying into her from the stage. I didn't use her name, just a "certain waitress" from the night before who was "a little cakey with the make-up." I don't remember the joke but I know it killed, and the mention of the make-up was enough. It was spot-on and I was sure it was something that would hit her in a vulnerable place. I was pretty good at being mean.

The story didn't end there like Patty and I probably both thought it would. Because I did well at Zanies meant I got booked back there not long after. Patty was still working there. A few cocktails after the first show back, we made peace. It was going to be a long week and, after all, it was always us—staff and comics—against the audience. We couldn't afford in-fighting. A few cocktails more at the bar around the corner and we were back in my hotel room. As I leaned her head out the window, she was bent over and I finished ejacualting into her anus. I waited two beats before leaning into her ear and whispering, "I just want you to know that I find you *completely disgusting.*" Her laugh confirmed that we'd be best of friends, and are to this day. We may have our beefs here and there, like when she will read this in a book, but we get past them.

Patty moved to L.A. with her two girlfriends and stayed for what seemed like six months but may have only been two. We were so drunk that whole time it could have all been a long holiday weekend. I was single and women were everywhere. Not satisfied, I still haunted Leann the Neighbor.

Leann or current resident,

I just wanted to say that—yes, I may not be the greatest catch for a lady—I'm short, balding, and out of shape. I am soft in the middle like baby shit, I smoke too much, I drink to excess to the point where my liver is sore to the touch. Yes, my ambitions in life are weak at best, and I am not one who can easily pick himself up by the bootstraps. Sure, you could say that I live like a pig, that my hygiene is lacking on the good day and my teeth are chipped and stained from a constant diet of coffee and nicotine.

You wouldn't have a hard time gathering that I am insensitive and certainly not a good listener. I am self-centered, possibly borderline megalomaniacal. You could look simply at the squalor I have my own Mother living in to gather how much I care about even those closest to me. You might even say I'm morally reprehensible for my lack of concern for others.

I may be a sexual deviant like some people have branded me. Yes, I need a veritable buffet of niche gutter porn and dangerous latex implements before I even can even achieve mild arousal. No, I am no stranger to erectile dysfunction, some stemming from my use of non-prescribed antidepressants and black market hair-growth products, some stemming from years of sexual practices that range from vulgar to gray-area illegal.

If someone told you I was a tragedy waiting to happen, I couldn't tell you they were wrong. A smart person might say to keep a wide berth from me, that I could only make trouble for you. Yes, I have tax problems and no respect for money. I may spend frivolously and God forbid you find me gambling. I'd go till I lost everything and then borrow from you.

It's true, I have no culture. I have no appreciation for music. I don't like television or films and you wouldn't find a book in my hand unless I was using it to prop up a wobbly chair. Nature is annoying to me and the beach just seems uncomfortable.

Fine cuisine is wasted on me and I wouldn't notice your new perfume from a strong chemical smell.

You may say that I have no respect for women, that my series of failed relationships that have left me a bitter hermit are no one's fault but my own. You could even say that I had it coming. My breath might be that of 1,000 unwashed asses and sometimes I may break out in tears in public places for no apparent reason. Children are aborrhent to me and I believe abortion should be mandatory. Some may fault me for my so-called "mercy killings" of barking neighborhood dogs through blowdarts and poisoned meat.

Others still could intimate that my hatred of God and country makes me a threat to society, that I am a sociopath with no chance of rehabilitation and that anyone associated with me will be dragged down into the muck with me and rot in a fiery Hell.

I can't remember my point.

Douglas from across the way

I'd sent half a dozen letters like this, and never received more than a smirk and a friendly roll of the eyes. Then, one day she came to the door and asked if I'd do her a favor. If she asked me to roll in dog shit I'd do it. She said that she was going on vacation to Mexico with her guy friend, and would I move her car for street sweeping?

Oh, absolutely!

I had my brother on the phone the next day as I drove Leann's mid-eighties Bronco down to Earl Scheib, famous for the slogan "I'll Paint Any Car for 99.95!" We were guffawing like stooges. Unfortunately, that old slogan was just that—old. The prices had gone up, and quite a bit more for the violent, metallic purple I'd envisioned. For that color on that size a vehicle it priced out at $600. That was just way too much. I called my brother on the way home and told him the bad news. We'd laughed so fucking hard at this idea just an hour ago. Hey, at least it was a funny idea, right? He said to me, "Remember what you always told me. It's only funny if you actually do it."

I paused for a half a second before banging a hard U-turn on Santa Monica Blvd. and went straight back to Earl Scheib.

Mother, Patty, and I were peeking through the blinds when Leann got home from vacation. Her car sat out front in the same spot she'd left it, now a shiny, sparkling Mexican low-rider purple. For added charm, there under her windshield wiper sat a street-sweeping violation, as though it had never been moved at all.

MOTHER SCORED A FEW MORE NON-PAYING ROLES IN INDEPENDENT films and started doing massage at some Korean massage joint. And, no. You're being racist just for thinking it. Not that I'm sure she wouldn't do it. Mother would occasionally throw out "I could always just go sell my ass on Sunset Blvd." comments. I couldn't tell if she was semi-serious. She'd told me she'd once taken a couple hundred bucks from a guy for sex just after she left my father. He was a friend of hers from AA and just left the money on the nightstand afterwards. She didn't say no. I don't think she was serious about selling herself now but I think she honestly thought she was still marketable at fifty-seven, with a guttural smoker's cough and tits like cinder blocks. I didn't point that out. That would be rude. And, as we were both technically former paid prostitutes, I'm sure there is some kind of code.

When I wasn't there, Mother had the gaggle of Chicago girls to hang around with. They'd go over during the day and drink Sanka instant coffee (like Mother didn't have the free time to brew a pot) and listen to Mother complain. She'd watch QVC religiously and was buying gemstones all the time with the idea of one day making her own jewelry again. Mother told Patty, "I'm your LA Mom" and Patty took care of her like she was her own. Mother seemed happy and I was happy.

Patty's friend Sarah who'd been staying with us was originally a Kentucky girl who'd also been a waitress at Zanies in Chicago. She was a stunning blonde, unbelievably beautiful and extremely

funny, not to mention twelve years younger than me. Her narrow
eyes put her somewhere between Maybelline and *Deliverance*. Patty
and I would occasionally mess around and now I was mixed up with
Sarah on occasion, all under the same roof. I was living a real-life
Three's Company. A *Three's Company* if Janet and Chrissy had always been drunk and Jack Tripper was actually sleeping with both of
them. And Mother was our Mr. Roper.

And seemingly within minutes of this paradisiac, low-rent Hugh
Hefner existence, with both ladies curled up on the couch, Renee
called and asked me to come see her. Her tone said that it was more
than a casual stepping out. I left within the time it took me to brush
my teeth.

I brought Renee to a gig in Salt Lake that Super Bowl weekend
in 2002. After the last show Saturday, we went back to the condo
and she told me she was in love with me and wanted to be with me.
I must have had really good shows. I protected myself by assuming
that it was the liquor talking. Renee always liked me a lot more when
she was drunk. In the morning, she said she still felt the same way. I
stopped looking for the catch. We drove like hell to get to Vegas—
my perma-grin never fading—to watch the game at my friend's bar,
Tommy Rockers. My New England Patriots were a 14-point dog to
the high-powered offensive juggernaut of the St. Louis Rams led by
Bible-thumping quarterback Kurt Warner. Nobody gave the Patriots
a chance. I was wearing my lucky t-shirt. It was just a plain black
t-shirt that was coming apart under the arm and at the collar. All I
remember of the game was that the Patriots were ahead most of the
game and won on a last-second field goal. I remember screaming at
the screen, "Where's your Jesus now, Kurt Warner!?! Where's your
Jesus now?!?"

The most beautiful girl I'd ever met and had fruitlessly chased
for years had done an about-face in a weekend and decided that she
loved me back. We were a full-fledged actual couple overnight. My
Patriots had pulled off a miracle and won the Super Bowl. I tore
off my lucky t-shirt like the Incredible Hulk in the parking lot of

Tommy Rockers and left it in a heap. I couldn't imagine there being any more luck left in it. For once, I left Las Vegas ahead.

We headed to Aspen for the US Comedy Arts Festival where I'd been named in the *Hollywood Reporter's* Top Ten Talents to Watch, a gracious accolade for sure, but I didn't care about getting noticed now. I was retarded in love. With Renee, I felt there was nothing left in life that I needed. My act was on fire with all the anti-patriotism material and I couldn't give a fuck who didn't like it. I did a show titled "Regarding 9-11" with the theme of how 9-11 has affected comedy. I opened with:

"Everyone keeps asking, 'When will it be OK to do comedy again?'"

"I put a lot of thought into that question. When will it be OK to do comedy again? The best answer I could come up with was this:

"June 8th.

"That's when it will be OK.

"Considering in the five months since the attack, the death toll has fallen from 6,700 consistently down to now 2,800, I figure at that rate, on or around June 8th, no one will be dead anymore.

"Then, let the jokes begin.

"Even today, when you consider the drop—6,700 down to 2,800—that's a difference of 3,900 people that are now undead. We have gained 1,100 more people than we lost. And they need jokes.

"Why do death tolls always start high and go lower? Because the media is a pessimist? No, because death, if it doesn't directly affect you, is entertainment. The more dead, the more entertaining, the more papers it sells. No one rubbernecks at a car wreck to make sure everyone's 'OK.'

"And if people aren't directly affected they will always try to attach themselves to the tragedy. Everyone playing Six Degrees of Separation from 9-11:

"'My sister's ex-fiance went to school with a guy who almost took a job at the World Trade Center and he could have been in there so that's not funny.'

"It's OK to do comedy now and it's been OK and comedy has actually occurred all over the place—in barrooms and at kitchen tables and in break rooms and all over behind the backs of the people who are truly affected or would just get cunty about it. Just because it doesn't fall into a network slot between *Friends* and Leno doesn't mean it ain't comedy. It's OK for Leno to do comedy again when the Geico gecko tells him it is."

————

NONE OF THIS WAS GOING TO GET ME A DEVELOPMENT DEAL. I didn't care. I was saying what I felt. I'd left my old managers and was now with Judi Brown, who'd brought me to that original festival in Vail. Now she was not only managing comics but also was in charge of organizing Aspen. Without her I might have been run out of Aspen on a ski pole. Renee wasn't making us look any prettier. Louis CK was headlining one of the showcases I was on. Renee was pretty drunk when I went on stage and I could see her drinking shots with comedian Vic Henly while I performed. Shots are not a good thing for Renee. Towards my close, she started heckling me. By the time Louis CK went up, she was soused and carrying on full conversations with the stage. I don't know how well-known Louie was back then to the general public but he'd always been huge to comics. He knew that Renee was my girlfriend so he didn't eviscerate her but I was mortified and had to half-carry her out of the bar and through a crowded lobby. Not the first time, not the last. In the morning, I asked her to marry me.

I was scheduled to go back to Vegas to do a show at Tommy Rockers the next month and figured why not just turn it into a mammoth blow-out farce of a wedding. Renee brought up the fact that I was still legally married to Dori from thirteen years earlier. Like taxes, divorce was confusing paperwork that I never found very necessary. But it didn't matter. We didn't need any kind of certificate or legal filings. We'd just call it a wedding and call ourselves married. We can call ourselves anything we want. We can call ourselves popes or colonels or Indians. We don't need anyone's permission. We'll just be married.

"But it won't be legal?"

"You're right. It won't be. We'll be doing drugs, too. They won't be 'legal' either but we'll still be high."

Sold. The invite went out in the form of an update on my Web site. Open invite to anyone who wanted to come. I got comic friends Andy Andrist, Henry Phillips, Sean Rouse, and Ralphie May to perform. I flew a friend named Father Luke down to do the ceremony. He was a former priest and now a long-haired vagabond poet I'd met in a comedy news-group. I hired Extreme Elvis as the band. Renee and I had once taken the train from L.A. to San Francisco to see him perform after I'd read about him on the Internet. He was a graphically obese Elvis impersonator of the GG Allin ilk with an amazing seven-piece band, horns and all. Nudity was just the tip of the iceberg with EE. It would get far worse. What a way to meet the in-laws.

Renee's parents both came with their respective new spouses. Her mom, from Colorado, was pleasant in a whole-grain and mountain-biking kind of way. Her dad was an active-duty Blackhawk chopper pilot. My act was at the apex of post-9/11 anti-nationalism, and that could present a problem, but her dad was also a drinker and that bond would overcome. They'd need to drink. They'd be sitting with Mother.

Renee was falling down shitfaced before they even got her into her dress. At the bar her friends jacked her up with ecstasy just to keep her upright. The best man was chosen by a high-hand contest on one of the bars video poker machines. My longtime fan and good friend Joe Vernon won with a queen-high flush in hearts. The show was chaos. The bridesmaids heckled every comic relentlessly. My set led directly into the ceremony. Instead of a ring, I gave her a Platinum Visa card in her name. That's far more commitment than a diamond. Extreme Elvis played us off and would continue to play the audience out. He was immediately naked and most of the band followed as well. I was thanking people for coming as he pissed into a pint glass and chugged it down, warm urine pouring out of the corners of his mouth and down his face. Tommy Rocker sat by, terrified, picturing his gaming and liquor license being burned in a bonfire. The quality of the musicianship was being overlooked, people focusing more on Elvis jamming two fingers up his own ass, then sauntering through the crowd, crooning while he gently swirled those fingers in their drinks. The in-laws decided to go hit a buffet just as Elvis tore the tampon out his backup singer's snatch, waved it around like a rat by its tail, before chewing it up and spitting it into a fleeing audience. Mother was already gone. This was Vegas and she had slot machines waiting for her. I'm surprised she even made it to the wedding.

Renee and I danced to a crushing rendition of "Suspicious Minds." Even I was naked by now and at the end I brought her to the floor and we rolled around on the dance floor now littered in piss and broken glass. You never forget those memories so long as you have pictures and a lot of secondhand stories.

The wedding was the beginning of a five-week road trip. In the mornings Renee would go out and buy fresh vegetables and hummus with fine cheese and crackers. She'd bring fresh-cut flowers to the room. We'd listen to NPR. At night we'd get raucously drunk. One night at a club in Lexington, Kentucky, there was a sparse crowd made up mostly of a large group of real estate women who obviously had no idea what they were in for. They'd come to see "comedy" as part of their function, having undertaken no due diligence as to who was performing. I paced in the back like a man on the green mile. I was facing certain death. Renee told me, "I love you. But if you make those people walk out, I will love even more." They were gone within ten minutes of my set, yelling at the manager for refunds out in the lobby. This was our honeymoon.

———

BACK IN L.A. WE HAD TO FIGURE OUT WHERE WE WERE GOING to live. Obviously Renee wasn't going to stay in a one-bedroom apartment with me and two girls I'd been fucking. Mother assumed we'd just send Patty and Sarah packing and stay there right beside her. That wasn't going to work for either me or Renee. Renee could make pleasant with Mother in short bursts but we were drunks and Mother could be overwhelming. If you stopped in for coffee she'd want you to stay for dinner, generally out of a can or from the microwaved package. If you stayed for dinner she'd want you to stay the night. She'd kept the bunk beds on the off-chance that company would come, even though the only people she knew were my friends, and the top bunk was stacked like a garage sale. There's no way I'd put Renee in a position like that every day whilst chasing off the inevitable morning fear of alcoholism. For now we'd stay in her tiny studio apartment in Santa Monica until we found a bigger place. Patty could keep my apartment. Mother was devastated. She acted like we were moving to Mongolia.

Renee's apartment was a single room with a kitchen that overlooked O'Brien's Irish Pub downstairs. The drunks would probably keep you up at night but not us. We were them and we didn't sleep so much as pass out. In the day it was cramped, and it didn't take long to start getting on each other's nerves. What you held in during the day would come out over cocktails that night. Road work would give us a healthy break. Unless it was a really cool place to go, Renee would stay home. I was booked in Dayton, Ohio. Renee stayed home.

I talked to her from a tittie bar Sunday night in Dayton. Monday morning I had a cab coming at 5 a.m. to bring me to the airport to head home. I called her cell from the airport and it picked up after three rings or so but with no greeting, as though she had accidently hit the answer button unknowingly.

I listened for about ten minutes, hearing the jabber in the background, sounds like dispatchers that made me think it may be a cab company. Renee was good for leaving her cell phone places. If I could hear the name of the cab company, I could track it down.

Finally, I heard a man's voice saying Renee's full name followed by, "No, she hasn't been booked in yet. Call back."

Fuck.

I called the Santa Monica Police and verified that she had indeed been arrested. Drunk in public, resisting arrest, and assaulting a police officer. The first charge I could see but the second two, while I am all for them, just isn't her forte. Bail was $2,500.

Needless to say, it was a very long flight.

Her brother had bailed her out by the time I got home and I heard the story.

She was crossing the street from O'Brien's in a crosswalk when a cop screamed through pulling a U-turn and almost ran her over. So she kicked its rear bumper. The cop slammed on his breaks, jumped out, and started screaming at her. She, in turn, told him to fuck off, that he'd nearly killed her.

He asked her name, she told him to fuck off again. She's good like that. Unfortunately, cops don't like it when you tell them to fuck off, even when it's truly in their best interest. This cop didn't like it one bit.

This cop, Officer Pace of the SMPD, decided that "fuck you" was the equivalent to resisting arrest and took her into custody by slamming her head into his pig-mobile, fracturing her cheekbone. What verbal abuse she couldn't come up with on her own during the booking process she could lift directly from my act. But she had plenty of her own material. The police report was very colorful.

"I like that uniform. I'd like to fuck you in that uniform. Then I'd take that gun and shoot you in the face, you fucking faggot."

Seeing her crying in the doorway, face swollen and lips broken and knowing that, short of a cop-killing spree, there was nothing I could do about it filled me with impotent rage. We had to leave for the Chicago Comedy Festival. I spent the entire first day there trying to find a dentist to see if Renee was going to require oral surgery. My act, already filled with anti-authority sentiment, just turned into hate-spewing vitriol without humor. It was Ice T's "Cop Killer" if the song didn't rhyme. The stage was my only outlet, and it wasn't enough. I melted down almost every show, walking almost the entire crowd headlining the finale at Zanies. Ron White was the only person that would even make eye contact with me at the after-party and eventually helped me to get Renee to a service elevator when she was too drunk to walk.

The mood was ugly enough after the arrest when she found out she was pregnant. There was no need to have the conversation. We both had no intention of bringing children into this ugly, fucking world. RU486, the abortion pill, was a miserable experience for her. It took several tries, and all resulted in an agonizingly slow miscarriage. It was unbearable for her physically and stomach-turning to have to watch. I scheduled a vasectomy as soon after as possible. I couldn't go to O'Brien's without staring out on to Main St., wondering if each passing cop was the one that had beat up my girlfriend and what I'd do if it was. Maybe living above a bar wasn't the best place to be anymore.

We moved to a one-bedroom in Venice, only about six blocks away. I rented a small single-room office directly next door to work. There was a homeless couple sleeping in the walled-off front stoop of the office when I got the keys and went to move in my desk. They apologized and explained that they thought the place was vacant. I told them that they were grandfathered in and could keep that area so long as they looked after it and didn't shit on the doorstep. They assured me they wouldn't. We'd eventually begin to hang out for cocktails with them most evenings. I was beginning to get noticed. I was named as one of *Variety*'s "Top Ten Comics to Watch" alongside Dane Cook. I brought Mother to the Laugh Factory for the affair. She seethed at Dane Cook like it was going to be a cage fight rather than a comedy show. She couldn't let it go. It didn't help that I'd take potshots at him onstage and on the Internet but there was no serious venom. Again, I used the Yankees/Red Sox analogy with Mother. When the game is over they hang out. Red Sox players don't have "Fuck the Yankees" bumper stickers on their own cars. That's for the fans to take seriously. If given the choice of drinking in an airport bar with Dane Cook versus a bar crowded with my biggest fans, I'm taking Dane any day. And Dane doesn't even drink.

———————

THAT SUMMER I WAS BROUGHT OVER TO DO THE EDINBURGH Festival by my now-manager Brian Hennigan. Edinburgh is the largest arts festival in the world and lasts the entire month of August. If you haven't heard of it, it's probably because you are an American. Something like thirty thousand performers are there, everything from street jugglers and sword swallowers to world premiere plays, opera and mimes and parades of bagpipes and kilts. What I'm saying is that it's mostly really fucking loud and annoying. For a month. I was only there for eight shows that first trip but it was perfectly timed. An American comic spewing anti-American, anti-government sentiment in the UK that close to 9/11 was like throwing out Mardi Gras beads. They couldn't get enough. It hadn't hurt that I'd been lambasted in a New York paper for just the same thing.

The column started with a piece about Tim Robbins and Susan Sarandon premiering a play at Edinburgh they'd written about first responders who died in the Twin Towers. As an afterthought they twisted some of my bits and web updates out of context and included in the piece that I'd also be in Edinburgh making fun of these same dead first responders. I got emails from all over the States, patriots, police, and firemen all threatening to boycott my shows. "Hey, you know that guy we've never seen or heard of? Let's not go see him!" For the record, the bit was making fun of all the hero pussy that cops and firemen were getting after 9/11. They spun that up with another bit about firemen in general being adrenaline junkies, and that your safety is just their excuse for risking their lives. That's how I was making fun of you. Not the 9/11 dead guys. And now I'm boycotting you for reading that shitty tabloid news and believing it. You can leave my house burning, thank you.

Brian Hennigan re-spun that bullshit into more press than I'd ever had in my entire career combined. I met him for the first time at the airport and immediately he was showing me multi-page full-color preview articles about me in major UK newspapers. The shows were fantastic and Brian would grab all the newspapers as soon as they came out, usually while we were still drinking from the night before. He made quite the production with presenting 5-star reviews, which were a few. I'd make Brian call Mother with every new review so I could read them to her on speakerphone. I didn't know how to dial internationally and I still don't. That's why I've stayed with Brian since.

Renee was with me and we took in all the sights, meaning we took one open-top bus tour and then hit the bars. Fuck the castle. That's all the way up that hill. We met shitloads of great UK comics and partied our balls off. I couldn't believe that these guys did this for an entire month. It's like doing four Mardi Gras in a row where you're both working and partying the whole time. I'm not ashamed to admit that I was well out of my league with that brand of stamina, even when chemically infused.

The brass ring of the Fringe Fest for comics is the Perrier Award (now called the Eddie) for best of the fest. You won like a billion dollars, some mineral water and scorn from your peers. I wasn't eligible as I hadn't done the minimum amount of shows required. I did my last show and as I left the stage, Brian held the audience. He made a long introduction to it but the gist of it was that the press had decided to make up their own award sponsored by a competing mineral water company—The Strathmore Press Award for Best of the Festival. I was the inaugural (and final) winner. It was significantly less than a billion dollars and came with no water, much less any scorn as it hadn't existed until then nor would it ever again. I posed for press photos outside the venue. They asked Renee what she thought.

"Well, it's no Perrier."

Funny cunt.

WE WENT HOME VICTORIOUS BUT IT DIDN'T LAST. I WAS BUILDING up a fan base online and trying to capitalize on it. Renee didn't use the Internet and was convinced that all the time I was spending in the office was taken up with watching porn or flirting with female fans. The tirades were ugly. She came in once when I happened to be reading a random email from none other than Maura, my grade-school girlfriend. Renee erupted into a wrath that I was online with my "ex-girlfriend." Goddamnit, we were nine years old! I could no longer give Maura shit about her husband thinking we had "unfinished business." The fight raged all night. I couldn't tell how much was residual from the police attack and the abortion. I tried to wait it out. We talked about leaving town. I didn't like L.A. I didn't care about acting. I was a comedian and my work was on the road. There was no reason to be in this shithole city. My manager called. Comedy Central wanted me as a new host for *The Man Show*.

I said no to the audition more than once. I'd seen *The Man Show* and knew it wasn't my sense of humor. I was assured that Comedy Central wanted it to have a new style. They really want you. They love you. And the old classic, "They want to be in the Doug Stanhope business." I knew it could be a huge opportunity. *The Man Show* was big. But I didn't want to have to audition. If they loved me that much, just give me the fucking job. Then Joe Rogan called me. He said that they approached him as well and that if NBC would allow him to do it at the same time he was hosting *Fear Factor*, that he was in and wanted me as his co-host. I took the audition.

There were ten comedians auditioning for the two hosts or one host should Rogan get the okay from NBC. Comics were paired up with one another to write monologues and perform mock run-throughs on a makeshift set to a crowd of what I assumed to be paid homeless people and detained immigrants.

I was first paired up with Patrice O'Neal. He was a huge, angry black comedian who I'd just seen destroy at Chicago. He'd followed me on a show there where I was drunk and rambling about killing cops while wearing a football helmet I'd found as a prop backstage, dying on my ass. Patrice destroyed. The viciousness of his set was the only catharsis I'd had in Chicago.

All I remember of our audition was him saying to me without so much as looking at me, "I don't work well with other people." He made no secret that he didn't want to be there. I was terrified of him. He died a few years ago and I'm still terrified of him.

Next I was paired up with Mother's favorite—Dane Cook. Well, how about that? How am I supposed to hope he sucks when our auditions depend on each other? I'm sure there was a way if I'd really tried but I didn't. We wrote some stuff together and did pretty well. Eventually, it came down to three of us—me, Dane, and Ralph Garman, an actor and local radio personality. My manager told me that she thought I had it secured and that it was probably going to be Ralph as my co-host instead of Dane. I didn't get my hopes up. Then Rogan called. NBC had allowed him to do it and he told Comedy Central that I was his co-host. Nothing is for sure in Hollywood unless Rogan says it for sure. I beat Dane Cook yet again. I won a show destined to be a piece of shit and he went out and released a platinum album on his way to super-stardom. Ha ha, loser!

THERE WAS NO WAY OF KNOWING HOW BAD THE MAN SHOW WAS going to suck. Rogan and I had grand ideas of all the weird shit we were gonna do, but it wasn't long before the dreams started slowly falling down like dead leaves. But before that could happen, my first concern was nepotism. I got my friend, comedian Andy Andrist a job as a writer even though I knew he could barely write an email. Then I started looking for ways to put Mother into bits. I finally got approval on "Doug's Mother Reviews Porn" segments. They'd film Mother in her apartment, chain smoking, coughing, and stroking one of her moribund cats while she reviewed a variety of hardcore porn. I wished it had been funnier. Mother had a weird thing when she acted of trying to hide her accent. Massachusetts was still thick in her voice and she tried to mask it but it would always come out at some point, and strong. I tried to give her pointers when they were shooting but it would only make her more nervous and snappy. "Leave me alone! I'm trying to concentrate!" I'd give up and leave the shoot. I knew she was afraid of letting me down. I wrote the segments with my own delivery in mind. I couldn't expect her to be me. Her delivery was the least of the show's problems and I was keenly aware of it. But it would be a while before the rest of the world knew that it was unwatchable dreck. So, in the meantime, why not live it up? Mother and I had a goddamned TV show together. A billboard went up behind the Del Taco where I always grabbed my breakfast burrito on the way to the lot where we filmed. Me and Rogan with our big heads all over Hollywood. I immediately ran and dragged Mother out of her apartment to take pictures. Moments like this are only this great the first time. I recently saw a bus stop sign advertising *Paul Blart: Mall Cop 2*. I doubt Kevin James was running out to take pictures with his mother. But the first time it's incredible, if only for me and Mother. There was nobody else to brag to anymore. Your enemies hoped you'd fail and your friends didn't know you were about to. Mother didn't give a fuck. Her son was on a billboard and everything he did was gold.

DURING TAPINGS, THERE WAS A LARGE GREEN ROOM WHERE industry execs and guests could sit and watch, out of the studio audience. Suits had no interest in watching. They didn't care. It was just a place to be seen and schmooze. This was commonplace in TV tapings. Only now they had the bad fortune of being in the same room as Mother, who didn't hesitate to loudly and repeatedly tell everyone, including my manager, to "Jesus Christ, will you please Shut the Fuck Up!" And they shut the fuck up. There goes My Hero.

Shit with Renee got to be too much. She was a star in her own right, simply by walking into a room and now the scales of attention were all tilted in my favor. The fighting I could deal with when I was just doing stand-up. Now I had a real job that lasted all day and into the night. I don't like to fight but when pushed into a corner, I have an ability to be amazingly cruel. And so did Renee. The show was already a daily fistfight trying to save any credibility in the face of bad comedy. I couldn't go home to more bullshit at night. I'd wake up to Renee already too drunk to walk in the morning and swearing she hadn't touched a drop. I'm sure that it was an exasperated sense of being left out, of not feeling as important. But I was too wrapped up in it all, in myself, to notice or do anything to balance it out. I shut off and she left to go live with her mother in Colorado.

Andy and I moved into *The Man Show* office and lived there semi-secretly. I slept on the couch, he slept on a cot. When we needed clean clothes we called wardrobe. When we needed food or booze, we sent a production assistant. During production meetings, we'd go through each segment and tell the props department what we'd need for set-up. No matter what the bit was, we'd always say that we needed two hammocks for it. Why do you need hammocks for a field piece in a nursing home? We never did get the hammocks. The lawyer for the production company made regular stops in our office to tell us we were not allowed to live there. It became a running farce. The more we insisted we didn't live in the office, the more we'd telegraph the fact that we did. We even strung up a clothesline and hung dirty socks from it. That's another book in itself. In fact, the title of this book could be "But That's Another Book in Itself." Andy and I continued to live in the office for the most part in the M*A*S*H-style quarters we'd built in our office for the entirety of the show. It was funny and we were usually too drunk to drive back to the Venice apartment by the end of the day. Besides, we had the homeless people to keep an eye on the place.

The show was a disaster that wouldn't end. We filmed twenty-two episodes that were so bad that they stopped airing them after eleven, and had us come back to reshoot parts for the second half to try to revive it somehow. They'd release it a year later as though it was a whole new season. But there was no saving it. That baby was blue and was going to float in the pool for a long time.

MOTHER GOT A FEW MORE SMALL PARTS ACTING. SHE PAIRED WITH dwarf comedian Tanya Lee Davis, playing grisly strippers dancing for

P-Diddy in a sketch for an MTV Carson Daly roast. She appeared in a Limp Bizkit video and did another movie with director Tamar Halpern, again starring *Breaking Bad's* Betsy Brandt. In that, she played a bull dyke security guard. Good thing she had the uniform. She still did occasional massage and her hoard grew to beyond its limits and started spilling outside. She was down to four cats, with one, Jimmy, quickly on its way out.

Jimmy had been waiting to die for some time but couldn't find a clear space on Mother's floor to fall down. Mother took him to a vet when she awoke to find Jimmy gagging up blood. Turns out he was just choking on a tooth that had rotted out of his head, but they did say his terminal state was due to diabetes and failing kidneys. They suggested some type of state-of-the-art life support system or transplant or some such funniness. Not on my dime.

Mother decided that before she put him down, she would bring him to an "alternative" veterinary type. She brought Jimmy as well as another cat named Stanley to this Dr. Angel for whatever Ouija-Board medicine he had on tap. Stanley had been losing weight, she said, and I tried to convince her that Stanley had gone Hollywood.

Mother called me afterwards and couldn't have been happier with the results. The cats were doing great. They are all "calm" and "mellow" and in a whole new space, all because of this wonderful voodooman. I must have missed the subtleties in the cats when I stopped by to see Mother. They always seem to be as calm as any animal trapped in a cluttered, fire-hazard one-bedroom apartment could be. The diagnosis?

Seems that Jimmy the Dying Cat was just carrying "guilt" from being trapped in that emaciated body, guilt that he was picking up from Mother. Mother was stopped in her tracks with this show of clairvoyance. It must have been like he could actually crawl into kitty's dying head! On a subsequent scheduled visit, Mother called to say she had an audition and would have to cancel. No worries, they told her, they could do it OVER THE PHONE! The thought

of her holding a phone up against a dying cat's head while this char-
latan whispers witchcraft into it without thinking you might be getting played all comes down to who's paying the tab.

Mother was so impressed with his techniques that she asked the
"doctor" in only half-joking awe—"Do you do *people?*"

"Of course, I do!" says Dr. No-Rape-For-The-Willing.

I'm in $1,500 already on this shitheel. Of course he takes people!
I bet for another $1,500 he'd agree to do holistic plumbing or trans-
mission work.

"The reason your engine is tapping is that it's sending you a signal
in Morse Code. It's saying 'Have the boy send money!' You haven't
been . . . revving it, have you?"

Remember that Mother has had her experiences with *alternative* types. The psychic in Florida, the healing crystals from QVC,
and who knows what else? Thank goodness she has finally found one
of the good apples in the Cat Whisperer. After all, the proof is in the
pudding. The fifteen-year-old cats are calm—aren't they???

Mother made an appointment the next day for her sinus, chest,
and back problems.

With a holistic veterinarian. It'll take time, he told her, and why
wouldn't it? You can't expect overnight results trying to cure forty-
five years of smoking menthols with tuning forks and aromatherapy
as much you can't remove a curse without burning dozens of Ben
Franklins.

Only now it's my Ben Franklins. Mother assumed that since I'm
on television, we must be rich. But Mother sounded so happy—and
the cats are feeling less remorseful, so who am I to be the buzzkill?

The voodoo didn't take for Mother or the cats. Jimmy died shortly
afterwards and Stanley kept shedding pounds. Every time a cat died
or was put down, Mother had a ritual. She would put the dead cat
out on a pillow in the middle of the room and allow the remaining
cats to sniff it and see its body so that they would understand it was
dead and have closure. Crazy. Like they'd think Jimmy had gone
to the store for milk and then beat feet to Palm Springs. Then, in

the morning, she'd put the dead cat in a Ralph's bag and chuck it in the dumpster. Not crazy. Logical. I'd have done the same with Mother if it were legal. There's no reason ever to spend money on a corpse. Mother had a beautiful way of vacillating between ethereal nonsense and cold rationality. Comedian Joey CoCo Diaz told the story of witnessing the dead cat laid out like a buffet for the other cats to mourn.

"And all the other fucked-up cats are doing laps around it, looking at this thing for parts! 'I need that eye! And I need that leg!'"

Spot on, Joey. Spot on.

18

Off the Wagon, Out to Sea

I'D NOTICED FOR YEARS THAT MOTHER ALWAYS HAD A MEASURED cup full of cough medicine out on her nightstand like it was an aperitif. With her waning lungs, I always wrote it off as a panacea, her pretending her gurgling hack was caused by something other than cigarettes and could be cured with shots of Dollar Store off-brand Robitussin. Turns out she had just been using it as a sneaky if distasteful way of getting drunk. Now that I lived elsewhere, she no longer needed to hide it and had moved on to Vodka. Vodka with a cough syrup back. I found this out from Patty, that she'd been diving in hard. Now it made sense that when I'd call during early evening hours she'd answer in her old faux-British accent. Mother had her old cheer back for the moment. I was sworn to secrecy. Patty was Mother's only friend and confidant. I couldn't out her for ratting on Mother. She was just worried about Mother and didn't know what to do. I wished Mother would have told me herself. If nothing else, it'd be kind of cool to get hammered with her after all of her years of sobriety. I found an opening.

Comedy Central had asked if I would go on a cruise from Ft. Lauderdale to Jamaica to film promo footage for the upcoming Commie Awards. Knowing that *The Man Show* had no chance of being nominated for anything, this was as close as I was gonna get to an awards show. And it included first class air and accommodations for two. Perfect vacation for Mother. We boarded the plane and sat in 1A and 1B. I don't know if this was my first time in first class but it was definitely hers and I was glowing with pride. Who cares if this came off the back of a dying mule? This was everything I could have ever wanted. The flight attendant came by with champagne. I took one and offered one to Mother. She took it without excuse or explanation and we toasted. We drank for the next week solid. When we got to the airport in Ft. Lauderdale, I noticed for the first time that she was running out of breath walking on flat ground. She had to stop for air repeatedly. I knew her lungs were fucked but I didn't know it was this bad. I hadn't seen her walk further than from the car to the apartment in years. I knew she was betraying a truth that she didn't want to admit. If there were stairs, even a few, I'd stop halfway up to tie my shoe or point out something that I feigned was interesting, knowing it would give her a chance to catch her breath. I like to think she knew I was making these bogus stops for her benefit but we never said a word. We both wanted to get outside to smoke.

We spent two full days on the ship, me working fourteen-hour days filming dogshit for commercial intro and outros, and her stuck with a drink in one hand and a slot machine handle in the other. We had the option of staying for the full seven-day cruise but opted out in Jamaica to get to a gig I had booked in West Palm Beach, Florida. My friend Andy was working with me, and that always meant, and still means, trouble. In Florida, that trouble meant cocaine. As I once said in my act, leaving Florida without a sunburn and a nosebleed is like leaving Thailand without the virus. You didn't immerse yourself fully in the culture. My friends had gotten Mother high like a dog before but given her predilection for chitchat, I thought blow might be more up her alley. Between shows on that Saturday, I hooked up and got a waitress to take her into the ladies' room and show her the ropes. I wish I knew who these random people were today. The only reason I have a Facebook page is in the hopes that someday I'll get a message saying "Remember me? I was the girl that

showed your mother how to chop rails on a toilet tank!" Whoever
you are, I send my regards.

Mother took to cocaine for the night like I occasionally like
to—just to keep you energized, chatty, and drinking longer. And
we drank for a long time. Andy pulled a gal from the late show. She
had come with her boyfriend but left him for comedians, drinks,
and blow. We went to the hotel. We stored what narcotics we had
left over on Mother. Our thinking was that if we got pulled over,
Mother would be the least suspicious. Even though we were in a cab.
Becker taught me that. It's better to be paranoid and wrong than not
paranoid and wrong.

Andy was sharing my room so I hung out with Mother, doing
bumps in her room until I thought Andy had had enough time to
wrap up with the lady. Then I went down two floors to our room
and some fumbling transition was made. He wanted more blow and
I wanted to get laid. She only cared about fucking the comics. You
could call it sloppy seconds. I like to think of it as Andy opening
for me.

I told Andy that Mother was holding, and without putting a
stitch of clothing on, he went to her room, deciding to take the
stairs instead of the elevator. Less likely to run into people in the
middle of the night, jacked up and naked. He was fucked up, not
stupid. I coke-dinked the girl clumsily as her phone kept ringing the
same way it had while Andy was fucking her. It was her boyfriend
calling for hours, screaming into her voicemail, accusing her of fucking the comedians. Meanwhile, Andy was upstairs, butt-naked and
doing blow with Mother while she chastised him for cheating on his
wife and lecturing him on the sanctity of fidelity. In the morning, it
was a breakfast buffet of regret. The girl's phone was still ringing off
the hook from her desperate boyfriend, the same way I had called
Khrystyne when she was off with her ex. Only now she was taking
the calls and lying poorly. Both Andy and I had that ominous feeling
like she might cry rape rather than take culpability. "I was drunk
and they took advantage." We were both stewing in post-cocaine

paranoia. Andy drove her back to her trailer park and then came back to take me and Mother to the airport. We were panicked for days. I wondered how many times I could have claimed rape because I made poor choices when I was drunk and my girlfriend was blowing up my phone. Mother didn't care. She was too hungover as well and not looking forward to more walking on flat ground through airports, bereft of oxygen.

After the paranoia left us, I could finally rule it a win. Mother and I went on a first-class vacation drinking and into heavy road carousing. So far as she knew, that was how every night on the road was for me. She wasn't always wrong but mostly the road was uneventful in comparison. That night stood out, and if she thought it was commonplace, all the better to let her. Unfortunately, Mother's good-time drinking days wouldn't last very long.

We went to the Commie Awards and were photographed on the red carpet. Nobody said, "Can we get a single?" It was a special moment and we looked sharp, both in black trenchcoats. Triumph the Insult Comic Dog raged from the dais, "Doug Stanhope is here tonight. Who the fuck is Doug Stanhope???" Mother leaned in and squeezed me backstage. I'm glad she laughed rather than rushed the stage. Maybe she just didn't have it in her. Mother ran out of gas, from her bad back, dead lungs, or too much booze, I don't know which, but I had to get her a cab before the show was halfway through.

———

RENEE CAME BACK IN THE SUMMER OF 2004. I'D RENTED A townhouse at the beach in Playa del Rey in an area called The Jungle. It was pricey but it was eight minutes from the airport, 50 yards from the beach, secluded and walking distance to some of the best dive bars in L.A. that the city wasn't even aware of. Oddly, on a side note, a few of those fantastic bars are pictured in the opening montage of the first season of *Bar Rescue*. No accounting for taste.

We were still filming for the revamped second half of *The Man Show* episodes. Andy had seen that the ill-famed ice skater Tonya Harding had made it small by going into professional boxing. He pitched the idea that I should fight her. The draw being that she was a professional trained Olympic athlete and I . . . well, I wasn't in much better shape than Mother, quite honestly. Andy had pitched this in the first go-around with Comedy Central and they'd shot it down. Now they were out of ideas, with their backs against the wall, and decided to run with it.

Mother would work my corner, feeding me beer and cigarettes between rounds. Renee would work Tonya's corner. All was set to go when Tonya showed up that afternoon to film. She was anxious and distrustful from the start, like there was going to be some kind of sabotage, that the entire show was going to be some prank at her expense. I guess she had every reason to think she might be the butt of the joke. I assured her that it was just a fight, nothing at her expense. Everyone's heart sank when she said, "Well, it's not a *real* fight. I'm not fighting a man!"

Uh . . . that's kinda what you were hired to do. She demanded that no matter how bad shape I was in, a woman couldn't ever beat a man. As for her own shape, let's say she wasn't in prime condition. She may have even been able to beat me in a weigh-in. So I caved in and agreed to fake the fight. The writers—Andy especially—kept trying to ply me with more beer to skip the fix and knock her out. It was tempting for the sake of the show, but honestly, I felt incredibly sorry for her. She'd been so vilified—right or wrong—that she was now a shivering rodent on a farm full of hounds, not knowing who was coming for her next. As far as she knew, we were no different than some morning radio clods waiting to exact some dated revenge on an easy target.

In the ring, she was dusted as soon as I was, if not sooner, no more than 20-30 seconds of lazy, misplaced jabs. I tapped once lightly in the head and then mumbled through my mouthpiece to ask if she was okay. She said, "No." Jesus. We can't even fake this fight. Between the first and second round, Mother fed me a cigarette while Renee fed Tonya her asthma inhaler. Between the second and third, Renee tried to block the camera angle while Tonya puked in a bucket. Like the rest of the show, the fight was a boring nonevent. I lost by decision as was planned. I should have knocked her out.

———

WITH RENEE BACK, I SAW EVEN LESS OF MOTHER. PATTY KEPT ME in the loop that Mother's drinking was even more out of control. She was stealing bottles of vodka out of Patty's freezer. Patty was doing her best to let it slide while playing both sides of the fence. One night I got a call from her letting me know Mother had hit bottom. Patty had been holding Mother's head over the toilet vomiting while telling her that she was going to kill herself. She made Patty promise that she wouldn't tell me. That's how Mother had become. Force someone to break her confidence in a situation where they had no choice otherwise. Then hold it against them later. Patty had to choose between calling me or 911.

Evidently, Tamar had called me with the same warning. I felt a bit shitty for not remembering. More so, I felt negligent for not even noticing how bad Mother had become over a short time, caught up in my own career, my own life, my own problems.

Again, continued from Tamar:

"Two years later, I'm gearing up for my second feature, Shelf Life. There isn't a role for Bonnie but I'm doing a table read and ask her to fill in as one of the male roles, Sgt. Knofelmacher, a fascistic rule mongerer out to save the public library from book theft. She reads it like a Jersey dyke and Sgt. Knofelmacher is now a she. Bonnie finds her security outfit and gets her hair cut dykey. It's a brilliant touch. People think I'm smarter than I am because of it.

While on location in absolutely gorgeous Bakersfield, I notice Bonnie is not on her A-game. She invites me to her room and offers me a glass of Hungarian wine she bought at the 99 cent store and, when I express my surprise, she tells me they also sell eggs there. While this is all news to me, having only been inside a 99 Cent Store once to film an actor walking around and asking how much everything is, the bigger shock is the wine. Not because it was rotgut and tasted like cough syrup, but because she was drinking it, too.

When I press her for details on how long she's been drinking, she tells me not to worry, she'd been twenty years sober and what's a little nip here or there. I beg her to at least consider some French table wine, pointing out that a decent bottle costs around twelve, but she ignores me.

About six months later, one of my producers lets slip that she's been supplying Bonnie with Vicodin. I third degree her and find out that it's becoming a constant request. I go to visit Bonnie. She's buzzed. And not in that oh-look-you're-so-much-more-sparkly-and-interesting-when-you-drink way. She was sloppy. She was depressed. I told her I was going to tell Doug. She begged me not to.

A couple days later, I called Doug, who at that point— other than the shoot and hitting a couple of his shows and that one time he sweetly offered to share his bed with me at a film festival—I didn't know all that well. I admired him and felt like I knew him through his comedy, but really, that was a one-way thing. Me laughing at his shows or playing his now second or third CD for friends so I can be the cool person who introduced them to a fuckin' brilliant comic. But calling him to say there's a problem with Bonnie? Weird.

But I did. And he was thankful. And he checked up on my story and clocked her into rehab in seconds. A big relief. And she came out fine."

Renee and I showed up at Mother's place in the small hours of the morning to find her in a worse-than-usual sprawl of filth, lying on her side on the bottom bunk, mostly passed out and moaning.

There was a Post-It note in the wreckage of her nightstand that read simply "PAIN IS TOO MUCH DOUG." Some people leave suicide letters. Mother left a suicide Post-It. What else did she have to say that she hadn't already complained about for years. We coaxed her through until daybreak and then found a detox for her. She agreed to go but dragged out the process for hours. She was ready but—oh, wait—she needed to find this or that amongst her piles of towering shit. She was like Steve Martin in *The Jerk*. She needed just one more thing and then another before finally trudging down the stairs in her filthy bathrobe to the waiting car.

"Stop at 7-11 first," she demanded, blubbering in tears.

"What else do you need??" I said, irritated.

"I need cigarettes. And lottery tickets."

"Lottery tickets??? Seriously? You feel *lucky* right now?"

Having Mother in detox gave me and Renee time to seriously investigate the extent of Mother's hoard, and it was frightening. There was no choice but to try to clean it out as much as possible. It took us three sixteen-hour sweltering days to clear through a roughly 400-sq-ft apartment, and that was just tearing down to start from scratch reorganizing. We could spend eight hours on just one corner. You'd end up uncovering a large dresser or other furniture that was impossible to imagine being that deeply hidden by the piles and crates that had entombed it. The cabinets were all virtual avalanches waiting to be triggered. *Dollar Store* shit. We'd count. Seventy-some toothbrushes, all in packages. Batteries in the hundreds. Crates of VHS copies of her play, *The Odd Couple*. Small tupperware with hidden booze or cough medicine. Chests of worthless gemstones from QVC still bagged with price tags that we tallied cost upwards of ten grand. Dozens of milk crates full of books, mostly self-help, and many multiples of the same title. We started a yard sale out front for the useless and redundant stuff. What we couldn't sell we left out for the Russians, and even they couldn't take all that we left.

By the time she was released from detox, we had everything cleaned, organized, made up, and livable. We felt like we'd completed a two-person barn-raising. Herculean to say the least. Mother left the facility in high spirits. She was even talking to the clinic about coming back to do counselling work there in her spare time. The closer we got to her place, the harder it was to contain our excitement, the look on her face when she saw how we had transformed that nightmare living junk drawer of an apartment into swanky, refurbished comfort.

Mother walked in and completely derailed. I was expecting a reaction akin to having a bow on a brand new car in the driveway at Christmas. What I got was anger and hysterics as though I'd robbed her blind. I assured her we didn't get rid of anything that could have any sentimental value or that wasn't easily replaceable. It didn't help. This was before the show *Hoarders*, and I was unaware of the severe psychological attachment people can have with seemingly worthless things. I just thought it had become too overwhelming to deal with cleaning out and was proud to have worked our asses off for her. And I hated her guts for not appreciating what we'd gone through to make her comfortable.

Renee and I talked more about getting the fuck out of L.A. I was getting enough of a following on the road—now in the UK and Europe as well as in the States—that there was no need for Hollywood. Everything I was doing in L.A. was ridiculous or uninspired. I hosted a *Girls Gone Wild* DVD just as an overpaid goof. Go out for a week or so and fuck with idiot sorority girls while they showed their tits. I hadn't factored in the idea that I'd be shown on every basic cable channel every fifteen minutes after midnight looking like an asshole, and that would last for over a year. It just seemed like a silly thing to do at the time.

The whole time I'd spent in L.A., I'd get TV pilots that you knew would never see the light of day, but that was another twenty-five or fifty grand of free money just for living there. I never calculated that L.A. expenses—much less the leaching effect on your spirit—made that free money a wash or even a loss.

———

ON MARCH 15, 2005, I WAS BOOKED TO DO THE UNIVERSITY OF Maryland with Mitch Hedberg. By this time in my career, it was clear to anyone that I was not a college act. Over the years I had become even more jaded where college kids were becoming dumber and purposely blinded. Hedberg could pull off the balance. I was more vitriolic and to the point. I knew that the only way any student-activities board would have let my act slip through the cracks was if Mitch had specifically requested me. And as usual with colleges, the money was great. I hadn't seen Mitch in years except in passing. I did my time to groans but no outright rebellion. Mitch destroyed the place. He was a full-on rock star. I thanked him on the drive back to the hotel for hooking me up with the gig and he looked confused. Turned out that he hadn't requested me at all. He was as surprised as I was. It just so happened that we were the two favorite comedians of the kid in charge of booking, the kid driving us home. The kid that was probably fired the next day for putting me onstage. Happy coincidence.

We went back to the hotel room, drank, and did a little blow while we caught up. We bemoaned the sober turn the industry was taking. When we'd started comedy, getting fucked up was as natural a part of the job as writing jokes. Now it seemed if you so much as slurred on a joke or ordered a shot from the stage you were looked at as some sort of problem case. People would get uncomfortable in their seats. I told him how I'd been spending a lot of time in Costa Rica, working less and trying to enjoy myself more. He said that he wanted to do the same. Mitch was a legendary warhorse when it came to the road. He couldn't say no to a gig. He remembered the days when it was all you could do to get booked. Now he felt like he was letting people down if he turned down an offer.

Two weeks later, I got the call that he was dead. I was shattered. Not because I would miss him in my life. I'd barely spoken to him in years. Nor was I surprised. We'd co-headlined a week at the Acme Comedy Club in Minneapolis back when I was filming the hidden camera show several years earlier. Mitch had jokes but there was always something real in them. If you know Mitch's act, you know he really did get free bread at Subway for a duck.

Mitch was riffing onstage one of those nights in Minneapolis. He had some bit that hadn't been part of his regular show that week. I'll do it hideous injustice but it was about having something you like but then when you find something you like better, you no longer like the thing you liked before.

"Like you like smoking pot. But then someone sprinkles some heroin in your pot and all of a sudden regular pot is no longer any good."

I'm sure I fucked that up but you get the gist. The audience laughed but I knew he wasn't kidding. Blasted out on coke in the green room after the show, I asked him about it. He stopped and said confidently "Stanhope, I got no intentions of slowing down." And that was the end of the conversation.

Mitch's proclivities were no secret by now, and when I'd just seen him, he looked like a sunken wax figure. I was gutted because if he could die, any of us could die. He was my age. His death made us all mortal for the first time. It was a wake-up call like no other. Not in my lifestyle but in how I chose to spend my time. L.A. could suck my dick. I was done chasing bullshit that I didn't even want. My lease was up in a few months. Now it was just deciding where to go. I was beginning to lose my mind in a way that I still consider good.

Not long afterwards, now-known actor Jason Sudeikis would play me on SNL in a spoof "Girls Gone Wild: Hurricane Katrina." Told you, Mitch. I was going to be "so real, people want to play me!" Yeesh. And to Gertrude Healy, who said in sixth grade that I may one day write for SNL, well, at least I was the fodder.

RENEE AND I HAD BEEN TAKING THE BACK ROADS THROUGH DEATH Valley a couple of years before and stopped at a place called Panamint Springs to have lunch. It was 26 miles from the nearest structure and was made up of a bar/restaurant, fifteen-room motel, and a campground across the street. Population: 9—just the folks who ran the place. We thought it was the perfect place to throw a party, so far away from any authority figure. Thus began our annual Death Valley parties.

I'd been on the road for over a decade at that point. Gypsy life. You meet really cool people, form brief friendships, and maybe you see them again in a year or two if you go back to that town. The idea of the party was to invite all these great people you've met on the road all to one remote location for several days of comedy, music, drinking and drugs—mostly hallucinogens. But more so just it's about getting to talk to people without the distractions of not just a drunken post-show audience, but without cell phones, television, or the Internet. That shit was unavailable in Death Valley. The main cabin had a porch that became a 24-hour stage for comedy, live music, or just bellowing your twisted, drug-inspired thoughts into the desert night. "Piss Roulette" was born there in Death Valley. Like Russian Roulette with two players only with squirt guns. Six guns, five filled with tequila, one full of piss. You'd pick them up at random and squirt it into your mouth until one of you lost.

One tripped-out morning, I walked out to find Becker in a lawn chair on the side of the highway. He had a fishing pole with a mousetrap baited with a sardine at the end. The trap was floating through the air on a giant helium balloon. I asked him what he was doing.

With eyeballs black as coal, he smiled and said, "I'm sky-fishing for raven." This was everything the party was built to be. If you wanted fun, you had to make it.

Year 3 of the party happened in late spring of 2005 just after Mitch died. My lease was about to be up in just a few weeks and we were leaving L.A. We still didn't know where we were going. We'd battled over locations. We'd considered Portland and Austin but weather and traffic shit-canned those in that order. Somehow, even Milwaukee was mentioned. I must have been drunk. I wanted to move to Reno but Renee said absolutely not. I still think Reno would be a funny place to live but Renee wasn't getting the joke. At one point, in frustration, I again threw a dart at a map, only this time it was a blow dart. Again, it hit rural Wyoming, just outside Cody. Maybe let's not follow this dart idea again.

Bisbee, Arizona was a town we'd found just after our wedding, killing a few days between gigs in Scottsdale and El Paso. We fell in love with it and went back as often as we could. It's a town of about 5,500 people in the southeast corner 100 miles from Tucson, the closest airport. I'd wanted to live in a small town but small towns usually mean small minds and yokels. Bisbee was not that at all. Bisbee used to be a mining town, and when the mine went bust in the seventies, artists and hippies moved in, giving the town a decent mix. It had great bars and I knew from the first time seeing it that, all things being equal, I could live there and never look back. But, as much as we fantasized, we considered it too remote and too far from an airport to move there.

I filmed one of my last go-nowhere television pilots in Bisbee just before our L.A. exodus. It was a travel show where I'd be hitch-hiking. When someone would stop, the production people would pull up, tell them what the show was about, and ask if they could put cameras in the car to film me interviewing them to the next town. They let me pick the locations where we'd film. It was easy. Any road going to Bisbee was accustomed to hitchhikers. We'd film from Benson, AZ, 25 miles to Tombstone for the first ride, then Tombstone to Bisbee for the next 25 miles. The gentleman that picked me up for the second ride brought me and the crew to the Copper Queen Hotel in Bisbee for Happy Hour drinks and introduced me around. A former state legislator from town told me that the best part of Bisbee is the secondhand smoke. It gets you high, he said. In passing small talk, I said that I'd always considered moving here. With that, someone at the table said that they knew the perfect real estate person and dialed her without me asking. I had just been trying to come up with stuff to say. I suck at polite conversation. I talked to the real estate woman, and when she asked what price range I was looking for, I lowballed it hopefully out of the market. She said she could only think of one house in that range and gave me an address.

We wrapped up filming in Bisbee and before we left in the morning, I went out and found that house just as a goof. I took pictures through the windows and of the outside. It was outside of downtown old Bisbee, and like a lot of this town it was a hundred years old and fairly decrepit but quaint, with a tiny guest house. I wrote down the realtor's phone number. As I drove back to the airport, I became convinced that Bisbee should be our new home. I called Renee on the way to the airport and told her we should move here. Somehow even this started a fight, something about not including her in decisions, which is precisely what I was trying to do on that phone call. After a brief blow-out on the phone, she acquiesced that we could at least talk about it. She loved Bisbee, too. She also just loved to fight as well. So we'd discuss it.

We were at the Death Valley party while Bisbee was still up in the air. Shortly before the party, I got an email from a girl I once knew from a weekend in Portland, Oregon. Her name was Amy Bingaman. We'd hooked up after a show when she was barely twenty-two and I'd horrifically romanced and sodomized her. She was a nice kid. She'd shoot me an email every year or two, once living in New Orleans learning the saxophone, another time while in Wyoming sowing her oats. This email said she'd just been released from a mental institution where she'd been 5150'd—locked up against her will—for several months. She said she'd seen me on a commercial for *The Man Show* in the nuthouse and yelled, "I fucked that guy!" but nobody believed her. Sure you did, Napoleon, sure you did. Since her release she'd been living in Tahoe at her parents' vacation home. She hadn't even spoken to anyone socially since her release. I told her that she should come to this party, that lots of drugs would be involved and that her doctors would warn against it but the invite was open. I never thought of it again.

On the first day of the Year 3 party, I was sitting with people on the front deck of the bar/restaurant when a girl walked up, thick-framed glasses and head shaved completely bald.

"Who is that??? That girl is wicked hot! No, I'm not kidding!"

And then, while I was distracted with cocktails and conversation, she disappeared into the ether. I assumed it was a wayward traveler coming in to piss or ask directions.

Later on, she came back when a group of us were standing in front of the makeshift stage, preparing that evening's show, whatever that might be.

"Stanhope?"

I stared, and after a beat:

"Bingaman???"

You could immediately tell she was straining to be social. Her eyes twitched and her mental illness was apparent if only just to me because she'd warned me. I had just assumed by the shaved head that she'd turned gay since I was with her. Not a shocker. So I put a lesbian friend in charge of watching out for her while I got back to setting up and hosting. But Amy spent a few minutes trying to focus her head before retreating back from people to her pickup truck and tent across the street in the campground. I made special arrangements for her to watch the shows every night from secluded areas and made sure nobody fucked with her. A few nights later she did mushrooms and spent the night speaking in tongues in the motel driveway. Different friends took turns staying with her so she didn't go sideways, or worse, fall prey to the Sausage Extravaganza of dudes that could have taken advantage. At the end of that night she crawled into bed with me and Renee, completely naked and looking like every artist's depiction of an alien and talking like one, too. The three of us fell asleep. Bingaman was gone when we woke up. She left a scrapbook she'd made during her time at the party, including a CD of a song she'd made just before being locked up. It was amazing. Just the fact that she could put it all together out there in the ground zero of nowhere during a party where I couldn't even put together a proper sentence. Her handwriting was unique like Hedberg's. Her song was a heartbreaker. I always look for genius in insanity. Here, it was bubbling.

———

HOME FROM THE PARTY, RENEE HAD JUST THREE WEEKS BEFORE WE had to head out of our L.A. apartment and still hadn't decided on where to go. Knee-jerk decisions usually work out the best. Follow your instincts. We're moving to Bisbee. I bought the house over the phone without having ever been inside of it. If Mother was thrown when I moved across town, she was hobbled by the sudden news that I was moving to some tiny desert town on the Mexican border in Arizona. I told her I'd look for a place for her there once we got set up. Right now, I didn't have time to fuck around with her problems. We sold most of our stuff on eBay and in a yard sale. It felt like the Fall of Saigon. I was still working weekends on roadwork at the same time. Chaos. We followed the moving truck with our stuff to Bisbee with our old friend Father Luke, arriving a few days before the deal closed and we could get our keys. I broke into the house. Fuck 'em. I'm too old to sleep in a car.

19

Bisbee, AZ:
What The Fuck
Just Happened?

RENEE, FATHER LUKE, AND I UNLOADED BOXES AT OUR LEISURE. The sunsets were bonfires with the monsoon clouds starting to come in. The silence of the neighborhood made you feel like every other house had been abandoned. Crickets. The cracking of a beer sounded like fireworks. Within days, that silence would be filled by shouts as the volatile drunken outbursts started again. Renee and I were poison. But now it was a small town, and as much as I loved her and still do, I had no more patience. This was never going to get better. I was determined that I was not carrying this shit to a new life. Renee left in a spat after only two weeks and drove off to Colorado with no warning. She could do that, thinking she could always come back. I thought I was in love with Amy Bingaman. I left for the Montreal Comedy Festival and flew Amy up to join me. I was right. I was in love with her. She moved in with me in Bisbee when we got back. Within the week I got another suicide phone call from a very drunken Mother. Father Luke, Amy, and I drove through the night back to L.A. to find her worse still than before the detox. We packed her necessities and remaining cats into her and my cars and evacuated her to Bisbee. In between, I'd crafted a well-versed email letting Renee know there was no coming back this time, I was in love with someone else. Yes. An email. I'm a cunt. I don't like to fight irreconcilable arguments, especially when I think that I might inspire someone to get violent. So instead of calling or flying out to tell her face to face, I emailed. Like my dad writing me a letter to tell me I was to be thrown out of "the nest." Don't mistake weakness for cowardice, I like to say.

My coherence was unraveling. Five weeks previously I had been leaving L.A. with Renee with great expectations of a new, peaceful life. Now I was living in Arizona with a defrocked mendicant priest-poet, a bald mental patient, and a drunken, suicidal Mother. Peaceful, indeed. I felt knocked out of my shoes like Lorca, only I'd also been the one recklessly driving the car.

I drew a hot bath when we got Mother back to Bisbee. We'd been up all night, through that day and into the next day. I tried to relax. Mother had already begun to nest on my couch. Everyone was slouched in the living room in exhausted silence. As I sunk into the water, Mother croaked without joking, "Do you want me to come in and scrub your back?"

OBVIOUSLY MOTHER HADN'T BEEN COPING WELL IN THE FEW WEEKS I'd been away. But in the whirlwind bullshit of my own life in that short time period, I didn't have the presence of mind to look any deeper than the surface circumstances. In my head, she was just a bad drunk who felt abandoned and didn't have the patience to wait for me to sort shit out. If anything, I begrudged her for the timing. I hadn't even unpacked all my boxes. Part of me felt like she'd gone overboard on purpose to get me to pay attention to her. I understood where she may have felt forgotten, and maybe she really had thought that I wasn't really coming back to get her out of LA. I never knew how much of her desolation she was keeping from me.

If there is hard evidence of a bottoming-out, it was in a printed-out email I found in her stacks of papers in the hoard. It was sent to her friend Jayne roughly a week before we came to rescue her from L.A. to Bisbee. Jayne was the only person I knew of that Mother kept contact with from her days in Florida. She'd visited with Mother in L.A. at the time Renee was scrambling to get our shit out of Playa del Rey and leave for Bisbee. This email was sent a few weeks after Jayne and our departure. Mother was a spelling and grammar nut. If I ever said, "Me and him went to the . . . " she would stop me mid-sentence to correct me, "He and I." I've left uncorrected her spelling, punctuation, and spacing in this email to show what state she was in.

"Monday . . . 9 a.m. LA time . . . checked this before send-
ing . . . 10:45 am now
I'm not dead yet.
I want to be...
Sorry I fucked up your wonderful trip....... I
SOOOOOOOOOO loked forward to it with you!!!
KNOW THAT!!!----------------- ˙
I think I'm detoxing from the vicodin that I have used to
keep me relatively........... and just
barely!!
away from pain.......physically.................
So....
last 48 ? + hours have tried to sleep.............. . . . as soon as I
lie down, my brain goes
into shit
I haven't remembered for years.......painfull shit!! Can't shut
it off!!
And I know that I'm just a spect of sand in the great cosmum
of everything----can't find the right word,,,,,,,,,but know YOu
know what I mean..............
So.................... Doug's new phone number........ in The
way to fucking hot Bisbee------------
is
520–432–XXXX

I'm not dead yet.

NOT!!!

:) :) :)

Wacky Begonia just won't fucking die!

So....

I'm almost feeling OK again.......... may be an illusion........

or temporary................

almost..........

wish you could know how much I have admired you....... and

envied you.....

your wonderful laugh... . . . your appreciation for the littlest

things in life......

yeah.......the fucking leaves changing color!!!! hee hee

hee......... . . . you and

Jeb crack me UP!!!!

So,,, sleep...

remember the wonderful smell, taste, feel of your trip....

those two great guys... . . . give them my whacky love.!!!!!

and don't hate me for fucking it up.

SOOO didn't want to do that.

You are SUCH a GREAT LADY!!!

As drunk as I was yesterday, went over to Patti's apt.......

Doug's old apt...........to check

on her cats.....

they were out of food......dragged my drunk ass over and fed-

,watered,patted them

then asked her for help last night.............

she had the fucking gall to be MAD at me!!

For putting her in a position of not calling

Doug......................!!!!!

She's 32.

7/15/whatever year that makes her 32 this year............

Cancer . . . needy. Sensitive . . . Aren't we ALL???
I'M NOT DEAD YET!!!!
Christ only knows how I wish I were! HEE HEE HEE funny
but serious.

Made a copy of this so if I'm not dead later on, I can read drunken
rambelings.......you gotta
    appreciate THAT!!
    I need a massage.
    My neck hurts. always been a mess.
    Mom told me SO many times how much she wanted a baby
girl.................10 years of
    trying..then finally pregnant.
    then told me SOO many times how she went thru 48 hours
of childbirth......that ripped her
    apart........2 weeks of having her breasts bound.........all he
went thru.....................
    so I've lived trying to please her.......NOT................. so
fucked up trying to figure
    that whole mess out..............needed to be ME, yet be the
good daughter...............
    gonna try to crash now.......
    I think Patti's gone somewhere...................I DO NOT
WANT TO SEE HER AGAIN!!!
    She's just close.................2 doors down.......so have de-
pended on her because of that
    closeness........
    OK!!!! LISTED TO THIS!!! DO IT!!!!!!!!!!!!
    Went to Doug's big deal Los Angeles PREMIER of "The Aris-
tocrats" on wednesday.......took
    Patti.......... so I wouldn't be alone..............what a phony
whore....
    ANYWAY!!!!
    It's a movie about a standard joke.....that all the comics seem
to know backstage..........and

riff to each other...a guy goes into an agent's office and says.I've got a great act for
you................

then talks about a family..............every comic makes up some bizarre

story..................and when the agent finally says...........
"What do you call it?"" .....the guy says....."The Aristocrats"

The point being.... that such a disgusting, sick, fucked up family....as much as each comic

can make it.............shouldn't be called "The Aristocrats"

Doug's at the very end......talking to a baby.......in his own, quiet wonderful way

ON THAT SOFA CHAIR YOU READ ON IN PLAYA..!!!!!!!!!!!!!!!!!!!!!!

.............with the sea breeze............

and after all the more famous comics................the well known ones........

as gross as they could be.......... trying so hard to be the funniest...................hee

hee heee

Doug ended the movie in his quiet, genuine, REAL way.........
talking to the baby........on

that chair!!..........quietly, honestly, genuinely, easily..........
(every Mother's nightmare!!

when you're trying to be a good mother)

.....don't even remember what he said....had to pee at that point and was afraid to go 'cause

I'd miss him.......

but he looked SO HANDSOME, and this mother's pride filled me......... . . . and I saw that chair and

thought of you.......and the sea........and how proud I was of him..................Jayne.....he's so wise....

I'm such a fuck-up. and he and Jeff have been gifts to me...............always have known

that.........
I'M NOT DEAD YET!!!!!!!!!!!!!!!!!!!!!!!!!
You awesome Lady, you...................
so long is my highest esteem.......and......I love your laugh!...................
it's LUSTFULL!!! IT'S WONDERFUL!!!!
OK. Whacky ain't dead yet.
You might be by the time you finish READING this!!!!
laughing in my own sick way..... hee hee
hee
I'M NOT DEAD YET!!!!!"

That email was sent roughly a week before we came to extract her. Mother's trash-talking of Patty was no surprise to me or Patty when I read it to her. Mother talked the same kind of shit about me to Patty when she was drunk. Patty sent me a long email about a year after Mother died. We'd drifted apart a bit around that time and evidently I forgot to tell Patty that she died. She found out randomly on the Internet. Patty was rightfully pissed off. Her email was slightly shorter than this book in detailing her highs and lows with Bonnie (as well as what an egotistical, selfish asshole I was for not telling her). In one excerpt, she said, "Bonnie was a bitter old jaded bitch of a broad. And I loved her for that as much as it drove me crazy. But that woman lit candles for me, cued up CDs of waves and wind instruments and singing dolphins, and put her hands on me and commanded me to let go of my worries and my pain in a way she would not have allowed anyone else to do for her. And does that make her a ridiculous martyr? Yes. But you and I both know, as far as martyrs go, there is no other kind."

If anyone was a "phony" in those dark times at the end of L.A., it was Mother. But Patty saw through her erroneous shittiness and knew the heart underneath. I have no idea what happened with the visit with Jayne, other than that it is obvious from the email that it went poorly and continued downhill after she left. I was frantic and unavailable in the lead-up to the Bisbee move, and then absent until I came back to pick her up off the floor. In my life as a drunk in a world of drunks, I felt no more than a barman picking up an old rummy out of a booth at last call. I didn't give any thought to everything that was underlying her condition. I'd like to say that if I'd known she had been that hopeless and despondent, I would have made more time, put in more effort and caring. With my own personal shitstorm rapid-cycling at that time, I don't know if I honestly could have.

From Tamar's email:

"When Doug had moved to Bisbee, Bonnie called me, terrified, unintelligible, weeping. I went straight to her and found a complete stinking drunk. Gone was the swagger, the wit, the true joy through the lens of pragmatism and dreams come true. It was the first time in my life I really understood alcoholism. I used to joke my mom was an alcoholic because she drinks daily. But her personality doesn't change, and she doesn't threaten suicide. Which Bonnie was. I didn't hesitate to call Doug. He jumped into action, getting her into rehab and moving her to Bisbee so he could be the eagle eye. With that, she was gone."

———————

NOW WITH MOTHER NEWLY IN BISBEE, I WENT OUT TO FIND HER a place of her own with the urgency of FEMA finding emergency housing in a disaster. Amy Bingaman—now nicknamed "Bingo"— wasn't stable enough to deal with Mother. She wasn't stable at all. Her meds worked like a broken clock. Finding Bingo walking down the street in broad daylight, butt-naked save for a painted head-and-neck while talking into a banana, thinking it was a telephone, was comical compared to finding her at night slicing vertical lines into her forehead with scissors. Hearing all of these strange, new developments scattershot and secondhand, my friends in the outside world were, to say the least, "concerned" for me. Renee was rightfully outraged and the phone didn't stop ringing. Neither of us would deny that our relationship was terminal. The idea that I conveniently pulled that trigger at a time when I had greener pastures is something I have to live with. Sometimes doing the right thing and following your heart are opposites. And doing both at the same time can make you feel shittier still.

Father Luke took it all in stride, cranking up his music and driving Mother into fits. When it all got to be too much, which was often, I'd just drink a lot until it got funny again. I had to focus on the humor. It was there in buckets if I scraped the layer of shit off the top.

Needless to say, Mother wanted to live with us and there was no fucking way that was happening. The guest house—a mother-in-law's quarters, as they call them—was now there for Bingo. She needed to stay there. That was a condition of her moving in. Her head was still too fragile, and when she went loopy she needed to have a private place she could lock herself away from people to play keyboards or paint her head. Make field calls on her banana-phone. Cut herself with scissors. She needed a safehouse.

The mental illness had been fun on paper and at the drug-diluted party. Now that everything was fucked-up, foreign, and out of control, I wasn't always sure I could handle it for the long run. Unlike an alcoholic who merely needs to stop drinking to make things close to normal, there is no guarantee that mental illness—schizoaffective, bipolar in Bingo's case—will ever get better. It can get worse. The people who treat it will tell you they really have no idea how it works, that it's mostly trial and error. The ones that don't tell you that are full of shit. That didn't take any arc off of my being in love. I wish my vocabulary held a better word than 'love' for all of the emotions I felt about her, how she made me alive. They don't live in a thesaurus. Still, as bad as she could get, I was afraid that I'd be hurting her by being the guy that was responsible. I wasn't qualified for the job. But nobody else had proven able to do any better.

I found an apartment for Mother across town. It was smaller than her Hollywood apartment but her hoard had been left in L.A. I took another trip back there to pick up important things, keepsakes and the like. She gave us a list. We told her we'd put the rest in storage. Most of it went in the dumpster, which we left overflowing. It wouldn't make a difference. Mother had two Dollar Stores and two thrift stores nearby to start back from scratch. And her new apartment didn't have any stairs so she didn't have to factor in her feeble lungs. She could back her station wagon right up to the door and unload.

The Man Show money was pretty much gone. I got paid around $400,000 over the roughly two years it aired. Sounds like a lot. Take out taxes, management, agent, lawyer, and business manager—basically an accountant who takes care of all your bills and tax bullshit—and that means that after 30K for a down payment on a house, I was close back to being broke. So much so that I actually got fired by that accountant for not making *Man Show* money anymore. They work on a percentage. I understand. But still, it felt like getting 86'd from your barber for going bald.

We weren't totally broke but I was preparing for it. We did what we called "Free Shopping," where I would call all the 800 numbers on the groceries in the cupboard to complain. I'd done this a lot over the years by writing fantastical complaint letters to companies just to see if they'd respond. They were outlandish and were mostly just for entertainment purposes, to post on my Web site. Now it was to actually get free food or sundry bullshit. Bingo was still in and out of the depths of crazy and was highly amused by extreme silliness so I would make all the calls like prank calls. I can't do characters so I did them all like the only goofy voice I could: Sol Rosenberg from the Jerky Boys. If you don't know who that is, Google it and come back when you know this voice.

"Yes. Hello? Thank you, then. Oh yes, I'm calling about your Rembrandt toothpaste. Yes? Thank you. I've been using it ever since back when I was asked to leave parochial school. I love it. I simply love it. But I just bought a tube from the local mercantile and it tasted all funny. I don't know what's wrong with it."

"What do you mean by 'It tasted funny'?"

"You know. It was stingy. It tasted almost tangential like it might have been left in the sun. You have to understand that I'm on a limited budget!"

The complaints were absurd but it made Bingo laugh and customer service would only try to pretend to understand for so long before relenting and sending you coupons for free product. They don't give a shit. They work in a call center and are happy enough that you're not yelling at them. After two hours of doing this for the first time, we ended up collecting about $250 worth of free shit. Keep in mind that a lot of the coupons require the checkout person to fill in minutiae with a pen. We filled two carts full on that first 250 dollars, and it took us almost 45 minutes to check out. The checkout lane spilled into the aisle behind us until they got a second checker to handle the overflow. Stares of hatred burned into the backs of our heads. Not a good way to ingratiate yourselves to the natives.

"Jesus, Douglas! We're trying to fit into a new town and this is what you do???"

Still, we were hooked on our new scam, mostly for the entertainment value of making the calls. Mother would sit in on a lot of them, just like watching me pitch in the old phone room days. We soon developed a system that made it easier and more profitable. Once I knew what different codes and dates on the packaging that customer service would ask for, we no longer needed to even have the product on our shelf. I could simply go to the grocery store, write it all down from the largest size of that product on the shelf along with the toll free number, and we'd get even bigger shit for free without ever having to buy it in the first place.

Free coupons would roll in like checks from our days of selling pens. Mother and Bingo would roar at the calls loud enough that they'd have to leave the room to not queer the deal. Without them as an audience, I probably would have never kept doing it. I jacked up Mother to start making calls herself. There aren't any real jobs in Bisbee for skilled people, much less for someone in her condition. Even if she were physically able at this point, the last thing a hippie town needs is another massage therapist. She'd been fired by the Korean massage joint in L.A. when "some cocksucker" complained about her incessant cough. She'd never cut it in this town of yoga and chakra healing. She could at least make a few bogus phone calls during the day to help offset living costs. She didn't even have to make them funny or affect the Sol Rosenberg voice. She just had to complain—nicely—three times a day and she'd have no grocery bills. If there was anything that Mother was skilled in, it was complaining. But she wouldn't do it. She was afraid she'd get in "trouble."

"You've always got away with this kinda shit. I know that I'd get into trouble. I'm different than you."

Ma. You're not going to get into "trouble" just for making a complaint. Do it fifteen minutes a day and almost never spend a dime on groceries. Times are precarious. There are four of us and I'm the only one with a job. How hard can it be? It was the easiest way I could find for Mother to contribute to the collective without having to expend any real energy. Still, Mother wouldn't even put in that much. I know a bunch of you will after reading this. Email me when you've paid for this book and more from that fun little pastime. Or just send me free coupons after you've stolen this book off the Internet. Either way, honor amongst thieves.

———

BINGO AND I WENT ON THE ROAD FOR MOST OF THAT FALL AND didn't get back until near Thanksgiving of 2005. Thanksgiving that year would mark twenty-five years since I'd first gotten drunk and smoked cigarettes behind Tatnuck School. So I decided that I'd quit both for the thirty days in between then and Christmas. Bingo hated to see me smoking especially considering the state into which Mother was deteriorating. On the fifteenth day of my "detox" and after a lot of broken inanimate objects, we figured we'd do some mushrooms. By mid-trip, not only was I drinking and smoking again but even Bingo had started smoking as well.

We still had plenty of mushrooms, and on Christmas Eve we convinced Mother that she should trip with us. This was a terrible idea for a woman with this much emotional baggage, but since she was still drinking—as were we—we overlooked the possible hazards. Unlike cocaine, Mother didn't take well to psilocybin. She just laid on our couch with her eyes closed, moaning and coughing and asking how long before it would be over. I went into a podunk security guard character, talking like Billy Bob Thornton's character in *Sling Blade*, who kept having to go outside with a flashlight to "check the perimeters." I never left character, and it kept Bingo in hysterics. Never try to explain why something nonsensical was funny while you were tripping. It just was. At some point, Mother came out of her half-coma and erupted with "I wanna get laid." She wasn't meaning presently, just in general. Again, sometime in life. She hadn't been with a man since Michael, maybe ten years or more. She just blurted it out, and then fell silent and wheezing again. But this declaration, for us on mushrooms, was very off-putting, lingering like a smell. It put the "ill" in "buzzkill." I went out to check the perimeter.

Father Luke was with us and he was a clean and sober guy, the kind that always seems to be tripping harder than you, regardless. Once Mother was over the hump and could move, we had Father Luke drive us around. This had become a regular pastime for us. Bisbee is a tripper's paradise even in the boring residential area where we live. All the houses are different, built mostly in the early 1900s as miners' shacks, and then further built upon. On mushrooms at night, under dim streetlights, they are amazing, like you've been shrunken down and put into the village of an elaborate toy train set. There's generally zero activity at night and Father Luke would drive us all over down these weird back alleys, dirt roads, and occasionally right through the police station parking lot just to scare the shit out of us. Tonight we dressed both Mother and Bingo in top hats, poured drinks to go, and took to the streets on a mushroom/booze-cruise of Bisbee. I played "Mother" from Pink Floyd's *The Wall* on the CD player. It was still religion to me from my first trip, picking blotter acid out of my own hurl. I could always find parallels with the movie in the years since, mostly the internal, emotional deadening of a longtime boozer. Oftentimes after a particularly hard bit on a drunken late show that queered the audience, I'd take a moment in the stunned silence or nervous titters before belting out the line from "In The Flesh"—"So ya/thought ya/might like to/go to the show" or just mutter "Is this not what you expected to see?"

The song "Mother" obviously struck close to home, and I thought Mother hearing it for the first time on our first psychedelic trip together would be a bonding moment. Mother just talked over it or told us to turn it down. I guess the lyrics are about an oppressive, cloistering mother but that's not what it meant to me. Either way, the sentiment was lost.

We wound up at St. Elmo's, a bar in Old Bisbee, and took a table in the back. After a few cocktails, Mother got loose and fun, and after a couple more she got downright maudlin. A strong mushroom trip can bring you straight down into melancholy. Mother, decked out in Father Luke's top hat and my long wool overcoat, had moved into the "When I die . . . " phase of conversation. She told Bingo, with a tremble in her mumbled voice:

"Before I go, I need to show you . . . the right way to cheap wrap and ship."

Nobody knew what the fuck she was talking about until we realized she was referring to the way she ships the merchandise she handled from my Web site orders. She said it with all the seriousness of an elderly Italian grandmother about to pass down the secret family recipe for the marinara. After a beat of looking at each other confused, we all burst into rolling, head-on-the-table laughter that didn't stop.

"Why is that funny??? There's a certain way to do it!" which brought even more laughs. When I was finally able to form words, I tried to explain that it was funny that she thought that that was all she'd gleaned from her life to pass on to her next of kin. This made her erupt into more tears, mostly because of the way I'd said it. It came out wrong. Maybe she really felt that was all she had to pass on from sixty years of living. Cheap and efficient forms of mailing

DVDs and t-shirts, rife with cat hair and nicotine. That was the only contribution she could hold on to that she felt she was making. And we shit on her just as she was about to let us in on it. I was hoping that mushrooms would give her some gravely needed insight, some higher perception of herself, or allow her to come to terms with some of her demons. I wasn't trying to divine how to cut corners at the post office.

––––––––

THIS NIGHT KICKED OFF ANOTHER TWO-WEEK BINGE PERIOD FOR Mother of heavy drinking and slurred, desperate, ending-it-all phone calls. It was her loneliness, her fear, her pain, and declining health. It was hard for me to accept that, first off, Mother was just a really shitty drunk. Not that all of her other problems weren't very real. It's just that alcohol seemed to exasperate them where, for me, alcohol hid my problems very well. I'm all for drinking away your problems but she was drinking them to front row center. I told her that. It was an intervention of one. There was no one else to fill the circle. She knew what to do about it, and wasn't doing anything but drinking and stewing in self-pity. I'd grown up listening to all of that AA dogma and watched her coach newcomers into sobriety my whole life, even when she was only vaguely involved herself. As much as I might find AA to be bullshit, she still believed in it. She'd made it work for her for twenty-some years. I asked her what she'd tell some-one who called her for help in a similar situation. She knew exactly what she'd say. This wasn't new territory for her. Get off your ass and follow your own advice. I can't be your constant middle-of-the-night savior from suicide. I'm already trying to figure out how to deal with mental illness, being a homeowner, and still be on the road most of the time. In January of 2006, Mother went back to AA, sobered up, and stayed that way until the night that she checked out for good.

Except for my short foray into AA in Las Vegas at nineteen, I have never made any serious attempt to quit drinking. Like anyone, I have those mornings where you question yourself but that's always short-lived. I enjoy drinking. I enjoy being in bars. Airport bars, and to a lesser extent, hotel bars are my favorite. There are no regulars generally in airport bars and everyone is there for a limited time only. You can be anyone you want to be and never have to live up to it down the road. If the guy next to you is a bore, you know he'll be gone soon. If you're shit-eyed and make an asshole of yourself, you'll probably never see those people again anyway. The only times I have stopped drinking for any length of time more than a couple days are on my attempts to quit smoking. I have to. Three cocktails is about the limit before I reach for a pack, with "Fuck it, you're gonna die of something!" dribbling out of the corner of my defeated mouth.

I made one of those many attempts early on after I moved to Los Angeles. Hide in, lock the door, don't drink, and don't have cigarettes anywhere near you. I don't know how long that one lasted. But I do know that I got a phone call shortly into my self-imposed rehab. It was from a comedian I knew peripherally. He said that he'd heard I was trying to kick alcohol and wanted to help. I explained that I was just trying to quit smoking and that, in the meantime, booze was just an ancillary habit that had to be shelved in the process. He didn't listen or didn't want to hear. He told me about his years in AA and that all I needed to do was reach out and he would be there for me. Then he started to tell me all the famous comedians he'd sponsored and help sober up. So much for the "Anonymous" part. But, still, he sounded just like an *agent*. He sounded just like the network execs who would try to woo me. He was *pitching* me. He dropped that he'd sponsored Bill Hicks like it was a movie credit. I didn't know how to react. I didn't know if that's just how everything worked in L.A. I hung up feeling like I'd just gotten an offer for a development deal from Alcoholics Anonymous.

Like church or witchcraft, AA is bullshit but sometimes bullshit works for people. It worked for my Mother for decades. Perhaps burning money in a voodoo seance would have worked as well. I've been outspokenly antagonistic towards AA in my adult life, on- and offstage. Like any child who grew up with a strict religious upbringing and never questioned it until they became older, I felt duped by it later in life. I believed everything that Mother was buying in those early years in AA. Looking into it as an adult with a reasoned head, it's quite obvious that it's a pile of malarkey. Both statistically and anecdotally, it has no more success rate than quitting on your own. Its doctrine is misleading, erroneous, and sometimes outright false to the point that it can be dangerous. But, like Jesus, it might keep a few gunmen out of a watchtower.

AA had worked for Mother, and on some levels I'd have to say it probably worked for me. There is no way to tell how much of my stand-up career was influenced and inspired by sitting in the back of those meetings at the edge of my seat listening to those provoc-ative, tragic chronicles of people at their lowest and still managing to get laughs and acceptance. As my own act turned towards more dark storytelling, I could imagine those same stories coming out in a circle of folding chairs in the basement of a church as somebody's "bottoming-out." To me, those stories aren't the bottom. They are the wealth. As a kid, I'd see people *kill* in an AA meeting and they knew it. They romanticized their lowest points, and they did it by design. The asterisk at the end about being grateful to the program for never having to revisit those times rang hollow. This isn't to say those people should not have quit drinking. Mother certainly sucked at it. But it's worked for me this far.

I remember when I used to drive without insurance in my early, flat broke days. Eventually, I was pulled over and cited for it. I re-member doing the math on the fine versus the cost of having insur-ance all those years. I made out like a bandit just paying the ticket. I feel that way about drinking now at this age. Should my liver ex-plode in the morning and I bleed out from yellowed eyes, I still come out well ahead for the good times I had. And I don't have to wrap my stories up in some disingenuous backpedaling of coerced remorse.

———

MOTHER WAS "SOBER" NOW, MEANING THAT SHE NO LONGER DRANK alcohol. What I hadn't known about is that she had developed a healthy Vicodin addiction, the roots of which are untraceable, possibly going as far back as Florida. Her back pain was constant, real and rapidly getting worse. But she was doing nothing to help treat the source of the pain. Just trying to get more Vicodin. The amount of pills she was taking was far more than even lenient Bisbee doctors were willing to prescribe, and she had no luck finding them across the border. Naco, Mexico, a few miles away, is ripe with Xanax and Viagra but shit for painkillers. She took to asking me to jack up my friends any time they'd visit. She knew most of them dabbled in this or that but I explained that painkillers were never a party drug people had around. That's like saying, "You do acid? Can you get me Lipitor?" When she wouldn't take my word for it she'd call them herself.

One friend who actually was a walking pharmacy of pills stayed at our house once while we were on the road and Mother sniffed her out. Our friend told Mother that she had some painkillers and would gladly drop some by her place. Most people would have just said thank you. Mother took advantage by having her stop by three different stores on her way with a long list of her shopping needs. You know, since she was coming anyway. She had been manipulative her whole life but now she didn't even try to be cute or cunning. She acted like things were owed to her. I had a hard time tolerating it. In 2007, I was gone for nearly forty weeks. She had to take care of herself. She needed to figure out how to get on to some kind of public assistance. Her body was failing her in every which way, not least her lungs. She coughed and wheezed like Ratso Rizzo in *Midnight Cowboy* and still smoked. It couldn't be my problem anymore. And it certainly couldn't be Bingo's.

The ironclad rule was that Mother was not to bother Bingo when I was out of town. Bingo is as malleable as Play-Do and is incapable of saying no even when her insides are screaming it. I could only imagine how badly Mother would abuse that weakness. Bingo was on her own roller coaster. Sometimes her meds worked and sometimes they didn't. If she was bad, she wouldn't come on the road. We wouldn't risk her having to be locked up in some fetid asylum in Rock Island, Illinois or Wilkes-Barre, Pennsylvania. If she spun out in Bisbee, we had people who could take care of her, and if she got locked up again it would be close to home. And it was only a matter of time.

I'd left Bingo home at one point when her meds were sketchy. Father Luke was gone by now and Bingo was left alone. I came home from the road to find she'd "redecorated" the house. Turns out she had gone into a protracted manic state and spent two days driving around town removing road signs of everything from mile markers, street signs, animal control, even the sign for the local airport. Now she'd covered every wall in our house with them.

I walked into the house and my jaw dropped with my bags. She was incandescent with delight. I scrambled like a cartoon to close all the blinds, horrified that the neighbors or the mailman might see or had already seen this. We already stood out as suspicious in this colorless neighborhood. Bingo looked like she was going to cry. In fact, I'm sure she did cry.

"You don't like it?" she asked like I'd opened a Christmas present, then thrown it directly into the trash in front of her.

I tried faux-calmly to explain to her this was a major felony. I was like Darrin from *Bewitched!* chastising Samantha for turning someone into a pygmy goat. There were thirty-four signs in total! I couldn't believe there were any signs even left in town. Some of them were huge. How the fuck she even managed to get them down and then up on the wall by herself can only be attributed to what was once called "retard strength." The illegality of it all had never dawned on her. She just thought she was doing something nice for me and thought I hated it. I fucking loved it, I was awed by it but we had to get these things back before she was put in jail, for fuck's sake. A missing stop sign could equal a manslaughter charge. "We're trying to fit into a new town and this is what you do?" as Mother had said back in Paxton. I spent the night taking them off the wall and loading them into the back of her pickup truck. In the predawn hours, I went out and left them on a dirt road that I knew Border Patrol used regularly and would find them. I'd considered just going to the cops and being honest, but this was before I knew Bisbee cops were actual people with names. I only knew L.A. cops smashing my wife's face in and wasn't quite comfortable that they'd be at all understanding in Bisbee. Border Patrol must have turned them over because every one of them was back up within days. I hope I've more than made up for any costs incurred through charitable contributions around town in the years since. Bingo is well-medicated now but back then, every day was an adventure, with Benny Hill's "Yakety Sax" theme song constantly playing in my head as I cleaned up in her wake. We assumed that another lockup in the mental ward was a possibility, if not a probability, but we both preferred that than to try leaving her in the hands of Mother.

I WAS ABOUT TO GO ONSTAGE IN COLUMBUS, OH WHEN I GOT THE call from Bingo from the back of an ambulance in Bisbee. She'd gone to the hospital when her mind started slipping hard. They were locking her up in Benson, about fifty miles away. They decided that she needed to come off one med while going on another—always a dangerous time—and in the interim they felt it safest to keep her confined and supervised. She was trying not to be afraid. But her problem was that they wouldn't allow her first to go home to get any clothes or necessary items. She was taken immediately by ambulance in nothing but shorts and a tank top for an indefinite stay. They'd probably take away her phone so she didn't know how she could get ahold of me when she was admitted. She didn't know the name of the place they were taking her. She didn't even have shoes. The fact that she'd gone to the hospital without shoes in the first place surprised nobody. It was amazing she wore anything at all. I took all this from the green room to the stage. It wasn't a very good show.

Greg Chaille, my tour manager, and I got into Louisville frantic the next day and immediately hit the thrift store to get clothes to FedEx to her. We walked into Goodwill, stopped, and looked around for a second.

"Okay, what exactly does she need?"

"Everything. She has nothing. She doesn't even have shoes."

And then our eyes locked as slow, evil grins crept up our faces realizing she was going to have to wear whatever clothing we sent.

We both grabbed carts and peeled off in opposite directions, grabbing everything and anything so long as it was completely ridiculous. Plus-size muumuus. Sequined ball gown. Acid wash denim vest. One-piece old lady swimsuit. Graduation hat. Rubber bathing cap with plastic flower. Winter parka.

Chaille and I were literally running through the store with separate carts like it was Black Friday. We were so giddy that we almost forgot the shoes. I had no idea what size she was but that was no issue. We found a pair of oversized novelty bedroom slippers designed to look like big cartoon sneakers, each one half the size of a bed pillow. We nearly had to stand on top of the huge shipping box to duct-tape it shut.

The Southeastern Arizona Psychiatric Health Facility was a small place and not part of any hospital. It was just a cinderblock box there in the middle of nowhere for the handful of crazies it could hold, maybe 15-20 maximum. I never saw the place. Bingo was out in a week or so before I could get off tour. But the image of her stomping around in a prom dress and giant Charlie Brown slippers trying to tell people she was no longer crazy kept us pissing ourselves on the road.

Bingo's mother Gay came down to take care of her at the house until I could get back from the road. Gay and her husband Ron are lovely people. They are retired professionals who live in Northern California where Ron—pronounced "Rhaaaaan" in Gay's thick Midwestern accent when she's yelling from across the room—runs his own hydroelectric power off a stream that goes through their yard. It powers their whole house, with excess left to sell back to the electric company. Clever fucker, this guy. He had to create a corporation for the enterprise and asked us for a name for the company. If it isn't obvious to you, it was to me. Gay Power. If you really love your wife and want to honor her, put that sign loud and proud in front of your house. Oh, did they laugh. But they never used the name. It's only funny if you actually do it.

In Bisbee, Bingo was full-tilt, self-destructive, out of her mind. It was like having a newborn where you are up and down all night. Only you aren't changing diapers. This is a newborn that believed it had invented its own surroundings, whose mission was to die and who had access to the knife drawer. You don't get a lot of sleep with that baby. In Bingo's few lucid periods, Gay had the pleasure of meeting Mother, who was evidently quite forthcoming with her tales of jerking off her cats. I guess she had to piss on her territory of being "not your average Mother." Gay actually is your average mother, Mother. You can relax. I don't know if Gay were more scared of her daughter's well-being or of Mother. Gay would be too polite to say.

Bingo was still in bad shape when her mother and I swapped out duties. I didn't know how to deal with it. I can deal with the crazy Bingo that was covering her entire bald head in blue Elmer's glitter-glue and then sitting alone in the balcony to watch my show like she was some character out The Fifth Element. But this was psychotic, depths-of-hell loss of sanity—self-harming, either by her own hand or loss of equilibrium. She fell onto the hardwood coffee table once squarely on her chin. The swelling made her look like Jay Leno. Until this bruising set in; then we called her Abraham Lincoln for a week. I couldn't sleep because she'd wake up like a stumbling drunk and fall into every sharp edge in the house. My house had an old wall heater that was directly between where she slept and the bathroom. She was so unstable that I thought she'd fall into it and brand herself. The closest I'd ever come to dealing with mental illness was trying to talk someone out of a bad trip. Bingo's mental illness, from what I know, is very similar. And if you've had one, rarely can someone talk you down. You just have to know it's a possibility going in, and if it happens, try like fuck to ride it out.

20

My Best Friend, Again

MOTHER'S DECLINING HEALTH WAS SPEEDING UP AS WELL. HER back problems were her lead complaint, but in the meantime she'd had to have a stent put in an artery, her blood pressure was fucked, she'd been diagnosed with osteoporosis and put on oxygen for either emphysema or COPD, which, so far as I know, are the same fucking thing. Autism or Asperger's, your kid still isn't in the debate club. She tried her best to quit smoking but even after being put on oxygen she failed. I've smoked for thirty-five years at this point. I am not going to say, "But if I ever got to that point, I'd quit!" I don't know that. But I hope like fuck I'd never continue to be the creator of my own demise and ask people to pick up the slack for me. The way an intervention is supposed to work is that those close to the person afflicted—or afflicting themselves—are told that if they don't change, they will be written off. It's too much heartache for the people involved. I didn't do that with Mother. Meaning, I didn't tell her. I just stopped trying to intervene. Quietly, I had to write her off.

From what I remember—which would be another appropriate title for this book if I hadn't had the good favor of friends who could fill in so many blanks—the write-off came when I got a call on vacation in Costa Rica that Mother had been life-flighted from Bisbee to Tucson. It had happened twice, this was her second time. We dropped everything and went directly to the airport in Liberia, Costa Rica. We finagled the most fucked-up flight home possible.

From Liberia, Costa Rica we flew to Miami and then, after customs, caught a flight to Dallas. DFW is such a stupid fucking airport unless you were brought up with the alphabet the same way their tram works—A-C-E-D-B. We were told to go from A gates to B gates, meaning we were stuck on the tram for its entire run around the airport. Fuck me and fuck Texas. We missed our flight like they must have missed Sesame Street. Instead, we got a flight to Vegas where we slept for three hours before going on to Phoenix and Tucson. Twenty-eight hours through six cities after leaving Costa Rica, I could only assume Mother was long since dead.

We went straight to Tucson Medical Center. Mother had a male nurse named Graham who immediately recognized me. I assumed it was because Mother had forced one of my DVDs upon him. Turns out he was also a fledgling comedian in the area. That gave me some sense of comfort. Comedians are better than all other people. That is fact. When we got in to see Mother she had a wide tube down her gullet and into her lungs, evidently sucking out gunk that was preventing her from breathing. Seems that when your lungs are that fucked, it doesn't take much of a cold to send you from wheezing to drowning in your own phlegm.

I don't like hospitals. I get queasy from all things medical. I didn't like to see Mother with a hose jammed down her throat. She was awake, and that made it worse. I talked to her with questions that only required yes or no answers as she obviously couldn't talk outside of nodding. I tried to keep it light. I reminded her that, if nothing else, she got a free helicopter ride. She had no recollection of it. I didn't have much else to say. I didn't want to be there. I told her about our Phileas Fogg travel odyssey and said we had to leave, we had to get home to fall down. I'd been flying so long my sunburn had already peeled off. She picked up her pen and paper she'd been using to communicate with the staff. She wrote down one word. "Vicodin!" was all it said.

I said with incredulous sarcasm, "What the fuck? Whattya want me to put it in your fucking IV?!!?"

She nodded a sincere and pleading yes.

I rolled my eyes, told her I loved her with only frustrated surrender in my eyes, and walked out. This wasn't something she caught from someone else's sneeze nor had it just creeped up on her. Before she'd even left Florida, she'd taken one of those tests where you blow into a machine to gauge your lung capacity. It told her she had the lungs of a 128-year-old. She thought it was kinda funny at the time. And this is how you wind up. I had looked at her in that hospital room, knowing that this was all caused by her inability to stop smoking cigarettes and that made me angry. And that made me want a cigarette. So I gave up and went out to smoke angry cigarettes all the way back to Bisbee.

When I say that I wrote Mother off, I don't mean that I cut off contact or deprived her of any financial support. I was still with her and helped out all I could. The write-off came in that I knew that I could no longer invest myself emotionally in trying to get her to help herself. Her time was now obviously limited and she was doing nothing in the way of slowing that down. I wasn't going to spend the rest of it harping on her. It was too late for any of that to help, even if she'd chosen to make the effort. I'd just try my best to enjoy her and make her comfortable while she was here.

Mother rarely left the house after she was discharged by the hospital although she did continue to smoke despite being on oxygen now. She was insistent that she was still able and wanted to be in charge of shipping my merchandise. It was the only thing left that gave her a sense of purpose. That came to an end when I started getting emails from people saying that they'd ordered things weeks ago and it still hadn't arrived. I'd ask Mother about it and she'd get irritated.

"Tell em to fuck off! It's like TV commercials always said—allow 6–8 weeks for shipping!"

That was the 1970s, Mother. You can't do that shit anymore. You may as well ship things C.O.D. on top of it. She was relieved of her duty. She cried and said she felt like she was being fired. That was her one job that made her feel like she was contributing. I assured her that I was only concerned with her health. God knows what a dick I looked like having my mother drag packages along with an oxygen tank into the post office. It was time for someone else to "cheap wrap and ship."

HER DEMISE CAME RAPIDLY. SHE'D KEPT DETAILED CALENDARS OR Day-at-a-Glance books going all the way back to the 1980s. While ones from several years earlier were dotted with auditions and classes, the last year were basically a cryptic chronicling of her downward spiral. Some entries just said "hot" or "cold" for the weather. Other entries read "bowels. diarrhea am & aft. back bad" or "can finally stand on my own." The rest were mostly doctor's appointments and oxygen deliveries. And always notations of when I was leaving town, when I had called, and when I was coming home.

I'd try to visit with her but I usually couldn't last more than a few minutes. The less mobile she became, the more vulgar her apartment became, but her hoarder instincts wouldn't allow me to touch anything. Spiderwebs climbed over stacks of old mail. Packaged food that had long since expired wasn't allowed to be thrown away. Soon she was using bedpans and missing the target more often than not. It was a horrible way to see her exist, especially in that it was completely unnecessary. Aside from dishes, she wouldn't let me clean up anything. She was afraid I'd throw things away. She was set in her ways and stuck in her landfill. Any casual suggestion to better her conditions just made her defensive and led to arguments. I had to let it be.

I flew my brother and his two kids out that summer of 2008 to see her for the last time. We went to an old seventies-style steakhouse in nearby Palominos, similar to so many she'd worked in when we were kids. Her only steps were labored from the car to a wheelchair. These kids didn't know it would be their last time with "Grannie B," but if they'd been any older, they would have figured it out on their own.

She was diagnosed terminal. She was placed under hospice care; caretakers would come by the apartment. When Jeff and I were kids, Mother loved to point out anyone in any state of disrepair—fat, stooped, or generally fucked—and say, "Jesus. If I ever get like that, kill me!" Now she was far worse than those people but I didn't bring it up.

I had to leave to do a five-week tour of the UK. I was told that she had a 50/50 chance of being alive when I got back. Mother and I were more easy with comedy than with the sentimental and I don't cancel gigs. Instead of some long heart-to-heart, I told her to try to stay alive until I got home. She said that she would. I told her I'd call her on speakerphone live from stage during every show to play "Mother, Are you Dead Yet?" knowing that if she were alive, she'd answer with the favorite line from our old Monty Python days of "I'm not dead yet!" Otherwise, a caregiver or paramedic might answer with bad news. Mother loved the idea. Vicariously, she'd get to be on stage every night, and there was gambling involved. Mostly, she would know I loved her. I gave her a SkyMall catalog and I encouraged her to buy as much shit on her credit card as she could. If you're gonna die, why would you die with $10,000 worth of Visa credit wide open? There's not going to be any estate that they can come after unless they want it paid off in old cats or expired Hormel Compleats meals.

I did that for most of the tour, explaining the story to the audience, and that we'd either get Mother on the phone or maybe the show is about to go sideways. If there is anywhere you want to find out someone you love is dead, it's onstage. Being on stage is like being in a fistfight. You never stop and say "I gotta take a shit" or get melancholy about an old girlfriend. I did have to stop a show once in Aberdeen, Scotland to take a shit but that was bad sashimi. But onstage, I was sure I could handle bad news just through sheer adrenaline. The audiences didn't seem to grasp that I was telling the truth and dealing with this in the best way I knew how. They were waiting for the payoff of the bit. There was no bit. I'd have Brian Hennigan predial so I would just have to hit send, still not knowing how to dial international. Mother would answer with her best faux British accent, saying "I'm Not Dead Yet!" and then I'd go on to ask her what she bought on her Visa. It generally went nowhere so far as comedy purposes, and almost always became a speed bump in the show. People were waiting for the punch line. There wasn't one. By the time I got to London, I was too afraid of critics so I cut Mother from the act. I still harbor some inner resentment towards the entire UK for that, even though it was me cowering to a handful of cunts. Mother thought she hadn't been funny enough. It wasn't you, Ma. Sometimes, Mother, it really is the audience.

She was alive when I got home. I kinda knew she would be and she said that she did, too. We high-fived. We knew it wasn't going to be much longer no matter how it ended. I knew she was in agony with shallow, gurgling breaths and there was nothing I could do about it. Now it was just a matter of waiting. It was a matter of whether she goes naturally before she had the chance to do it herself. Her history of suicide attempts or threats ranged from age fourteen into her drinking days in L.A. and into Bisbee, and were rooted in depression. But in between those, she had always made clear, unemotional comments that she'd kill herself before she'd ever live in any terminal state. In 2004, I released a DVD that included a bit about Mother's eventual suicide, imagining her going out as a suicide bomber. The premise was built on "when" Mother kills herself, not "if." She'd always been aware and open to the possibility that this day might come. In her present state, I'd be foolish to think she wasn't considering the option.

———————

OUTSIDE MY HOUSE WAS A CLUSTERFUCK OF CONSTRUCTION WHEN I got back from the UK. Bingo had decided to "surprise" me while I was away for the five weeks by having a six-foot corrugated metal fence built around the entire four lots to the tune of $17,000. She'd got a puppy who was burrowing under the old 3-foot picket fence and decided, rather than train the fucking dog, we needed a new fence with a underground foundation. Surprise! They'd originally built it in even more garishly off-setting 8- and 10-foot slabs of rusted metal until, after a complaint, the building inspector came and made it be cut down to 6 feet, citing city codes. Nobody here has a house that is up to code. I don't know how to impart to you how difficult it is in Bisbee to have someone complain that *your* house is too weird. But they did it. The mailman came by when I'd just pulled in and asked me if I was trying to start my own Third World country. I'd just got back home and was thinking the same thing. I didn't try to explain because I didn't know either. I had worse problems to deal with.

Bingo's parents showed up to visit. They're wonderful people who give you hope that not every gated-community person is a fuck-head. Maybe they are just as afraid of juvenile delinquents as I am, since I was one. They didn't know what they were walking into. In the best of times, coming home from a tour like that is where the work really begins. There are bills to pay, paperwork, and getting all your shit back together. Unpack, repack. Call people back. Pet your pets. Reconnect. Do laundry. Now there's construction in the yard, in-laws, and your mother who is about to die. How do you handle it all? Cocktails, goddamnit! And quick! No time to try to reinvent the wheel.

When I got the call from Mother's caregiver that I "should come over to talk," I'd already run it over in my mind so often that I was numb. I went over to her place like a plumber going to work. Mother's timing was perfect in that the in-laws were already planning on leaving that night. Once I determined that Mother wasn't fucking around and would be at the house at any moment, I told the construction people to take a long weekend.

Bingo's parents were now informed that Mother was on her way over to die. They were not weaned into this information. They were not told to "sit down, we need to talk." There was no time for that. We told them flat out and they took it in stride. They'd already planned to be taking off that night but now even offered to stay around and help. They were more than courteous, or possibly they didn't want to be seen as fleeing a sinking ship. Either way, I knew the last thing Mother wanted while she was at her gurgling worst was trying to make pleasant with the in-laws she barely knew. So I frog-marched Bingo into the kitchen. No time for indirect hinting or insinuation. The parents had to be told to be on their way. I am sure that secretly they were very relieved to hear this though they'd never admit it.

Nevertheless, the Bingaman's sense of manners and awkward decency meant that there was going to be a happy hour cocktail before they shoved off, the drinks being in consideration of us as they don't normally imbibe. Mrs. Bingaman made some lovely amaretto-based concoction that we all stood around and sipped like we were waiting for Santa Claus, everyone ignoring the iron-lunged elephant in the room.

———

THE IN-LAWS LEAVING MADE EVERYONE WHEEZE A SIGH OF RELIEF. Bingo, Mother, and I could rise to the occasion so long as we didn't have to put on a fake face. I honestly love Ron and Gay but I wouldn't have wanted to be there when they had to tell their daughters why they were getting their first period. This wasn't a time for that kind of intimacy either. From that point Thursday evening until Saturday night, the house was largely peaceful. Mother would doze off now in mid-sentences and then wake up later with some smart-fuck remark as though she'd been listening to our conversation the whole time before drifting back into a morphine haze. She'd still be surly with Betty when she made her rounds. She'd spring to lucidity in order to excoriate whatever guests were on *Maury Povich* or whatever nonsense TV she'd have on, as though that was of paramount concern. Maybe it was. Those people are morons and maybe Mother felt it needed to be pointed it out one last time.

And the rest of the email from Tamar:

One day, I emailed Doug to tell him how much I enjoyed his book about trapping pedophiles online (which Bonnie had sent me after I sent her the awards from Memphis Bound and Gagged for her new apartment in Bisbee). Doug replied, adding, "Mother would like to hear from you. She's not doing so well."

I got on the phone and she said simply, "I'm dying. But don't worry about it. How are you?" I told her about my third film and how it was being considered for a film festival in Tucson. If it gets in, I told her, how about I visit? She was excited. Before we hung up, she said, "I'll wait for ya."

Wait! She also asked me if I had any narcotics. I laughed it off nervously, but true to Bonnie form, she was serious. I stammered I might have two or three from a car accident years before somewhere in the medicine cabinet. "Send them to me," she said. When I tried to argue, she told me she had terrible back pain and because of the rehab she couldn't get any good prescriptions and why the fuck not, she's dying after all. I sent the three measly pills in the back of my medicine cabinet the next day.

A month later I called to say the festival had accepted the film and I was coming out. "Great!" She said. "I'll wait for ya." I ask if the pills helped. No, she said, they were too old. I apologized.

I call her from Tucson to make plans to come down the next day. She says she's just moved into Doug's house, but doesn't say why exactly. I tell her I'll be there midday. She responds with a cheery, "I'm waiting for ya!"

I arrive, wholly unprepared for the hospital bed in the middle of Doug's living room, the oxygen tank hissing into the double set of nose tubes she's wearing, the tiny, skinny woman who jokes that I wasn't ready to see this, but here she is, and "look at how my fake boobs are still huge! That shit don't shrink when you're sick!"

She still has two or three cats but one of them is hiding under the bead hyperventilating and the other disappeared out the front door, so Bonnie has me canvassing the Bisbee desert neighborhood calling out "Bottoms!" Or "Hankie!" or whatever the missing cat's name was. I'm out there for a half an hour peeking under cars.

I get back and Bonnie and I review every memory of every moment we've shared, including that one cunt actress. We talk for hours, with Bonnie taking breaks to pull her oxygen tubes out of her nose so she can hoover down a cigarette. She's small, like concentration camp small, but she's still hilarious and honest. She asks me how long I'm staying and I say I need to be back in Tucson for a late dinner with my family. She says she wants me to stay the night. The people in Tucson aren't dying. She actually says that and I say okay. She dozes off and I retreat into the kitchen where Doug and Bingo have an envious collection of airplane booze. They make me a drink. And then another. As I relax, I realize I am an interloper. Doug is losing his mother in his living room.

Bonnie wakes up when the hospice nurse arrives. She demands we all watch Bad Santa together. She dozes off after and I'm back in the kitchen. I tell Doug she's asked me to stay the night. We discuss it and instead I kiss her on the forehead and tip toe out. I get a speeding ticket in Tombstone and by the dawn Bonnie has left, taking all the pills she's squirreled away."

People die. Rarely do people have the opportunity to die knowingly, surrounded by their loved ones and nearly counting it down like it was New Year's Eve. I don't know anyone who's had the fortune, freedom, or fortitude to die like Mother. That's not to say there was no fear or sorrow in her or in us. But with Mother there was humor. There was outright belly laughs, for fuck sake. How could that possibly be wrong? Everybody dies. Maybe we're just different. When I die, I don't want to be surrounded by a bunch of morose cunts praying and rubbing beads.

That Saturday night when Mother decided to exit the stage for good was the most courageous I'd ever seen her, ever seen anyone.

She simply quit. Like the way you quit a job that sucked for too long. Throw off the apron and tell the boss to go fuck himself as you feel that freedom and empowerment envelop you as you walk out the door. Mother quit living like it was a shitty day job. She just decided one day she'd had enough and that was that. Hit the bar for a drink and a smoke, a few good laughs about the old days, and we'll see you out there somewhere. And in the morning she was gone.

————

THERE WAS NOBODY I COULD THINK TO CALL. MOTHER WAS SIXTY-three years old and had burned out or run away from all of her friends by this point in her life. Aside from my brother and his kids, she had no other family. There was no need for an obituary. If I'd been inclined to write one, it would have just been a litany of everything she hated and everyone she complained about in Bisbee. And that would have been funny but I didn't think of it until it was too late.

There was not much in the way of tying up any loose ends. Her body was donated to some foundation that does something with dead things. Scientific research, cadavers for medical students, Moroccan food. I don't have any idea. She wouldn't care nor did we. They sent her ashes back months later. I tried to sell them on eBay, with all proceeds going to The Humane Society but the auction was shut down within hours. Seems selling dead people is not only against eBay policy, it's against federal law. Feds must not like cats like Mother did. So now her ashes are in a drawer or a box somewhere around here. Not quite sure. I've become a bit of a hoarder myself.

My father died with a cemetery plot bought and paid for—coincidentally just across the street from the old house where we lived with Mother and John Kirk in Paxton, Mass. We talked about putting a gravestone on the plot with the old "I'm With Stupid" finger pointing towards the sky. Never got around to it. Like Mother, he's still just a bag of ashes somewhere in my brother's hoard. Years ago we talked about mixing his ashes in some cocaine and snorting him. Just for the story value. We laughed like pigs. But we never did it. Not long afterwards, Keith Richards made international head-lines by saying he'd done that very thing with his own father's ashes. When you have a great idea, get it out there before someone beats you to the punch. It's only funny if you actually do it.

Mother didn't have any estate aside from her last cat Georgia, who lived for another disheveled year and a half. Mother's bills could all gather spiderwebs now. All Bingo and I had to do was clean out her apartment one last time. I thought it would be easier now that she was dead but it was even more difficult. The minute you die, so many of the things you cherished in your life become im-mediately worthless. Mother's framed certificates from massage and nursing schools hung on the walls. I kept them but had to ask myself why? I will never hang them on my wall nor will my brother or his children. Am I supposed to leave them in my own crawlspace and make them someone else's problem when I croak? Yet to just chuck them in a dumpster that quickly seemed even too callous for me. Best to just keep them for a while and eventually give them to the thrift store for some other hoarder. They will use the frame someday for something. And for only $1.50.

The infuriating thing about the dump that Mother left behind was that, although she considered it "organized," there was still no rhyme or reason to it. I'd go through stacks of old electric bills dat-ing back to the nineties, and just before I was about to throw the whole fucking box out you'd find an envelope full of sequentially-ordered 1976 two-dollar bills straight from the Mint or my great-grandmother's original birth certificate from Scotland. That means now I'd have to go through every slip of paper to make sure I'm not throwing away something valuable. And I'm glad that I did. I wouldn't have been able to write this book had it not been for her keeping the boxes I saved. All of her old weekly planners, calen-dars, records, resumes, greeting cards, pictures, and letters helped me piece together so many holes in my memory. I know that the cost of my delivery where I was born at Fairlawn hospital was $251.58.

She'd kept the cancelled check. I now know that I didn't use my credit card on 9/11. For some reason she kept my old bills in her boxes. I can hear her saying "I told you so" from the grave. Or from some drawer somewhere around here, as it were.

Mother lived a life rooted in fear, frustration, and loneliness with bouts of great bravado and boldness. Towards the end it was mostly remorse, reflection, and regret. Being around her in those later years was trying, but also cathartic. I was slowly becoming like her. Everything I carped about to her about were things I was tacitly telling myself. Get outside, eat healthier, stop complaining about every fucking thing. Find something positive. Enjoy yourself. All things I could stand to be improving more on in life. I was understanding her insanity. I was seeing my own Ghost of Christmas Future in her. I still do, and even when it's just finding myself mimicking one of her eccentricities or shortcomings, I miss her.

I had a couple of shows on the East Coast that following weekend after she died. I don't cancel shows for dead people. And anyone familiar with my comedy knows that recent devastating loss or personal tragedy isn't going to dampen the spirit of my performance. That's generally already woven into the seams. The first show after she died was at an awful (great) punk rock bar called the Milestone in North Carolina. My musician friend Mishka Shubaly was opening for me. In the green room before the show, he asked me tentatively how I was holding up. I don't remember it but he does. He said that I just stared off into the distance and said softly that I didn't have anyone to call anymore now when I had great stories to tell. Even at the worst of times, she was always the only one I was playing to, onstage and off.

In the hoard, there was an undated yet timeless Valentine's Day card she sent to me. I don't know if it's from her hoard or my own. The text inside the card reads:

This is an invitation to Remain close to me always. It's my way of expressing The beautiful feelings that You've awoken in my heart. I want you to know, I will follow you wherever you go.

And Mother continued after the sappy sentiment in a spiral around the card:

. . . I will follow you to your bathroom, your kitchen, your bedroom. I will hire a bagpipe band to serenade you through your worst hangover. I will spout dirty limericks at the top of my lungs until I get you to understand that you are an incredibly wonderful human being with a tender heart, a fascinating, inventive, imaginative mind, a warm and fun and funny guy and one of the two greatest gifts God gave me. I love you, my son!

Ma

This is a love story.

Acknowledgments

TODAY IN THE MIDDLE OF A PERFECT DAY—DRUNK ON THE DAY this book is going to print—my editor emails and says I forgot to submit my acknowledgments. Oops.

So obviously I have to start with him. Ben Schafer. He was kind enough to actually invite me into his home only for me to realize that it is also his one-bedroom office. Perhaps the Da Capo printing press is in that apartment building's laundry room. But that's none of my business.

This book would have never happened without the cruel and relentless badgering over a course of 7 years from my friend and partner Brian Hennigan. And an agent, Marc Gerald, who finally realized it might be sellable years after we submitted it.

Also to Alex O'Meara and Adrian LeBlanc, great friends and writers who were my go-to people for advice and for filling me with false confidence. I feed off of it and you were always there. Except when Adrian was away for months with no cell phone reception trying to finish her own book.

It'd be easy to thank J. Depp but Deuters probably deserves more credit for busting Johnny's balls to get it in on a deadline.

I bothered everyone still alive to fact-check or reminisce repeatedly but nobody more than my brother Jeff whose cell phone only worked outside, always at night in his underwear.

There's other people to thank but fuck 'em. They understand I forget shit.

The title of this book is and always has been "The Long Version of a Suicide Post-It Note: A Love Story."

All the higher-ups rejected it. But it is always the title so far as I'm concerned.

Two weird fans just showed up at my house while I'm writing this in the middle of a day-after party. They could be dullards but sometimes you just open the gate and take your chances.

Their names are Adderal Jack and Rebecca Jean.

Maybe they'll be in the next book. But probably not.